WHERE IS SER

IS SER

THE BRAVE LION

RIVER RAINBOW
O'MAHONEY HAGG

Black Rose Writing | Texas

The author grants the final approval for this literary material.

Second printing

This work is based on the author's personal experiences. Some names and identifying details may have been changed to protect the privacy of individuals

ISBN: 978-1-68433-919-8
PUBLISHED BY BLACK ROSE WRITING
www.blackrosewriting.com

Printed in the United States of America
Suggested Retail Price (SRP) $20.95

Where is Ser is printed in Sabon

*As a planet-friendly publisher, Black Rose Writing does its best to eliminate unnecessary waste to reduce paper usage and energy costs, while never compromising the reading experience. As a result, the final word count vs. page count may not meet common expectations.

This book is dedicated to:

All those who have gone before me, and for all those who will go after.

Most of all, to Peace.

GLOSSARY

Agir- Fire

Azad- Freedom, masculine

Azadi- Freedom, feminine

AK or AK47- Soviet made automatic rifle 7.62x39

BDU- Battle dress uniform

Binadar- A wounded person

Berxwedana- Resistance

Bixie- a belt fed soviet made heavy machinegun 7.62x54

Bixfing- a Rocket-propelled grenade

Biji – Great diversity

BMB- home-made armored truck

DELTA- The 1st Special Forces Operational Detachment–Delta (1st SFOD-D), commonly referred to as Delta Force.

Canton- A division size element of the SDF or YPG. A division is a large military unit, usually consisting of between 6,000 and 25,000 soldiers

CLOX- trauma treatments include advanced bandages that rapidly stop lethal bleeding and dressings designed to quickly seal wounds that penetrate the chest wall.

Embichem- go to

Fermander- Military commander

Giving Set- the IV line that attaches to the bag of fluid and needle in the arm.

Heval- Comrade, brother in arms, member of YPG

Hevala- Comrade, sister in arms, member of YPJ

Hypotension- a decrease in systemic blood pressure below accepted low values. It becomes a concern once pumping pressure is not sufficient to perfuse key organs with oxygenated blood.

Hypovolemic shock- a condition of acute peripheral circulatory failure due to derangement of circulatory control or loss of circulating fluid. It is marked by hypotension and coldness of the skin, and often by tachycardia and anxiety. Can be fatal

IED- Improvised explosive device

IFAK- a compact, versatile individual first aid kit

Jin- Female

Jiyan- Life

Midclavicular line- An imaginary vertical division on the anterior surface of the body, passing through the midpoint of the clavicle

Military time- Instead of having a twelve-hour clock that resets twice, you work with one clock that starts with 0000 at midnight and runs all the way until 2359 hours (11:59 p.m.)

Nava Min- Name mine

Nequshani- Hospital

NPA- nasopharyngeal airway, also known as an NPA

Nocta- base of operations or place you are staying

Orientalism- Book by Edward Said that has been highly influential and controversial in postcolonial studies. In the book, Said effectively redefined the term "Orientalism" to mean a constellation of false assumptions underlying Western attitudes toward the Middle East

Overwatch- is the state of one small unit or military vehicle supporting another unit, while they are executing fire and movement tactics

Peshmerga- A Kurdish militia in Northern Iraq.

Rojava- Western Kurdistan located in the top half of Syria

SDF- Syrian Democratic forces

RPG- Rocket-propelled grenade

Serkiftin- Victory

Sehid- Died in battle

Sehid Namirin- (Heroes are never forgotten/ Heroes of the people never die)

Ser- A brave or noble lion.

s- A small 's' in front of a name stands for sehid

Taboor- a platoon size element of SDF/YPG/YPJ consisting of about 15 to 20 male and 15 to 20 female.

TCCC- Tactical combat casualty care, can be divided into three phases. The first is care under fire; the second is tactical field care; the third is combat casualty evacuation care.

Tekoser- Revolutionary or outlaw of the people

Woop.de.woops- The big bumps on a dirt-race track.

YPG- Peoples Protection Units (men)

YPJ- Peoples Protection Units (woman)

Zoo or Zood- Hurry

5.56- the ammunition adopted in 1980 by NATO as a standard service round.

WHERE IS SER

THE BRAVE LION

Chapter 1: Iraqi Prison

Chapter 2: The Beginning: My Name

Chapter 3: The Genesis of a Partisan (part 1-9)

Chapter 4: Free Fall

Chapter 5: Detained

Chapter 6: The Crime Scene

Chapter 7: The Call

Chapter 8: The Safe House

Chapter 9: Hitchhike to a Gunfight

Chapter 10: No Friends but the Mountains

Chapter 11: The Battle for Shaddadi

Chapter 12: The Grunt Medic

Chapter 13: Airstrike Baptism

Chapter 14: PTSD Flashbacks Suck!

Chapter 15: The Monster

Chapter 16: The Front Loader Ambulance

Chapter 17: Refugees

Chapter 18: They Call Me Doc

Chapter 19: Binadar Heval Ashti

Chapter 20: PTSD and THE DMV

Chapter 21: Rocket Panzer

Chapter 22: PTSD and The Balloon

Chapter 23: Tal Nasri

Chapter 24: The Storm Inside

Chapter 25: Hard Target

Chapter 26: The White House

Chapter 27: The Chicken Factory

Chapter 28: The Dancing Hevals

Chapter 29: PTSD Dreams

Chapter 30: The Devils Belly

Chapter 31: Hevala Berxwedana

Chapter 32: For a Few Hours More

Chapter 33: Where is Ser?

CHAPTER 1: Iraqi Prison

When they let me out of Iraqi Prison, a black SUV zoomed up, stopping in a small cloud of dust. A back door was opened, and I was quickly shoved in. The door shut. The SUV zoomed off... and that is exactly how long it took for my life to change, forever.

Two FBI agents escorted me out of prison that day. As we were walking down the long hallway away from the warden, a twisted, hateful man named Major Serwan watched. One agent said, under his breath, "Keep walking and don't look back. We're not out of here until you clear the front gates!" Even from that distance, I could feel the eyes of the major burning holes into the back of my neck. His eyes follow me, like watching a fish come off the hook at the boat, only I was the fish. The major was not happy they had forced him to release me. He didn't like me. He knew I was lying. He wanted to make me stay in his prison. But I am American and with that comes privileges. In this case, they were the kind that forced a powerful man like the major to let someone like me go.

Every breath drew me closer... all the way to the door, one agonizing step at a time. It opened with a hiss into the bright day. I stepped through it, into the light. My heart pumped adrenaline as my feet carried me outside. I heard the loud bang of the door closing behind me and for the first time in my life it represented freedom. The best damn door ever to shut on me.

I still didn't turn to look. It seemed as if the major could somehow see through the walls. I just kept my eyes forward. My destination was in front of me. Across the long empty courtyard was a huge solid black gate. A guard house stood in front of it, butted up to a twenty-foot-tall stone wall. I could feel the prison looming behind me. I knew how the inside looked. That was enough. I did not need to look to see the outside to know that it looked the way torture sounded. My heart raced; my lip was sweating. I was gripped by an overwhelming fear of being returned to the grim reality only steps behind me.

Back inside the prison, guards dragged inmates out one by one. The men who seemed randomly selected were pulled, kicking and screaming, "No! No! No? Please? Please!???" The men were begging, feet and hands trying to find purchase on the cold smooth stone floors. Squeaking like dry rubber across glass and about as effective, they slid uselessly out the door.

KAAABOOOM! The cell door slammed shut with a terror and finality as only it can in prison. Hope was locked out like the last sound heard inside a coffin. The first scoop of dirt hit the lid and with that, they buried us alive.

It was hard not to panic being locked up in a foreign country, a place where I hardly speak the language, and no one knows I'm here.

Outside in the hall guards were laughing over yelling, then *THUD! THUD! THUD!* I heard the sound of blunt objects striking soft flesh. Grunting, gurgle... "No!" and for a moment there was silence... Then I heard a sound like someone dropping something like a coconut on the floor... followed by the two guards laughing and the sound of them dragging away a heavy object.

Sometime later, a terrible screaming could be heard, but it was far away, and in another part of the prison. The chilling echo filled the halls. It was a piteous howl of agony, repeated over and over, for hours. I didn't know a person could make that kind of sound. I tried not to hear it, we all tried not to hear it, but it was impossible not to hear down the halls that cared less. So, into our ears, the sound slipped. A terrible whisper saying, "You're next... You're NEXXTTTT." We could not help imagining the unseen terror and pain being inflicted on our cellmate while we sat all crammed in our own version of hell in silence, sitting on concrete and waiting our turn to confess.

The sound faded from the loudest howl you have ever heard from a man all the way until hours and hours later, a trickle of water was louder, but still audible... and then silence. At long last, silence. And in the quiet, I felt guilty at the relief of it.

Sometime later - hard to tell how many hours it had been in a place without any clocks -- shoes squeaked down the hallway. The sound of keys scraped into the lock. The two guards, grinning cruelly, dragged the unconscious man back in, dropping him like a used-up sack. But our cell was so crowded, his body would not hit the concrete again this day, as we were the floor. Our hands caught our brother as his hands caught us, and in this way, in this place, there was a commonality amongst us that transcended borders or ideologies. The guard laughed, pointing. "You!" And the next victim was grabbed and dragged out.... How can you describe the sound of fear in places deeper than hearts know?

There were ninety-six of us stuffed into one sixteen- by thirty-foot cell, packed to the point not one more would fit. We were let out once in the morning and once in the afternoon for thirty minutes, to a small courtyard in the center of the prison. We would do laundry, exercise, walk and shower there.

I never knew sitting on concrete all day would be so painful. Inside, we were not allowed to stand except to pray. So, we would sit against the walls or back-to-back for upright support. You could not lie down during the day because it took up too much room.

During mealtime, a long plastic sheet was rolled down the length of the cell and the food was handed down it to the end first, and then back up to the front. We ate together off the plastic with our hands and bread. Five times a day, everyone prayed, but no clerics or mullahs ever came to visit the inmates.

I felt guilt in my heart at the look on their faces that day when the door was opened, and I was unexpectedly freed. So many of them had spent years here for nothing. They spent lifetimes behind these bars, here endlessly for just being in the wrong place at the wrong time. They had the wrong ethnicity/religion or just the wrong last name or were simply in the way. There was no justice in Iraq, no speedy trial, no innocent until proven guilty. And even now, as you gaze at this page and absorb these words, these innocent victims are living ghosts, buried alive behind six-foot-thick concrete walls that block all sound in and hope out. This is the place where the disappeared aren't missing.

The innocent, and the forgotten, are not just random names or numbers, but people. Sure, there were a few murderers, thieves and definitely some ISIS fuckers in here, but at least 90% of us were innocent of any wrongdoing.

The old man Mostafa was here because he refused to sell his house to the son of a rich local politician. Then one-night Mostafa was dragged from his house by four young men and beaten half to death. They rolled him up in a carpet and drove him here in the trunk of his own car. Mostafa had been here ever since. There are no charges against this man. He has never seen a judge. He is in the twilight of his years, seventy-six. There won't be a new house, or time for him to start over, if they ever do let him out.

Injustice is an ugly truth and a hard pill to swallow. But here you don't have a choice whether or not you can take it. It's just crammed down your throat day after day. My heart was heavy for Mostafa, the end of his life spent smashed in a cell, with sore old bones on cold, hard concrete floors.

Malath is twenty-four years old. He had been studying abroad in India in his third year of pharmacy school. He had come home to visit his mom. When he was leaving to go back to India for his last year of college, Malath was seized at the airport. They told him it was for how he dressed. For his flight back, he had put on a pair of black traditional baggy Indian pants. That was his only crime, black baggy pants.

The Iraqi authorities wanted him to sign a confession saying he was ISIS. When he refused to sign it, they tortured him repeatedly using a hose and electricity. One time he said the interrogator told him they had injected him with AIDS, and he would die in two days if he didn't agree to cooperate. The interrogator told him only he had the antidote, and Malath would die a horrible death. But Malath knew they were lying about the AIDS. He said to me he would never admit to something he was not. So, on orders from Major Serwan, the cops arrested Malath's little brother; he was only sixteen. Despite that, he still wouldn't sign the confession. So, in the end they crushed his right index finger with plyers. I could see the angry pink scars on his weirdly bent, gnarled finger.

Malath laughed it off and said, "Now I cannot sign it. So, they leave me alone. Someday they will let us out. And when they do? My brother and I will leave this country and never come back!"

Malath knew that a confession was a death sentence for him. All convicted ISIS in Iraq at that point were being executed. This prison cell had been his and his brother's life for the last two years.

I thought they kept him in prison, though, because he spoke such good English. That way, when they arrested foreigners, it was like having an in-house interpreter. I wish he would have never spoken English. I bet they would have let him out two years ago.

There was Ali. He was seventeen and had been here for a year and a half because his father was wanted for bad debts and fled. They imprisoned Ali in his father's place. They robbed him of his youth to pay for his dad. Malath had been teaching him English, so we would work together on things like the ABCs and other basics - it helped pass the time. I wish it would have made up for the years he missed in school, but it's better to do something than nothing.

I tried not to think about home too much, but it was hard not to. I wondered how long it would be before I saw my own daughters again. I missed their sweet little faces and loving eyes. Not the hard eyes of kids of war. Not the scared faces of kids who have been shot or blown up and are crying in pain. Not the sad eyes of Ali, who had been raised by convicts in this jail.

I missed seeing the sweet, innocent, loving eyes of my daughters. Those are the eyes all kids should get to see the world through.

The lights clanked off, one set at a time. I could hear the ballast shut down one by one with a metallic *CLUNK...CLUNK...CLUNK...* Another day here. My soul was tired. My body hurt. There was no freedom from this prison, not even in sleep could one escape. The floors were concrete covered by thin blankets, each of us pressed into the man next to him, and him into him, into him, on and on. We were like human sardines stacked head to toe, three rows deep. The acrid taste of injustice blended into the sorrow and fear of the ninety-six of us confined helplessly in this sarcophagus.

Before prison. Manbij, Syria: We were living like rats, scurrying from one bombed-out house to another, going weeks with no running water, bath, shower, bed, or any other kind of modern comfort. We had no food to eat other than what we picked from the dead burned city. The smell of rotten corpses strewn randomly amongst the rubble stung our noses. On the streets, the sight of the freshly killed ISIS fighters being eaten by starving dogs was constant. There is a way the dogs tug at the face first, snarling and fighting each other for who gets to eat the eyes, the tongue, the lips, and the most prized of all, the brains.

Apocalypse is not a concept in an old dusty book; it is a reality and it's called modern warfare and modern warfare isn't fucking modern at all. It's insane. It's draconian. It's running house to house fighting ghosts that kill in a tangled concrete landscape that's prone to exploding at random! War is landmines, IEDs and shit falling from the sky, dropped or shot by jets or drones from both sides... hiding at night and in the morning, plundering the dead bodies for more bullets to kill each other with... climbing through and over smoldering rubble... mouth dry, heart pounding, dust in my eyes, scraped hands and knees... never knowing where death is coming from. War is this, over and over, day in and day out, the feeling like it was the end, only it was just the beginning.

Iraqi Prison: I stood at the gates while they slowly opened in front of me. At last, a dream I didn't want to wake from: walking out of this hell. That word so long dreamed of, now almost on my lips, "Freedom!" I stepped out from the shadows into the sunlight, through the last open door of the prison. "Free!" What a strange word to hold in the mouth of my mind. It was like an unfamiliar language from a different world. The unimaginable now a reality... Out of one door and through another...

Inside the SUV, its soft, smooth, black luxurious interior contrasted my minutes earlier experience beyond description. I was completely and instantly removed from the horror happening just behind the sordid walls I was leaving, or worse, just across the border from here in Syria...

I felt like it was super slow motion at 1000 frames per second, like I couldn't move fast enough. It was the dream where you can't run no matter how hard you try, a punch that lands soft as a feather no matter how hard it's thrown.... Time??? Time is the eternity spent in-between heartbeats. Will the heart beat again? I waited for the SUV door to close, for us to depart this nightmare...

How horrible it would be to be dragged back in, just on the edge of freedom. Dragged back inside to the belly of the beast... It didn't happen though; the door *POOFFEUFFED* shut, trapping in the AC and smell of leather. The car was shifted down to drive... I could hear the three distinct sounds of the shifter on the column, *CLUNK, CLUNK, CLUNK.* The black SUV lurched forward with alacrity, through the gates without slowing. Laying on the horn, the driver swerved into traffic like a shot entering the bloodstream, only I, the drug, shot back into life, the body. I was leaving!

Outside the prison gates, Erbil traffic seemed so busy, so crowded. It was like jumping to hyper-speed on the starship USS GTFOH. Everything moved so fast... the cars, the people, the sounds. I was completely overwhelmed. The dark SUV wove in and out of traffic through the busy Iraqi streets. This felt safer than anywhere I had ever been in my life. There was an AK beside the driver, so I instinctively looked for mine. I guess by now that just seemed normal.

The farther from the prison I got, the more real the word "*home*" sounded. The car stopped. I got out. The safe house was nice. Gus was a British-sounding dude; he was in charge. He told me to make myself at home. What a nice word. There were all the amenities one could want: TV with every channel, fridge full of food, full weight room, large deluxe showers. In my room I found a soft bed, nightstand, window with a clean full white curtain. I set the AC to 72. It was luxurious to be cool. I turned around in a small circle, taking it in. I wasn't far enough away. The dread returned. I panicked. I had a flashback and for a second I thought Daesh was coming into the house. I hit the floor and rolled under the bed, wishing I had my rifle. "What the fuck is wrong with me?" I came out from under the bed feeling foolish.

I stripped naked and walked into the shower, turning on the hot water, the steam rising, looking up at it like I've done all my life. My eyes closed, the hot water streaming onto my face. "It's ok now," I told myself. "You're ok. You're free now. There is no Daesh here." I took a big breath in and exhaled it slowly, trying out the word again in my mind.... *free...*

Twenty-four hours later, I was nervous, really nervous. I tried not to shake visibly. I was escorted through the airport by a fixer my friend Ricky had hired to get me out.

He smiled easily. "Remember, just smile, nod, and repeat what I told you on the way here. OK?"

I nodded up and down, "OK! I got it." Maybe it was easy for him to smile, but for me, it was the most dangerous part of the exit.

The customs officer looked at me hard. "For why you come?"

My fixer stepped in and fired back a sharp-sounding rebuke, but I couldn't understand what he was saying. All I could hear from the poetic Arabic was the word Peshmerga.

I was then treated very differently and ushered along until the last gate, where my fixer smiled and said, "Next time you come to Iraq you will have to come eat with us! It would be a great honor my friend."

I smiled back at him, knowing there was no way in hell I was returning here anytime soon.

On my way to Iraqi prison, as seen in the documentary, "The Volunteers, part 2." I smuggled in a GoPro camera with me. They found it at the end of this bus ride at the main prison.

CHAPTER 2: The Beginning: My Name

I remember the moment now, like someone knows his own face. I know its mine, but if I stare at it for too long, it looks like a stranger standing there staring back at me.

I was in the YPG/YPJ foreign volunteer academy: the commander's office, Rojava, Northern Syria, February 14th, 2016. The clock on the wall read 1936. I was sitting propped against the wall on a long cushion with some pillows. Sitting opposite me were the commander, Heval Sasoon and his lead instructor, Heval Jonser. After pouring me chai, Heval Sasoon leaned back comfortably, and asked me in his soft voice, "Mister, please. Why have you come here? Why do you wish to be YPG?" He pronounced it YiPeGey. He leaned back, awaiting my answer. The way he got comfortable seemed to suggest he was not interested in the short answer. Which is a good thing, because anyone who knows me knows I love to talk.

It was the last interview, and I didn't know it was happening until I was seated here. The last obstacle, if you can call such things that.

I had never answered this question honestly until then. Seated here with these two men from the mountains, I found myself telling my life's story because the one question didn't just have a simple answer.

When I finished, they sat quietly for a moment. I wasn't sure what they would do next. They spoke to each other intently for a short time before Heval Jonser looked at me and said, "Your new name is Heval Tekoser Azad."

Heval Sasoon nodded approvingly at the name. I tried out my new name like meeting myself for the first time. "Nava min, Tekoser Azad," I said out loud, trying to cement it into my memory. One's own name is a very important thing to remember. I mean, whom will you ask later if you forget it?

Heval Jonser smiled at my mangled attempt to say my own name, saying, "Your name, Tekoser, means Guerrilla or Outlaw of the people/Brave-Lion; Azadi means, Freedom!" He paused for my reaction. I loved it.

Heval Sasson nodded approvingly "Yes this is a very good name for you, very good. Here let us have some tea before you go." When you first join YPG, they give you a new Kurdish name, or as they like to say, a new "Code name." It doesn't matter your ethnicity, religion, gender/sexual orientation or country of birth; once you join YPG/SDF, you are a Partisan. A twisted irony: a war for peace, for democracy, women's rights, ecology and religious freedom. It is a war where those who fight for such things are the outlaws, all the way down to the new name and busted-up old rifles.

Me in Manbij after a gun fight

CHAPTER 3: My Answer to the Question

Part 1: The Genesis of a Partisan

Why did I go to Syria in 2016 to join the YPG? (Yekîneyén Parastina Gel, which means People's Protection Units.) To really understand this decision, you must first understand the fear of a child being abused. On the schoolyards of my youth, being called a "Stupid Hippy!" or "Fag!" constantly picked on, pushed around and tormented. Maybe it was because I liked to wear dresses? Back then, I just wanted to be like my Big Sissy. Big Sissy was my hero, my protector, my best friend. This was before we were wrongly taught that sissies are sissies.

My sister and me

It was 1982, Charlottesville Virginia. we had just moved there from Arcata, California.

The small coastal town was tucked up in the ancient Redwood trees - dusted by fog, sky light shafts through the grandfather trees, dappled dramatically and splashed across the forest floor. Contrasting rainbows hung in the sky, dangled beneath rain-shrouded dramas. An out-of-the-way place, for out-of-the-way people. Arcata was about as opposite to Charlottesville as I was, it seemed.

My name, River Rainbow O'Mahoney Hagg, completely and immediately misaligned me from a community I desperately wanted to fit into, i.e., the 2nd grade. Up until this point, I had been raised in a non-binary way. Now I was dropped into this very binary world. As a kid, I was completely unprepared for any of it. I quickly learned from the hate directed at me that "I sucked" and I was "a freak." All of it made me weak, and weak on the schoolyards of my youth made me an easy target.

There were many days spent hiding from my tormentors, running across the playground only to be tripped and laughed at. I would be left on the ground crying with skinned knees or pushed when I was peeing in the urinal, so I got pee all down my pants. I had to go back to class, pants wet, walking bow-legged, because no one can stay in the bathroom forever, not even if he wants to. The sound of laughter can be the meanest sound you ever hear.

The first day was always the worst. In every new class, there was that awkward moment when roll was called, and the teacher thought my name was a typo or a practical joke. She would say, off the roll sheet in a hesitating voice, "Ri... Ver? Rain... Bow?? Omaaa? Hag? Huh? What the heck kind of name is that?" The class would erupt in laughter.

I didn't know "boys" didn't wear dresses. Just like my long hair, I liked my dresses. Right after we moved, I wanted to wear one to school. Mom warned me some of the boys might be threatened by me in a dress. I didn't understand what she meant. If it threatened them, then maybe they would leave me alone! After I came home from school, Mom held an ice pack to my bruised face and said, "The bigger man will just turn the other cheek, honey. I am soooo proud of you!"

I threw all my dresses away that night. I didn't tell anyone. I just snuck outside and shoved them all in the trash can. A few days later at Bobby's house, with the help of his dad, I shaved my head. My mom cried when she saw my fresh cut. I didn't care what Mom wanted. I did it for survival.

It didn't matter though; the damage was already done. School was worse than ever. A free punch on "River Liver! The Fag Hag! Rainbow!" I would fall down after they hit me and cry, because I didn't know you could fight back. No one ever taught me how. I was scared. So, year after year it went on, until as many states as moves later, I had enough of Mom's bull crap pacifist horse shit. I had it! And I wasn't gonna take it anymore.

It was Hilo, Hawaii; I was in the 8th grade. I was pushed into the urinal for the last time. I spun around and yelled, "I'll SMASH YOU!" I attacked the laughing bully. Swinging wildly, he stepped back, grabbed my hand and spun me around, punched me in the back of the head. I bounced off a stall wall and struggled to keep my feet, screaming. I charged him like a wild animal. He kept on punching me, but I just kept on coming until he finally quit. I didn't care if I lost! I yelled at him as he bolted out of the bathroom with his three asshole friends, "Quitter!!! I win!" And for the first time, I felt free of that fear I had always known. I tasted my blood and laughed there alone in the bathroom. I wasn't scared anymore.

I got into an after-school boxing club. After six months at the club, I knew no one would ever push me around again. My coach Rudy was even talking Golden Gloves for me.

The thing is, it's hard not to get lost as a young man. I didn't understand the difference between defending and attacking. The line between right and wrong blurs quickly when one looks to inflict harm on another person. Sadly, sometimes there are people in this world that will take whatever they want from you unless you stand up to them and put them down. They will take until there is nothing left to take. I detest violence, but sometimes because of the sickness of humanity, a sickness that breeds bullies, racists, rapists, and killers, someone has to take a stand. The problem is when you begin to like it; and if you don't like it, how can you live with it? And that is a question, my friends, that has no easy answer. So? Who kills a killer? Who stomps a bully? And what is the cost? Sheepdog or Wolf? Or both? These explanations? This dilemma? They evade my best explanation.

Part 2: All I Ever Dreamed of

I became a father young; I was 21. I put away childish things. I was now a man, a provider. I joined the Navy as a firefighter. It felt good to serve others. For me, the Navy was a place where I could put my fighting spirit to better use, i.e., running into burning shit that others were running out of. I would be decked out in my FFE (firefighting ensemble), running to an inferno. This time I got to be the rescuer, and I loved it. So, I trained hard. Until that point in my life, I had never felt truly proud of myself.

I became a fire investigator, a top qualification for a firefighter. It meant I was the first one to a fire. I went before they sent in a team to battle the blaze. My job was to direct the resources to the fire. I was basically the dummy who ran blind into thick smoke to figure out what was happening, so no one else had to go in unknowing. I was never happier than at the tip of the spear.

My job meant I was going in blind, but it also meant action. I loved that. Most importantly to me, it meant I got to respond first to real fires when they occasionally happened. The rest of my shipmates had to sit all geared up, waiting for me to call back whether to roll in or not.

I took an additional course to become an EMT. When I got out of the Navy, I planned on joining the San Diego Fire Department.

It was Sunday; I was on watch. At 1723, an alarm went off. This was not a drill. I was running to a fire alarm. Over-excited, I hit the deck wrong, coming down the ladder. I felt a searing pain in my knee, but I was almost to the space where the alarm blared, so I kept going. My knee felt like someone had stuck a board in it. I was sweating from the pain.

I got to the fire; white smoke spilled out of the cracked hatch. Carefully, I felt it and the bulkhead for heat. Feeling none, I radioed in and I entered the space. Breathing through my mask, the cool air sounded like a scuba tank.

I located the fire quickly. It was just a small electrical panel with a short erratically sparking. Some flames had started around the plastic wiring, but mostly it was just thick white smoke. I hit it with CO_2 and radioed it in.

The bridge immediately cut power to the space, completely putting it out. The red safety light kicked on. My head lamp acted as a laser light in the dark and the smoke.

I found a desk to sit on while I waited for help to arrive. My knee was hurting like hell. One of the ship's electricians and a damage control expert eventually showed up and posted a fire watch on the now cold panel, until it was to be repaired. He relieved me of my fire watch, but as I limped out of the space and down the ladder, my knee buckled and I went head over to the deck, knocking myself out cold.

A few weeks later at Balboa Naval Hospital, the doctors told me my firefighting days were over. It seems I took one step too many after I was hurt and did irreparable damage to the cartilage, patella and ligaments. They did a surgery, but the doctors were right; it was never the same. I was crushed. No fire department. I would never run normally again, let alone drag a hose up to a fire.

I was lost and confused - what was I going to do now? My lifelong dream ended. I was twenty-five with no education, a wife who was not working, and a small child. They all depended on me for rent, food, and everything else. It was a dark few months until my discharge.

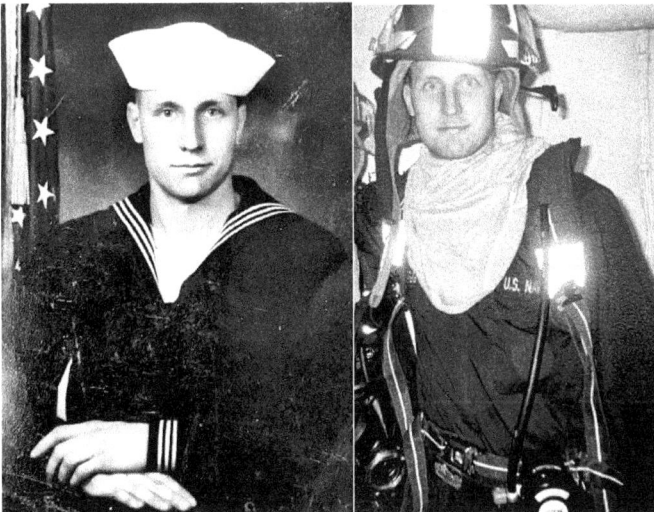

Me in the U.S. Navy

Part 3: Starting Over

I hit the civilian world broke and broken. I considered myself lucky, though; I got a job on a used car lot. This ended after a month - I never sold a car. So, in a fit of desperation, mixed with mania, I bought a vx2000 Sony video camera and a Blue iMac on credit. I put an advertisement in the local paper. I called my company "Moonlight Video." It was an awful name, and I had no clue what I was doing, but I kept at it. I went to a used bookstore and picked up a few old college film textbooks. I started volunteering for the San Diego Media Arts Center.

No one thought I would succeed, including myself. All the neighbors in our apartment building had put up a betting pool on how long it would take me and my small family to get evicted. I had no TV experience to speak of. I had only taken videography for one year in high school, but I always loved cameras. I guess I had a natural gift for seeing the world through a lens. With nothing left to lose except our apartment, and with only a few more days to make rent, I got hired to film the Goldens' bat mitzvah. They gave me a four-hundred-dollar deposit, which covered the rest of the 1200 dollars we needed for rent that month.

I worked hard. I never said no, even when it meant I worked for free sometimes. I started freelancing more and more, but mostly I got lucky.

Looking back, I don't know when I "made it." I just know at some point, after years of struggle, I had become very good at what I did. I had gone all over the world filming for the Department of Defense and others, from war zones to tropical paradises. I had filmed or produced everyone from A-list celebrities to reality TV zombie hunters to rogue fisherman. I lived in a world of "people are profit," where your personality is the commodity. It was a never-ending chase for ratings, and it was the golden statue that was somehow so important for me to have.

Now, all these years later, when I look at myself in the rearview mirror, I don't see the success my friends perhaps see in me, because I have the inside view. So, all these things ended piled up behind my eyes, hidden away in my heart, locked up. Stashed with the memories of childhood bullies, fighting back, and running into things that were on fire, I was miserable, and I saw no way out.

Part 4: Burned Out

One of our cast members' father died. I was there when he got the news. He lost it because his father's passing had been really unexpected. The poor guy broke down crying, doubled over like he got hit in the guts. I felt awful for him. We had spent years working together on a reality TV show and I knew how close he and his pops were. Unexpected death is the worst, because you never get closure, never get to say goodbye. It was a long, tough day on top of an already long, tough season.

When I got back to the hotel late that night, actually closer to the morning than the night, I dragged my crate of gear and media into the production office. When I walked in, it surprised me to see the executive-executive producer (EEP) there. He was the EEP, as opposed to the EP, because just one executive credit wasn't enough for the big boss. He had freshly arrived from LA and was slightly buzzed from the first-class free booze. He looked excited to see me.

"Why tonight?" I thought.

He held out both hands as if ready to accept some sort of package from me.

He said, "I heard the mate's dad died! Tough for him, you know! Tsk tsk tsk! But man! That's great TV! Tell me you got it?... Right?" He was smiling from ear to ear, but there was a tone in his voice that meant, "You better have got it."

I was tired. I felt terrible for the mate. What the hell was wrong with these people? But I'm a working stiff, you know, and it's not my job to tell the EEP he's a dick. It's my job to give him what he wants. That's the only reason I have a job. All those years of being picked on were finally paying off, because I sure knew how to take it.

So, I just took a deep breath, slid my media in the intake tray, and said, "Of course I got it, Boss." My EEP excitedly slapped me on the shoulder, telling me what a great job I did, blah blah blah. I was h is number one shooter/producer. My footage makes great TV compared to other producers. Then he told me the same thing he told me at the end of the prior year: "Next year! Next year! There'll be good things in store for you!"

I, the sucker, believed him again. I felt better for a moment with his praises. But when I left, as with all fake shit, it didn't last. As the door shut behind me, all that was left was the unpleasant aftertaste in my mouth of cruel optimism.

Me filming the fishing show

Part 5: Our World Earth

When the fishing gig ended, I headed to Los Angeles to see my kids at their grandparents' house. It was just before dinner. I was in the den with my two daughters, Alyna-Rose and Arcata Rainbow; they were one and six.

From the kitchen, I heard the girl's mom fighting with her parents. They always fought. It was normal for them; it's just how hateful people show love.

I ignored the ruckus from the other side of the house and focused on my daughters. I had missed them terribly. An advertisement came on TV for the show I had just come back from. I perked up because it always stoked my ego to see my work being advertised all over the world. "My payoff for all the hard work and bullshit," I thought, smiling. The ad is like, "This boat against that boat. blah blah blah... Episode Blood on the Decks, Blood on the Docks!"

I smiled from the comfort of the den at this year's payoff, a fancy edit and my shots in the cut. On the TV screen, the rocket fish surged violently past my camera. It was something I could be proud of, even if someone else gets the credit, I got the shots! The ad cuts to the captain, shrouded by exploding ocean, as the tiny boat backs down into a monstrous sea. He is yelling in slow motion as if produced on some Hollywood back lot. This is also, my shot. I smile proudly, because I am done now, and it's always easier to look back than forward.

The TV went back to the news. I looked down at my daughters. Fuck the news! I intentionally focused my attention on this perfect little baby clutching my finger. She had grown so much; she gazed up at me. She had such perfect little tiny fingers, such clear eyes. Her sandy-haired sister next to me curled up like a little raccoon munching on Cheetos.

The TV reporter got into my mind, though, as I became conscious of his voice. He was saying something like, "What we are about to see might be disturbing to some viewers," and he repeated something about the Syrian Civil War.

I looked up, my eyeballs a slave to my own morbidity. You know, the TV host tells us these things, not because he wants us to turn the channel or actually look away, but rather because he really wants us to look up, watch and pay closer attention. So, I did, and I saw a little baby washed up dead on some beach far away. I sat there frozen. My heart wanted my brain to tear my eyes from the TV screen and unsee it. But my brain refused; so, my eyes took it all in, every detail: the water, wet sand, red shirt, still little face... all cold... all dead.

I looked down at my own daughter in my arms. For a moment, I saw this little dead baby in my arms. He felt cold and somehow heavier. I was overcome with such a terrible feeling. My eyes welled with tears. I shook my head, looking away and then back down... it was my daughter again. She was looking up at me, a concerned look in her little eyes, as if she could sense my weird brain malfunction.

I was shaken deeply, though. For that second it seemed vivid, so real. I took a deep breath and squeezed her a little extra. I was so happy it was their baby who was dead on that beach and not mine. "Not My Daughters! Thank YOU, GOD!"

My next emotion was overwhelming shame. How can I see my children as so much better than anyone else's? How can I see this wrong happening and pretend it is not? Looking down at my own daughters, I was ashamed that I had been so happy it was their baby that was dead and not my own. What is this world we live in that allows death to such innocent little people in such a cruel and scary way, that allows a little baby who can't swim to drown in the cold ocean?

I picture that moment in my mind, the moment at sea when hope went from dim to none. It's night. The ocean is rough; the boat is tossed around violently. People are terrified, some are sick. The boat takes on more and more water. Everyone is wet and cold; the boat capsizes with an enormous wave out of the darkness. I see this baby slipping out of the hands of his panicked parents.

Underwater bubbles swirl like miniature whirlpools, made by thrashing hands and feet. The baby chokes right away. He is lost in the confusion; he sinks deep beneath the black surface, thrashing at first. Deeper and deeper he sinks, the struggle over before it began, and he is still. Suspended in the ocean, he drifts silently, dressed as his mommy and daddy had dressed him for their big trip. Days later, he is finally delivered by the wind and tide to the shores of freedom, where his body lands, though his soul could not make the journey.

The power of a photograph to convey a story in one image smashed the glow of my now seemingly fake reality TV ego. What did I do compared to that? What did my work change? Petty name calling? A fake competition that celebrated who could kill the most beautiful rocket fish for TV ratings and bragging rights?

This one photo landed on my life like a 10,000-pound brick. Shaking my head sadly left and right, speechless for a moment, I looked away and down at my daughter in my arms and then at her sister. They only saw Daddy, their hero, love, protection, and I could see that in their eyes... but in my heart I shrank with guilt... because to me I was none of those things... but I wanted to be.

I had this epiphany inside of me right then and it said, "Enough!" I looked back up at the TV, the commentator still soberly talking... I didn't want to be ashamed anymore of who I was, or what I had participated in before.

A plan began to form in my mind. I had a good friend, Ricky, who was very connected. We had been in Afghanistan together. All I had to do was make that call. My heart was pounding, my mouth dry. I set my daughter down next to her sister and stood up. Taking my phone from my pocket, I looked at it...

My three daughters, Mariluna Sunset, Arcata Rainbow and Alyna Rose

Alan Kurdi

Part 6: The Conclusion of a Moral Deficiency

My mind and heart are at war, fighting between all the reasons not to act versus outrage and the need to act. My conclusion: my daughters will have a good life. In America, they will get the chance to grow up in a comparatively safe society, go to school, college/trade school, have families of their own, and only if they CHOOSE to, and NOT if they don't. My kids will not be bombed at home by fighter jets, turned into war refugees, or drowned at sea fleeing madmen with machine guns and machetes. My children can do so many things with their lives, but most importantly, for now, they just get to be kids. I am not saying life is easy in the United States, especially for women and minorities, because it's not. What I am saying is that in some other places in our world, it's a whole hell of a lot harder.

Part 7: The Cage of Nationalism

Gagged by my own guilt, I just shut up. For years, I never would say what I am about to say. I wouldn't because I am guilty as a participant and that shame is something that has hung around my neck like a noose.

I know what happened in Iraq, because I was there twice before: The first time was in 1999 on a WESPAC deployment in the US Navy, and the second time was 2005, where I was embedded as a combat cameraman with the Third Reconnaissance Marines, 1st Platoon and 3rd Platoon.

I am sad to say that I bought the misinformation campaign about the Middle East we were all sold. I didn't even know I was prejudiced against Middle Easterners. I didn't realize it was a bad thing to hate Muslims. Everyone I knew did. Ignorance made it easy to hate, and 9/11 revenge made it all seem justified. So, in the beginning I took what they said as truth, but it was not truth, not any truer than the Weapons of Mass Destruction were. So, in the end, when the lies wore off, my eyes wide open, I knew I never would escape my participation in the birth of ISIS. None of the USA would... only most of you didn't realize it yet....

Me in Fallujah, Iraq, 2005

Part 8: The Middle East Explained

It seems like everyone I know thinks the Middle East is so complicated, but it's not really that complicated. It goes like this: about a hundred years ago, the Middle East as we know it today was divided up by the French and British after winning WWI - after wiping out the Ottoman Empire. They then divided the place up like a pie at an eating contest (Sykes-Picot Agreement) and it's looked like it does now ever since. Different ethnic minorities are forced to live partly together, partly divided, strong in one, weak in the other. Some ethnicities, like the Kurds, didn't get a country at all. Their ancestral lands were just divided into quarters, with part in Turkey, Syria, Iran and Iraq.

The goal, it seems to me, was to keep the Middle East unstable and so, easily exploitable. Now, a hundred-plus years later, the fight rages on just as it was planned.

At home (USA), ten years after the second invasion of Iraq in 2003, the very same people who first beat the war drum to invade Iraq were tired of the war, Democrats and Republicans alike. Now, all these years later, we've become weary of the nightly roll call of fallen American heroes somberly listed on the national news. Now we all know, one hundred percent, that there were no weapons of mass destruction and there never had been. This made it difficult for the politicians who watched over the endless sacrifice to get re-elected. Each flag-draped coffin acts as a reminder to us all of how much their lies cost us.

The new political solution to the old "Iraq Problem" is GTFO, regardless of consequence, wishing to absolve this national shame as if it could just be out of sight and so out of mind. A new political administration, the same old political strategy, deflect it onto the "others," and so the new US policy emerged: "End endless wars." This new policy really stands for abandon the ship and let it sink.

What was left behind when America split? A living Hell? Life under ISIS or as they are called by everyone else in the Middle East, "Daesh," which translated means something along the lines of: Fake Muslim, Fraud/Pretender, Suck-Face, Lowlife, Scumbag, Piece of Shit.

It was clear all we had "won" in Iraq was a deep sense of failure. And you know who got to shoulder the load? It wasn't the president who stood on a U.S. Navy ship and declared victory years before we actually lost. No, it was the Iraqi people, the veterans, and most of all the families of the fallen. At last, a commonality shared... all for nothing, and nothing for all. Like used-up condoms, the excitement over, tied in a knot and tossed out, we lay discarded in the dirt lot of our country's turnaround.

Part 9: The Devil of Our Own Design

Knowing everything I knew; I was compelled to action because I could no longer live in my own skin if I didn't take a stand here and now. I made up my mind that I was going to Syria to shoot a documentary on foreign volunteers who were joining the Kurdish militia, the YPG. I didn't know how I would accomplish this, but I knew I was going to go and that was the only thing that fit in my mind from then on.

I needed money to go independent, though. Money, I didn't have, so I pawned my motorcycle to my aunt and uncle for 10K. It wasn't enough, but it was far more than the bike was worth. It's not like I had much of a pay-back plan. "Hey Unk, I am headed to Syria, can I borrow 10K?"

My Uncle Chris was not too enthused, but he said to me, "If it's what you need to do, son. You have always been your own free soul... crazy kid." He paused, and in a serious note he added, "Don't go and get yourself killed, God-damn-it!" He reached out and tussled my hair like I was still twelve years old and begging for a ride on his chopper.

In the coming days and weeks, I thought a lot more than I probably should have about how hard it is for someone like me with no backing, no media connections or network affiliations, to pull any of this off. I was just a man with a medic bag and a camera trying to get to where the war was the worst.

The thing is, usually war makers don't like cameras too close to the killing because they don't want the world to actually see the carnage and real business of war, aka wholesale murder for profit. But that is exactly where I was aiming to go and what I was planning to do. I just hoped I could make something impactful. Something that mattered - that made a difference. But most of all, I hoped I could pull any of it off and not get killed doing it.

I knew everyone said I was crazy to go. But it didn't matter anymore because in my mind it was all set and that was that. I would go or die trying. Life, kids, career, houses, relationships... I pawned them all for an addiction to my guilty conscience.

What hope does one have to make real change in the face of so much madness? Still I had to try. With so many opportunities for failure, I pushed all negative thinking away from my mind and just followed my heart. When I really listened to my heart, it didn't matter if I made 'it' or not because, as I learned before, success is in the doing, not the end result.

When people would try to talk me out of going to Syria, I would just nod vacantly at them saying "yea yea yea" as if I meant it. Anything I said at this point was an excuse, or a rambling line of bullshit, all aimed at propelling me to get where I wanted to go. I actually didn't know what the hell I was doing. But sometimes, it's better to be 'lucky' than smart. I cashed in all my years of frequent flyer miles from production; it was just enough for a one-way ticket to Erbil, Iraq. My life was now a Hail-Mary pass at hope, one longshot of doing something great with the mediocrity that was my life.

As one might expect, there was no fanfare when I departed for Syria, no special lunch or send-off, no crowds, bands or parades.

In the end, it was just me on the curb of LAX watching my daughters speed away, peering out the back window of their mom's red minivan. Left there wondering if I would ever see them again, I hoped their last memory of Daddy was not this moment, as they merged into traffic and disappeared. Standing there on the edge of the world... I turned and stepped off.

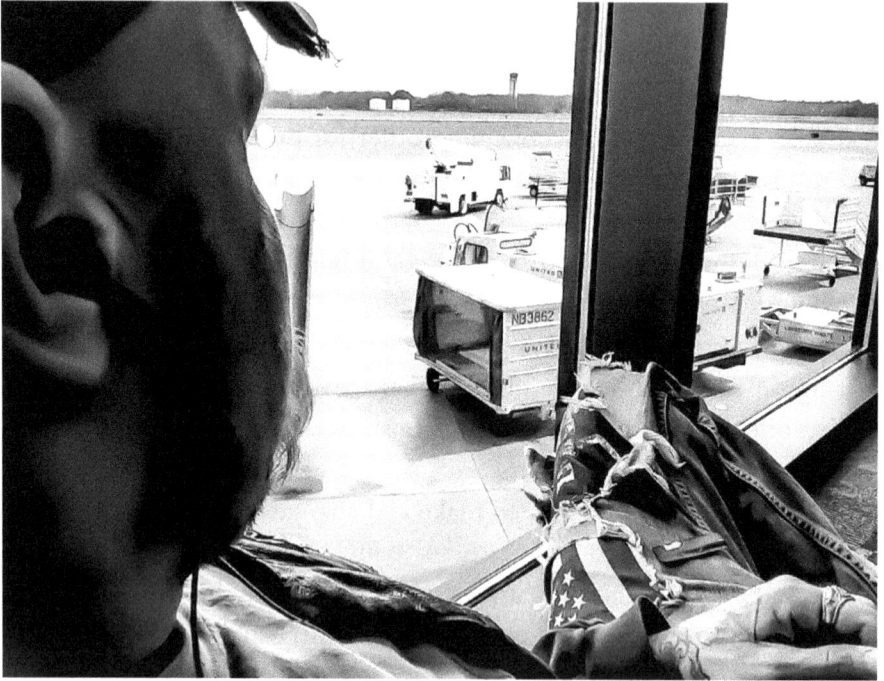

CHAPTER 4: Free Fall

On a jet 45,000 feet high, drinking heavily, the curvature of the earth was ringed in brown, dappled with stratospheric clouds. The sun had already set behind the airplane's twin contrails, the earth was passing below at 540 miles per hour. We hurtled into the waiting darkness.

I pushed the seat back, staring out the small oval window to the fate that awaited me on the rim of the world. I closed my eyes, a fitful, awkward, mouth open, head back, drank too much free booze, plane sleep.

The bump of the landing gear woke me. I felt like there was lint in my mouth and a hammer in my head. The seat belt light dinged off. People all stood at once. The quiet murmur rippling through the plane as they collected carry-ons and shuffled off one by one reminded me that I am eighteen hours in, with twenty-three to go...

I staggered off the plane to the men's room, where I threw up in the last stall, an acidic green foamy bile that burned and tasted like chewing on aluminum foil. Forlorn, shaking, and weak, wiping my mouth clean with a tissue, I muttered, "Fuck it!" I exited the stall and washed my face. The cold water brought temporary relief.

Collecting my thoughts, I looked up at the bleary-eyed stranger looking back at me. I saw death in the room with me. The stranger standing there just stared back at me. I shivered as if a hand brushed my neck. "Screw that!" I said to myself. I shrugged it off and walked out into the flow of people. Some of them were going on vacation, others to work. I could see their excitement, or relief to be escaping the mundane, or the opposite, stressed out businesspeople running, late again, toward an always closing gate.

It seems to me we put up with all this crap in life to get away on vacation for what? Ten days out of a year if we're lucky? The idea of success, "the two-week European vacation." Back at work after your trip, you'll be "the envy of the office!" You know, it seems to me there is a serious dilemma in the morality of the human condition. Our world has never been so small. So, is it OK to go on some fantastic vacation if you fly over a country of starving people to get there? Or what if your resort itself is surrounded by starving people, the private picturesque white sand beaches protected by a three-mile perimeter and 1000 armed guards? Should you have to fly over it to care? Does anyone in the world, a world where so many have so little and so few have so much, care anymore?

I was conflicted between desire and conscience. The surrounding tourists chit-chatted happily while waiting. They have worked hard in life; they deserve a delightful trip! I am such a grouch. Clearly, I am the only one here conflicted by this.

I shook my head at the irony of having made it to beautiful Vienna, hung over in an airport, alone and going somewhere terrifyingly dangerous, somewhere I might never come back from. I gazed out the window at the European countryside. It was surreal to me in some vacant way. I watched it all, trying to memorize normality, knowing that in hours or days this place would seem as unreal as my destination does now.

My hopeless optimism was drawing me nearer to a fate not of my own understanding, but I could feel it pulling me closer by the moment.

I found a wall near my next gate and sank against it, only twenty-two hours left. I didn't have any extra cash but that was OK; where I was going, cash wouldn't matter.

CHAPTER 5: Detained

Flying into Erbil, Iraq, outside my window I could see rugged snowcapped mountains and below them fields of lush farmland that stretched out to meet the city. We were about to land. I heard the whoosh of the plan dropping down and the sound of the landing gear. I felt nervous. I hadn't been here since 2005. I braced myself. The wheels hit the tarmac with a squeal.

Outside, the airport was loud and crowded with people all trying to come and go at the same time. I don't speak Arabic or Kurdish. It was a chaotic rush of traffic and people moving like blood in veins as if beating by an unseen petrol heart. I tried to get to the curbside with all my bags, struggling through the dense crowd.

Just as I hailed a taxi, I heard, "MISTER! MISTER! Wait!" I turned at the English spoken. It was the customs guy who let me through. He was running after me, fighting his way through the throngs of people. I couldn't pretend I didn't see him -- he was looking right at me. My heart skipped. This was not not good. I waved the now impatient cabbie on to someone else. I turned, waiting for the customs guy to get the last ten steps to me.

He was almost out of breath. He said to me, "Yes! Mister! Please, I am sorry, but you need to come back with me."

I took a deep sigh. So close, but so far. "Why, is something the matter here?" I asked.

He said, in a serious tone, "Yes sir, it seems you have some contraband!" My heart was racing. I could see two Iraqi police officers armed with AK47s also making their way toward us. There was no escape. I did my best to look horrified and innocent as I was led back inside by the three, back past the security check line, I had been so happy to clear. Back past the main security checkpoint and in through a frosted glass door, I found myself in a small room with a long metal table bolted to the floor. I waited there, my mouth dry, heart racing. After a time, another man came into the room. He was wearing a suit and tie. I wanted to vomit. In his hand, he had a clipboard and was writing on it.

Looking at me, he smiled, "Mr. Hagg, is it?" Tilting his head, a little to the side, he continued, "Why have you come here to Iraq?" There was a slight squint in his eye. "I see you have lots of... um... military type equipment with you? And this, um, drone? Why do you have such military equipment?" His smile had a dangerous edge to it.

As calmly as I could, I offered my best explanation, saying "I am here to film a documentary on the Peshmerga (the local militia). I brought some stuff as gifts for the commanders and also for personal use. You know, if I am able to make it to the front, that is?"

My dice were rolled and my bet placed "all in" on the game table of life. I had no Peshmerga contacts, and no plans to work with them, either. The Peshmerga did not let foreign volunteers in to fight, and they also had the backing of the Iraqi army: jets, tanks, drones, and thousands of boots. ISIS had almost made it to Baghdad but was at last stopped by an international military coalition. Across the border, the Syrian Kurds had none of those luxuries but were nonetheless still putting up a fierce fight and beating ISIS back. In fact, there was an embargo against northern Syria's Rojava, so the resistance was a homegrown backyard resistance of sorts.

That's why I was going to have to sneak across the border. If the interrogator asked, I wouldn't have any back-up, no Peshmerga contact, no return ticket. I would be screwed because he would know I was lying. I would definitely be detained, maybe even put in jail.

The interrogator smiled at me. "Yes, I have seen your press credentials. They are not very impressive. It looks like you printed them out at home."

I felt like a mouse just cornered by the cat who is playing with his food first, only I was the food and he was the cat. In a slight panic, I opened my photo folder on my cell phone. Saying, "Here, look," I shoved the phone toward him. A nice production still of me with my camera on my last boat. "See, look, I tell you I am here to make a documentary. This is the last show I filmed!" I flipped through some more recent pictures, me holding a camera on set and posing with different famous cast members from rock stars to adventure reality stars.

"See, that's me! I'm telling you the truth!" I was desperate to try to save my ass here with legitimacy, even though legitimacy was the last thing I had. He nodded, smiling at me now.

"OK, I believe you... Hahaha," he laughed a bit of a fake laugh. "I thought you might be Daesh/ISIS trying to sneak into my country to fight, but I see this is not so. But nonetheless, drones are not permitted here. You may keep the rest of your equipment though."

I started to protest, but he looked up sharply at me. "It could go very differently if you wish," he said.

I shook my head, "No sir, I understand."

He smiled at me. "Ahh, very well... Let him go then," he said to the two guards still in the room. Turning, he left smiling, wheeling out my drone case with him. I was fuming, but I was more scared than angry. So, I took his suggestion, and I got the hell out of there before they searched deeper and took more.

CHAPTER 6: The Crime Scene

I hailed a cab at the airport curb again. I was fuming! I had big plans for that drone! I couldn't believe the assholes kept it! I barely noticed the taxi driver as I got in the cab. I don't know if I was madder they took my drone, or happier they let me leave? I only took the taxi a few miles, and I dumped it. I didn't want to be followed.

When I got out of the cab, I drifted aimlessly for a while, just taking it all in. I walked in and out of the streets and alleys through bazaars and past apartment buildings and official buildings.

A very unexpected thing happened then. This deep shame came over me. I had never seen this part of the world except through the porthole of the American military or Orientalist media warp. My chest got tight; my throat constricted a little. I felt completely out of place, but it all felt so familiar. Then it dawned on me: It was like returning to the scene of a crime so many years later. What had my friends died for here? My friends like:

Marine Lance Cpl. Holly Charette, 21
Navy Petty Officer 1st Class Regina Clark, 43
Marine Cpl. Ramona Valdez, 20

Holly, Regina, Ramona

They were almost done with their seven-month deployment and were already making plans of BBQs and reunions back home on their SAT phone, which they let me borrow whenever I wanted. It had been a long hard deployment for them, and I knew they could almost taste home by now. Time was short - they were due to rotate home in three weeks. Just three weeks left. I was on an operation the day they were all killed. A car bomb hit their seven-ton truck as they were coming back to Camp Fallujah in a convoy. The explosion ripped the truck to pieces and fire slowly finished off what the VBID started.

We drove by the tangled wreckage of their seven-ton truck on our way back to Camp Fallujah. I remember being disturbed at the sight of the newly twisted and burned steel skeleton shoved off the side of the road. I felt a deep pain in my heart knowing a scene like this meant more flag-draped coffins were headed stateside to waiting broken hearts.

I didn't put it together until later, when I was back at my trailer, which was just across from theirs. We were at the end of our row of four units. In between our two huts was a small open-ended concrete bomb shelter we shared.

At last, back at the trailer, I knocked to let my friends know I was back in the wire. The door to their trailer swung open slightly. It hadn't been latched. That's weird, maybe they forgot to lock it? "Hello?" I said - there was no response. I peeked inside. It was completely empty and cleaned out. What? No!?... There wasn't a single sign of them ever having lived here. I looked around - a sinking feeling in my heart. There was no trace of them except a small pink carpet they had washed and hung on the clothesline between our two huts outside. I guess that's why the packers didn't take it? The carpet now swung abandoned in the light afternoon breeze, an endless gentle flapping back... and forth...

I didn't have to ask to know what happened. All these years later, I still tear up at the unfairness of it. It stings deeply. But because they were such lovely people, I don't want to leave you here with my last memory of them and that carpet, so I will share with you the second-to-last memory I have with the three of them. It's better to remember them this way.

It was the middle of the night. We got hit by rockets. I didn't always go to the bunker during attacks, but these rockets were hitting pretty dang close to us. The loud shriek and following explosion rocked my little trailer. And then we heard the telltale sound of another rocket as it screamed overhead just before it hit again. Close! Too close! That was all it took to get me up and out to the bomb shelter - I was the last one to the bunker. Regina had little tabs of C-4 that she lit and was currently toasting marshmallows. She laughed at me as I scooted into the bunker and in her sandy voice, she had said to me, "Well, just like a grunt to drop in just in time for chow!"

I laughed and joked back innocently, "Who me?"

Regina just laughed and handed me a S'mores, and then another rocket hit, but it was farther away. In the end, the S'mores tasted a bit like plastic, but what the hell! She was right, I was just in time. It was good for some laughs while Regina, Ramona, Holly, and I waited for the all clear. There had been no casualties that day, so it was easy to laugh.

Today, I am the only one who is alive to remember this moment. Their faces and smiles might be forgotten by time, but not by me or those who still love them.

The sound of loud honking broke me from my thoughts. A truck was turning right and had blocked a driveway; a car was trying to exit. Avoiding the yelling between the two battling drivers, I crossed the busy street, walking in and out of moving cars that didn't stop. I just paused on the dotted white line and crossed one lane at a time, easily stepping through the moving traffic speeding by inches away from me. When I reached the other side of the street, I saw a taxi. I waved at him. He pulled over and waited. Approaching, I leaned down to the open window. "Salam," I said.

He said, speaking English well, "Salam, hello, where may I take you, my friend?" He got out of the cab to help me with my bags.

Giving him my rucksack, I said, "A decent hotel that isn't too expensive, please sir."

He laughed, "You're American?"

"Yes" I said

He smiled "Very good!... I love America! America is a land of opportunities!"

I laughed, looking for a compliment in return. "Yes, this is true my friend, but northern Iraq is also very beautiful."

He popped the trunk open. Smiling, he said, "Kurdistan."

Fitting my bags in tightly, he closed it with authority. I got in the cab. The taxi driver smiled largely at me, saying, "I will take you to a nice hotel. Very good price. Yes?"

I nodded "yes" to him, and we pulled into traffic. I rolled down my window. It was a beautiful day outside indeed. I would be lying if I said I didn't feel distrust, though. There was an enormous price on westerners here. I was worth enough for him to never work again should he sell me out to ISIS. But he was smiling and put music on, loudly singing along. I smiled and let it go. I was here! No turning back now!

I guess the hardest thing about letting go is the enormous amount of trust it takes to just let go. No one is going to hold your hand or lead the way for you as you freefall backward through the infinite blackness of the unknown. The only way to land is all the way through it to the end. If you make it out alive, that is. I wondered if the reporter Chris Foley thought about that before ISIS caught him and ruthlessly chopped his head off. I cringed at the thought of the video and how those fuckers had turned his life into a spectacle of terror. The news cuts the video off just before the hand begins to hack with the dull knife. The act of brutality fulfills every Orientalist fantasy ever instilled in me.

(Orientalism is a book published in 1978 by Edward Said that has been highly influential and controversial in postcolonial studies. In the book, Said effectively redefined the term "Orientalism" to mean a constellation of false assumptions underlying Western attitudes toward the Middle East.)

I pushed it from my mind; it was already too late to turn back. I only had a one-way ticket here and 300 bucks left over to eat with. Make it or fuck!! Because there is no 'else.' There is no fallback plan, no magic way back home. Maybe that makes me stupid. I think it makes me determined.

Waiting at a traffic light, a car, one lane over, rolled down the window. The driver was looking at me, smiling and waving. He yelled to me, "Hello!! Hello!!! My friend!!! Where are you from?"

I waved back at him, and called out, "I am American!"

He got an even bigger smile and now waved with alacrity. "Yes! YES! Ameriki! Welcome." The man was still smiling at me like I was his long-lost best friend. He was my age: late thirties or early forties. "I am from Fallujah. I am terrorist! Welcome to Iraq," he says, grinning.

I was surprised by his response and I yelled back, "No! You're joking?! You're not a terrorist!"

The light changed; the man's car disappeared into traffic. I didn't expect that answer. I thought about this man... was he really one of 'them'? Was he joking? He must have been. Why would he say that? I never felt more conflicted than that moment, seeing my old foe now all these years later. Try as I might, I found no hate for this man in my heart. We, each on opposing sides, represented the yin and yang of our own hate and riotousness, the opposite ideology sold to each side as the ultimate truth.

Outside my window, I kept looking for those I was so angry at before. I kept looking for "Hodgies," but I didn't see them, no matter where I looked. Instead, all I saw were people trying to live just like we all do. I saw people going about their days, going to or from work, school or shopping. I did not see one person worthy of any hate, not even the man who drove by yelling out his window.

It's strange to be back in a place where I once had been so scared. I don't know what I expected returning here all these years later. I hadn't really thought about this part of it when I decided to come back, the shame of it.

My commander in the Navy had told us, "One needs to keep the mission in mind, not the politics!" We blew up a lot of stuff on that deployment. On the list was an apartment building. We blew it up with a smart bomb. I guess it wasn't so smart after all. I saw the footage as it fell from the sky onto the city below. At the time, I had the weird sensation of falling myself as I watched the video, transfixed in fascination and horror. The video was played on a loop five times in a row over the ship's TV system.

On the video, the city turns into a city block, into an apartment building, and then into the roof of a little shack. A man comes running out. The screen goes white. It was supposed to be a SAM missile sight. It was not.

Below is a list of civilian deaths and casualties from my Persian Gulf WESPAC in 1999 and some links to my sources.

28 July 1999: Eight civilians killed and twenty-six injured in northern Iraq.

21 July 1999: Seventeen civilians killed and eighteen injured, near Najaf southern Iraq.

18 July 1999: Fourteen civilians killed in a raid on southern Iraq.

13 May1999: Twelve civilians killed in a residential area in the north of the country.

https://www.historyguy.com/no-fly_zone_war.html:

"Since the beginning of 1999 through August 1999, Allied pilots launched over 1,100 missiles against 359 Iraqi targets. That number equals nearly three times the amount of ordnance used in the four-day Desert Fox strike. Also, the pilots in the Iraq War have flown two-thirds of the number of missions as NATO pilots in the 1999 Kosovo War. By all accounts, Iraqi forces continue to target their radar and fire missiles at Allied warplanes despite the punishment inflicted from the air. The estimated, unofficial cost of this war to U.S. and British taxpayers is around $1 billion per year. As of August 1999, over 200 military planes, 19 naval ships and 22,000 American military personnel are committed to enforcing the "no-fly zones" and to fighting Iraq."

http://news.bbc.co.uk/2/hi/middle_east/1175950.stm

https://www.wsws.org/en/articles/1999/07/iraq-j21.html

CHAPTER 7: The Call

I paid the taxi driver and checked into the hotel. The manager was Kurdish. He gave me a discount because in Iraqi Kurdistan everything is a little negotiable. So instead of $75, it was only $50 a night. I paid for three nights in cash.

The room was simple, a small bed against the wall, a nightstand with an old-style hotel phone on it. I picked it up and dialed a number. An Australian voice answered the other side. "Yea, hello this is Jake, leave a message I'll get right back atchaa… *BEEEPPP.*" I answered, "I am here bro, I need that number for your friend in the YPG - the other guy didn't call back." I gave him my call back number and lay down looking at the phone, trying not to wonder when it would ring. Overhead, the ceiling fan was slowly going around and around. It was hot. I was exhausted; I closed my eyes and waited.

I was passed out. The phone rang. It startled me. The room was dark. What time was it? My wristwatch said 0013. Fumbling for the receiver, I answered the phone groggily, "Hello."

There was a scratchy connection on the other line. It was hard to hear "Y--h i—m- -at-, I -m on --e Sat phone. I c-n't talk lo-g or I will b- -targeted by --e T-rks. I am over here in Rojava now. You got a pencil and paper?"

I nodded through the phone, relieved the connection had at last smoothed out. "Yeah, I am ready," I said, fumbling with the hotel pad in the dark as my friend Jake gave me the digits two at a time in a big hurry

"Listen mate. This guy Erish he's a bit paranoid. Just tell him Aussie Jake gave you the numba and I am here at the academy waiting for you. He took me over last month. OK, mate! He'll know what that means!"

I nodded to the phone. "Yeah, I got it! Thanks Jake, I owe you big time, man!" But the phone was already dead.

Jake was my last hope to get over the border to Syria from Iraq. I looked at the number on the scrap of paper. I put it on the bedstand table like a loaded gun.

In the morning, after I woke up and got over my nausea of self-doubt and fear, I picked up the phone and dialed the number. It rang three times and then a man answered. "Yes, hello. Who is this?" Smiling at the phone because I know it will come out in my voice, I said, "Hi, is Erish there?"

He answered, "Yes, this is Erish. Who is this?"

Still smiling at the phone to ensure my voice reflected my friendliness, I said, "Yeah, this is River. Aussie Jake should have told you I was on the way. He said you would help me get over to the other side. They are waiting at the academy for me."

Erish sounded confused. "Yes, hello? Who is this? River? I don't know a River. Who is this Jake you speak of?"

I wanted to hang up before he says no. I realized I needed to get to the pitch. The first rule when dealing with smugglers is that as soon as they say no, it's a hell of a lot harder to get them to say yes later. So, with that in mind, I said, "Yeah, Aussie Jake gave me your number. You got him across a month ago. I am in Erbil right now, but I can get a cab to Sully and be there by this afternoon. I will call you when I am there. Yes. OK." The second rule of dealing with a smuggler is to use yes and OK in your sentence to get their mind also thinking yes and OK.

I finished up as quickly as I could, saying, "Thank you very much for your help, sir! I have to go now; I will call you again when I am in Sully." He sounded a bit confused, but he hesitantly said, "OK." I hung up.

Six hours later, I arrived in Sulaymaniyah, Iraq. The shared taxi pulled over at its last stop. I was now deep in the heart of the old city. In the beginning of the trip there had been three of us; I was the last one left. The driver said to me, smiling, "This, now stop you." His English was a lot better than my Kurdish. He was eager to return to Erbil - it was a four-hour drive for him. I nodded, smiling, "OK, yes, thank you!" I stepped out of the cab. I was on a busy street on the side of a hill; there were lots of little shops and traffic was congested. The city is a beautiful place surrounded by high snowcapped mountains. The minarets of the various mosques poked out of the city like cat tails. There was an ancient feeling to a place that had been lived in for thousands of years. I got my last bag from the cabbie. He smiled, waved, and walked back to his car. He had a long ride in front of him. He pulled back into traffic and quickly disappeared. Well, it looked like I was staying here either way. I sure hoped this Erish guy would show up. I dragged my bags over by a wall and waited.

There was an icy wind in the air here that made me shudder. I pulled out a parka from my large bag and put it on. I felt small here, standing on the sidewalk alone in a completely different part of the world from anything I've ever known. "No turning back now!" It's not just a saying anymore. There quite literally was no way back for me. Leaning against the wall wondering what the hell I had done; I pushed the consequences of failure from my mind. There was no way to hitchhike home from here, that's for damn sure. I shrugged it off and lit a smoke while I waited. Erish would show because my gut told me he would.

Out of the foot traffic moving up and down the sidewalk, a tall, clean-shaven man with short cropped dark brown hair emerged. He stood looking at me for a moment before he approached me. "River?" the man asked. I crushed out my cigarette. I was instantly on alert, studying the man for any malcontent. Nodding to him, I replied, "Yeah, that's me. Are you Erish?" He nodded and looked me up and down. His eyes stopped on my camera. "What is this?" he asked, pointing at the camera in my hand. I said, "Yeah, I told you I am here to film a documentary on the YPG." I had not told him that.

Erish looked up, suddenly alarmed, "No, no, no! This is not OK. I do not take press! Only YPG volunteers! Only those who will fight! Sorry I cannot help you, my friend!"

My heart dropped out of my chest. This was beyond bad for me. "But," he said, smiling, "If you join YPG for six months to fight, I will take you over the border, but not unless you join to fight and are willing to stay the whole six months!"

My heart panicked - six months! That was way too long. I started to protest to see if I could make a deal - a compromise, "OK. I will join YPG. How about for two months?"

Erish shook his head - he was not in the mood to play games. "No! This will not do my friend, I am sorry, I cannot help you." He turned to go and in a desperate moment of all or nothing...

"OK! Wait! OK! I will join for six months as a volunteer." He stopped and turned around, a big smile on his face.

"Are you sure?" he asked, looking into my eyes. I nodded. I had all this doubt and fear just disappear when I said yes. It was like it was my destiny, as if there was such a thing. But it felt that right and I was suddenly at ease.

"I am sure!" I said with conviction, "I will stay for six months."

He smiled, nodding, "Yes. OK. I believe you. Very good! We have a deal." He stuck out his hand. I shook it in return. Sealing a deal made in more than just words; this deal was made with very life itself.

Erish, now smiling easily, said to me, "Come, I will take you to the safe house. We have a few days to wait before we cross into Rojava." So, it was done. Just that quick... handed over for the grand total cost of nothing. My life had just been given away trustingly to a complete stranger on a street corner in Sulaymaniyah, Iraq... the best decision... I ever made, in my life...

Chapter 8: The Safe House

Around a corner at the end of a narrow street sat a house surrounded by a high concrete wall with broken bottles cemented on the top and a small dirt yard with a detached garage. The house was a faded pink. Inside was cold. In fact, everywhere here was cold. I could see my breath inside the house like I was smoking. Upstairs, down a short hallway, was a corner room with shag green carpet and a well lived-in feel, perhaps because it was warm. Stepping into Erish's office at least felt hospitable. There were posters on the walls with a yellow background and the face of a western volunteer looking down at us. The name under the picture was in Kurdish.

Erish indicated for me to sit in a chair opposite his desk. He asked for my passport and travel documents. I felt strange handing them over to him. It was as if I somehow lost control of something I had always taken for granted. "My passport, my key!" I nonetheless acted without hesitation and produced the requested documents. It was a gesture, it seemed, that was not lost on Erish, who for his part just nodded, smiling, and took them from my outstretched hand.

The scanner/printer had a door missing and was just wired to the wall. There was no outlet receptacle. Erish scanned my passport and from his computer printed a document. When the printer spit the paper out, it was hard to read. The ink was out.

Looking at the paper, he said, "I have some ink to refill the cartridges."

It's a crappy job if you've never done it, but I had, so I offered, "I can help you if you want."

Erish smiled easily at me now. "I can tell you will make a good heval."

I laughed even though at the time I didn't really know what he was saying. We filled the inks. He put them back in the printer. It spit out its pattern print page. Taking it, he seemed pleased. Turning back to his computer, he hit print again, and it produced a page. Taking it, he put it on the desk in front of me, and then handed me a pen. It was a half-page enlistment form in English and Arabic or Kurdish. It was very simple and short. It stated I would stay for six months, follow my orders, and the YPG rules/protocols. At the bottom was a miniature scan of my passport photo page.

"You must sign it," is all Erish said.

I took the pen and signed the document. I joined the YPG officially. There was no swearing-in ceremony, like when I graduated from boot camp for the Navy, no march, parade or band. Erish just smiled, nodded, took the paper, and placed it in a manila folder and put it in a large filing cabinet against the wall.

Outside his office, it seemed even colder than it had been before. He led me downstairs, showed me the kitchen and bathroom, down another hallway to the front room. Opening the door inside, there were two hardened looking soldiers sitting against the side wall. Both looked to be in their late forties or early fifties. One was stocky with a giant mustache and the other was tall and wiry with a chiseled face and salt and pepper hair. They both looked like there were dropped right out of a WWII movie. They were going over gear, marking each item off on a checklist. The two stood as we entered the room.

Erish introduced us. "This is Fred and Cheenook, this is River." They smiled at me.

I smiled back and said, "Hi."

Erish continued, "They're French, they don't speak English, but this is no problem we teach you Kurdish at the academy, so it will be fine." They both stood up. The tall, lean Frenchman, Cheenook, nodded at me, smiling. But then he immediately spoke - demanding - sounding French. Erish, just shrugged and didn't appear to understand.

Erich said, "I will be back late. But be ready to go anyway because we will leave any night now."

The Frenchman, Cheenook, looked at Erish angrily and muttered something in French that sounded a lot like "bullshit!" But Erish had already turned and gone. It was just me and my two new friends.

Fred had one of the warmest smiles you've ever seen as he eyed me up and down, slightly nodding at me.

"Bonjour," I said, smiling, and shook both of their hands.

Cheenook smiled, "Bienvenue! Ravi de faire votre connaissance!" I smiled and shrugged. I had no clue what he just said.

I made my way to the back wall and set down my packs. They watched and tried to talk to me in French. I don't speak French and they don't speak English. It must have looked comical as we tried to carry on a conversation using a universal language of grunting and gestures. It worked enough, though. From our conversational attempts, I understood Fred and Cheenook had both been with the Peshmerga but had left after a month because they would not be sent in to fight ISIS. They were extremely upset about the Paris attacks and both of them were former French Legionaries. That's about the most I could gather from them.

I showed them a few pictures of me filming in Afghanistan, my kids, and a few photos of the rocket fish. They both were impressed with the giant pelagic in the picture next to me. It might have been awkward with two different kinds of people, but the two of them were easy to get along with. I showed them my Unit One Pack. Cheenook was excited and opened his large sea bag. It was stuffed full of medical supplies. He started firing away in French again. I just laughed and shrugged at him, not understanding a word, but definitely impressed with his assortment of hemorrhage control and airway management supplies.

Introductions over, I unpacked my bed roll, which was an inflatable backpack style air pad and an ultra-light sleeping bag, REI's finest. I kept my jacket on and took out a battery to charge my heated long johns. There was something amiss in the cold house, which felt abandoned despite our presence.

I had a lot on my mind; I wanted privacy, so I lay down, tipped my hat over my face, and felt happy for the warmth of my bedroll.

The two French men seemed nice. I was glad for the company. I wished they spoke English, or I spoke French. Well, whatever the differences, there was a commonality that reached across the spans of cultural divide. We now shared the same lot on this crossroads of choice, our fates intertwined.

Sometime later, I heard a door close and the floor squeak. I tilted my hat up to look. As I did, the door to our room opened slowly. There was a large figure entering our room. I sat up. He looked over sharply at the unexpected movement.

Seeing me, he smiled and said, "Oh! Hey, I didn't see you there. I'm Albert." He walked over toward me, sticking out his hand. I was happy to hear American English. There was something so familiar about his Midwest accent, just the sound of it brought a smile to me.

Getting to my feet, "I'm River Rainbow," I said, sticking out my hand.

Albert smiled, "Cool name!" he said, shaking my hand in his bear paw of a hand.

I smiled, "Thanks, you know that was Mom's doing though, bless her heart."

Albert laughed, "OK Sue, how do you dooo?!" Then we both laughed because Albert was funny and there was no better ice breaker than laughing together.

The two Frenchmen stayed outside for a few hours. Albert and I talked in depth. He was from Cleveland, Ohio. A former Marine, he was working as a cook when he was home. He was like a lot of us vets; he was pissed that the troops had all been pulled out of Iraq and ISIS was born in the vacuum left behind. Albert had a lot of friends' back home who supported his decision to come over here, so he felt like he was representing Cleveland, Ohio, but his sister wasn't a fan of the decision. Albert said he didn't blame his sister for not liking it. They were all they had, but she was a grown-up and he had to do what he had to do. This was his second trip to Rojava.

It made me feel so much better to have an experienced person to break down what I would expect as a volunteer. And even though I had only been away from home a short while, being in such a foreign environment, I was grateful to have Big Al tell me so many things about Rojava and the YPG (male) and YPJ (female) Peoples Protection Units. He explained things like I would get a name when I crossed over. His Kurdish name was Cekdar Rojava. He told me about the academy all foreign volunteers had to attend, which did not sound at all appealing to me. And most importantly, he talked to me about the Kurdish culture so I would not offend anyone by accident. When he was finished, he slapped me on the arm and said, "SerChava, Haval (nothing in my eye, comrade)." I laughed and tried to repeat it.

The two Frenchmen came back inside. Albert stood up and said, "Hevals, let's go get something to eat!" He was motioning with his hand to his face in the universal gesture for eating. Fred got an enormous smile and said something in French that I could only guess at but by the way his eyes sparkled, I figured he was all in. I expected us to cook our own food in the cold kitchen, but we didn't. Rather, Albert just opened the door, walked through the courtyard, and stepped out through the big black gate onto the street. Oh snap! That was cool. I didn't know we could just walk around. I had kind of thought of it like I was imprisoned in the safe house. Outside in the street, the smells of dinners cooking wafted by us and I was suddenly starving. Walking down the street with my three new hevals, we went into a little store. Albert picked out the dishes, and we all split the total. We ended up spending three days at the safe house. We explored the city. I found a place to buy some beers so we would walk down through the ancient bazaar with beer cups like two tourists on vacation. What an ancient city Sulaymaniyah is, too, surrounded by snowcapped mountains and filled with colorful people. But we weren't meant to stay here - so two nights later at 0100, Erish came in, waking us. "OK, now is time to go."

I sat up, instantly excited. Erish had all our passports in his hand. Opening the door, he walked out, and we could hear a car start. He came back in. I was hastily stuffing my bed roll back in my bag.

"If there is a problem, let Hossan do the talking. He will be the one taking you from here. Good luck!" is all Erish said as he handed each of us back our passports and me my camera. I shouldered up my bags, and we walked out through the gate into the night.

The ride was tense and very, very uncomfortable, with all of us shoved into the compact car and all our gear smashed into the trunk and/or riding on our laps. We were leaning slightly to the side to fit us all. It was awful. I needed to pee... fucking beer! One does not realize how long one can hold a pee until a time like this. The throbbing agony, tempting to squeak out one drip at a time. I was shaking, almost crying, by the time we stopped for a head break. I ran/walked to the bathroom, trying not to piss myself. It was the best pee I ever took in my life. I peed for the whole pee break and everyone was already back in the car when I returned. Albert laughed at me about it, but other than that, there was no talking. I put my head against the window and slept. I was jolted awake when the car stopped, and then we got in a new car with two Peshmerga fighters.

Hossan said, "These men will take you from here. Good luck hevals! Serkiftin!" He kissed us each on the cheeks and then left.

The other two men were nervous. It made me nervous. They had three uniforms but not a fourth, so they put Cheenook in the trunk. The rest of us changed into Peshmerga uniforms (Iraqi Kurdish militia, not friends of the YPG). I got in the SUV. The man in the passenger seat turned to us. "Say nothing at the checkpoint, just smile and wave when we wave. Good?"

"Yes?" We all agreed.

Albert was happy. "Last time I had to swim a damn river and climb a mountain! This is sweet!"

The French man Fred laughed happily, saying something in French. There was a muffled cheer from Cheenook in the trunk, and I laughed.

An hour later, we drove up to the final checkpoint. The border guard put up his hand for us to stop. He spoke rapidly to the driver and the passenger, who replied easily and sat back nonchalantly. The border guard stepped back, his hand on his AK. Using his other hand, keying his radio, he called us in. The driver and front passenger looked nervously at each other. My heart raced. If we were stopped here, we would definitely be sent to Iraqi prison. Also, being dressed as a Peshmerga might make them label us as spies. They would hang us for sure. I hadn't considered this before now. My lip began to sweat. The check point guard looked at me. I smiled and made a little wave gesture. He smiled and did the same. Then his radio crackled. He listened briefly, nodding, and then waved us through.

Postscript note* The next trip across the border a few weeks later the two Peshmerga smugglers were arrested with everyone in the car. The border was sealed shut for months afterwards. Sadly, Albert and Fred both fell sehid (killed in action) in the battle against ISIS.

Albert and me, in the safe house.

Albert A. Harrington KIA Rojava Syria, 25 January 2017 USA

Fred Demoncheaux KIA Rojava Syria, 7th September 2017 FR

Dressed as Peshmerga (Iraqi Kurdish militia) as we were smuggled across the Iraqi border. Left to right, Albert A Harrington, Fred Demoncheaux and myself.

CHAPTER 9: Hitchhike to a Gunfight

I felt like I had been spun in circles, blindfolded, and kicked out of a plane backward. I was at a YPG/YPJ base called Chalak Nocta (The Cow Base). I had only been in Rojava three days now and to say I was in a little bit of culture shock would be putting it mildly.

I had not stayed at the academy for foreign volunteers more than a few hours. After I had been named, they immediately assigned me to the new combat medic team that some of the other volunteers had just started; we left that night.

The Calak Nocta (Cow Base) was just outside of a town called Til Tamer. It was named the 'Cow Base' because before the war it had been a massive dairy farm with over 600 cows. The concrete structures of the dairy had been heavily fought over and battle scars were everywhere, but in the end, Til Tamer had been where Daesh/ISIS's advance was stopped.

I was in a long hall that used to be a concrete barn. It wasn't a barn anymore, though. There were fourteen men in it, eating quietly at a long table in the middle of the room. Guns and rocket launchers were neatly stacked against one wall. A tension hung in the air like an unspoken secret.

The leader, Servan, stood up, saying, "OK, listen up, men. We are moving out tonight at 0100. The assault on Shaddadi is beginning and we are the tip of the spear."

There was a shuffling in the room and an added zing - a murmur shifted around, heard but not. My heart took two extra beats... Servan spoke again after pausing briefly for it to settle in. "The medics stay here. They haven't trained with us and we can't take any extra bodies."

There was another murmur of agreement and one or two dissatisfied grumbles. My heart sank. "Well FUCK HIM!" I thought angrily. The big Kiwi, Dil Sauz, saw me looking pissed. He quietly nodded his head side to side as if to say, "stand down." So, I just looked down and finished my chicken, eggplant and rice.

After dinner, the small taboor (platoon) prepared for battle. AKs, RPGs, heavy machine guns, sniper rifles, grenades, bandoleers of bullets, land mines and baby wipes were all packed into the backs of the two waiting trucks.

I watched it all sulkily. The tension in the air was alive with excitement for them, but I was fuming at being left behind. Whether or not we had just arrived at the unit, it was all bullshit. I mean, who leaves behind the medics? FUCKER!

As 0100 came and the taboor left in their two trucks, the three of us medics were left standing outside, watching the brake lights glow fainter as they drove away.

Chalak, without looking away, said, "Godspeed brothers."

Dil Sauz, patting the much shorter man on the back, said, "Don't worry mate, ol' Dils' got a plan."

I smiled at the new hope. Dil Sauz was an ex Kiwi/British special forces operator. His broken nose and 6'8" stature told of surviving more than one scrape with death. So, when he said he had a plan, I believed him.

Chalak laughed at that. He had an easy laugh. It reminded me of fried chicken and waffles. "I bet you do, big guy. I bet you do," he said.

The next morning at the motor pool, all geared up, Chalak and I waited off to the side while Dil talked to different drivers. I could easily see that they were all struggling to understand Dil's Kurdish and strange request, something about doctor soldiers and fighting. I began to lose hope, but then Dil seemed to find someone who would help. I watched him talking and nodding, then pointing, more nodding, and Dil waved for Chalak and me to come over. Dil talked to the driver and pointed. I could hear him say British! Amerki! doctor. heaya, tamam, Shaddadi embichim. (We are soldier doctors, take us to the battle of Shaddadi). I am pretty sure that's all the driver understood too, because soon enough, he pulled up and motioned for us to get in the back. I climbed in the flatbed excitedly.

Dil Saus gets us a ride

*Dil Sauz, Chalak and me in the back
of the flatbed on our way to the gunfight.*

CHAPTER 10: No Friends but the Mountains

In the beginning, the YPG command didn't understand what we were talking about. "Medics were not needed on the front," we were told. To the YPG, doctors were far too rare and valuable to be anywhere near the fighting. There really wasn't a word in Kurdish for combat medic, so we used the term "Askir Doctor/Soldier Doctor," which created a lot of confusion at first; the situation was very much confounded by our own inability to communicate in Kurdish.

The YPG/YPJ did not start out as an advanced military force, but rather a home-grown resistance, born of the very need for survival. One could not, at that point, compare YPG/YPJ to a trained and equipped military, because it was composed of entirely civilian volunteers who took up arms to defend themselves, their families, their homes.

Before the civil war, these partisans were herders, farmers, and tire changers, but not by choice. They were confined by the Asaad regime's systematic oppression of ethnic minorities. The Kurds here were forced into the lower ranks of society and held there; Kurdish residents were denied basic citizenship, even in their own ethnic homelands. Kurds in Syria could not have passports, drivers' licenses, and could not teach in their own language. That is…. until the Arab spring happened.

Still, I couldn't really get my head around the lack of support for a combat medical unit here... I thought once we explained it to the commanders, that would be that, but it was not.

Sehid culture at first made little sense to me. But the longer I stayed in Rojava, the more I understood it.

Think about it. In battle, when medics and doctors are not available, you are probably going to die if you get wounded. It's not debatable, it's a fact. And when there is no choice but to fight, what do you tell those who willingly walk into death's way? There is only one thing to say to these heroes, "Martyrs never die! Martyrs live forever. Sehid Namirin."

Talk about a rock and a hard place. What happens if you're seriously wounded and by some miracle you survive losing a foot, leg or arm? Once recovered, there is no societal support for wounded warriors like at home in the United States. There is no VA or Social Security Disability to take care of you. You are returned home broken and shattered, not a hero but a burden; so, in this way it was not sehid by choice, but by the lack of it.

CHAPTER 11: The Battle for Shadaddi

The solitary truck clawed its way over the eroded mountain dirt road. Holding my AK47 with one hand, the other hand bracing myself against the jarring, it was a rough ride as the tires met potholes on the tattered road.

Looking out across a cavernous valley dotted with sheep in the distance, one would never know that war was raging here. It was strange that this beautiful valley would know such hate as war. The violence of murder did not seem to fit in this place, with the gentle slopes of green, dotted with wildflowers. But war had touched here. The crater in the road acted as a testament to all who saw it; even in this tranquil place, the soil knew the taste of blood and gunpowder.

I felt small compared to the towering mountains above us. Huddled against the chill, I peered out from under the brim of my cap and took it all in. Our truck's engine complained as it clawed its way up a particularly steep grade and through a narrow crevasse between two scraggy peaks. As we went through the pass, the truck swerved hard to the left and then right, winding its way past large chalk marks in the road indicating active land mines. Every once in a while, we passed deep craters in the road, or just off the side of it, denoting either an air strike or a missed chalk mark.

"Glad it's not raining," I thought wryly to myself... wondering if Sabotage (the mine crew) would come back and clear it here before it did rain.

Yanking hard to the left, the truck swerved around another giant pit in the road. I eased to the right some to make my bullet-proof vest more tolerable. Damn thing hurt; I was still not used to wearing it. I knew in a few weeks it would feel like a second skin, but right now I was still breaking my body into it, like a new pair of boots. Only I was the boot, not the foot.

At long last, our ride came to a dusty halt in the single-track road. We were in a small valley backed up to the high mountains. Short grass like carpet stretched away and up the foothill in front of us. This hill was now all that stood between us and the violence awaiting below.

I had a headache. My wrist hurt from propping myself up for so long. I had to pee, and it was cold. The excitement had worn off by half past now. But upon stopping, my heart beat faster and I again could feel the weight of my AK in my hand. Waiting for instruction, I looked over at the other two in the back of the truck with me, Dil Sauz and Calak. They looked at ease, but alert.

The driver appeared around the side and in Kurdish said, "The commander is there." He pointed at the ridge line. A single dirt track led up and stopped just below the crest line. A truck was parked there, and some soldiers were near it.

Dil nodded and started to get up. "This is our stop," he said. I climbed off the back of the flatbed truck and Calak helped me drag my bags over the side. I helped him get his. Dil dragged his own bag out.

I was struggling just to get up, like someone doing a deadlift at the Olympics... just a fraction of a pound shy of failure. My kit must have looked a bit like someone stacked the dishes too high. "Whatever." One, two, I rolled over onto my hands and knees. Trying to get to my feet, like some kind of Frankenstein, I jerked left... right... and then I got a leg under me. The leg didn't buckle. "Hell yeah!" Each time was a bastard, but whatever.

Once up, I was functional. Everything in my bag was mission critical. I could feel the eyes of curious hevals on me, but that didn't matter at the moment. What mattered was the hill in between us and permission. "Welcome to Rojava," I muttered to myself as we climbed the hill toward the top and the commander.

Dil indicated for us to drop our rucks at the base of one of the little pine trees. I flopped my two bags down, getting a bit stuck between my AK strap and my camera strap. It probably looked rather comical, but I wiggled free. My cheeks burned a little red and not just from the heavy load I was carrying.

All around us, the curious eyes of the hevals watched us closely. They were whispering to themselves, some of them laughing. It was not threatening, but more like we were exotic pets brought to school for show and tell. I felt very self-conscious at the attention, but I was determined not to show it. Grabbing our rifles, we headed out.

As we climbed the hill, the hevals I passed were, for the most part, a hard-looking bunch. They carried their weapons low and with ease. Each was loaded down with ammunition, bandoleers crisscrossed and draped with grenades. They were of all ages, young and old, male and female, because age and gender aren't disqualifiers here.

The kid soldiers stuck with me the most. They looked like any kid back home in the USA, but their youthful innocent faces, once full of excitement, now hid behind war-hardened eyes with little joy in them. These were the eyes of combat veterans, not kids. Here, instead of prom dresses and tuxedos, the youth were adorned with AK47s, rocket launchers and 1,000-yard stares… A hevala jin (female fighters of the YPJ) with a heavy machine gun, not more than five foot one, walked by going down the hill. She was smiling and gave a friendly wave to us. I waved back and flashed my best smile.

We kept trudging up the now seemingly endless hill. The pine trees had fluffy branches that reminded me of the tail of a mad cat. The trees smelled like the ponderosa back home in the High Sierras, especially when the smell of campfire mixed in. I took a deep breath, savoring it like one smells wine perhaps… but despite the familiar smell… it didn't feel like home. Home what a strange word… "Home," I tried it in my mind again, as if saying it out loud would jinx it… I thought about my girls; I hoped they were safe… I hoped they would never have to be gathered below the pines just below Mt Shasta, or outside of Sacramento, California, preparing to storm over the top and take on Daesh bullet for bullet.

It was so cool to see Muslims, Christians, Yazidi, Jews, Alwite, Atheists, men, women, young, old and foreign volunteers from all different corners of the world. All of us stood here together, all of us willing to lay down our lives for each other on this day in the name of liberty and freedom. All of us waited for the same thing… orders to attack the slave trading, head chopping fascists. We might not have had the best gear, guns or uniforms, an old AK from 1973, Chinese grenades from who knows where or when, but there was pride in this group, a pride only those who selflessly defend others know.

The three of us started to climb in earnest. Each step acted as a reminder that I had perhaps skipped one too many "leg days" at the gym…

Dil led the way through the trees. On the other side of them we climbed the rising hill toward the truck parked just below the ridgeline. As we approached, I could see there were two men and a woman. They stood and greeted us. The three had all been sitting, drawing in the dirt with a stick, when we approached. Dropping our packs, Dil, our de facto leader, stepped forward to explain our situation.

"DemBas (good day)," Dil said to someone we assumed was the commander - the man with the drawing stick in his hand. Dil was ignoring the woman completely.

The man greeted us in return. "DemBas," he said. But I happened to look over at the woman and I saw a hard look in her eye as she looked at Dil Sauz, who still hadn't acknowledged her. I just faded back a little. The YPJ woman now motioned for us to please sit. The other heval offered us chai from a small burner and tea pot near the front of the truck. I sat the furthest from the conversation, but happily accepted the cup of hot steaming chai when it was presented to me. Dil tried to explain to the man what we were doing.

He said, motioning to us, "We're combat medics, we want to advance with your troops and provide medical care."

Dil could see the English wasn't working, so switched to Kurdish, but he was having a hard time explaining what we wanted or who we were. None of our Kurdish was worth a shit, but mine was the worst, being the newest. The dude just looked at us skeptically, not understanding, shaking his head. What I gathered he said was, "If we were doctors, we needed to return to the hospital. Doctors did not belong on the front; it was much too dangerous."

None of us realized that the woman was the one really in command here; she let her lieutenant commander talk to us because that's who we wrongly assumed was the commander.

There were so many differences in Rojava culturally, including that women played an equal role in all aspects of life. This commander was not only the YPJ force leader but all YPG and SDF's leader for this phase of the operation.. It was no wonder she looked at us so skeptically. Dil didn't know or assume she was the commander, nor did I, but she was.

It's sad to say, but in America and the west in general, most girls are taught to play with dolls, have long hair, paint their nails, and use beauty products daily to look beautiful as a product of desire. Girls where I am from are not taught to be military leaders or commandos. Really, even though we 'think' we come from countries (USA/ UK/ EU etc.) that have "women's rights," when you are in a country that really does have women's rights and the equality that goes with it, then let me tell you it's a big difference. Even though I would have never thought that I was sexist, it was moments like this that changed how I saw the world/myself and realized just how fucked up I was. How fucked up most of us are... we should have included the woman, but we did not.

The man scoffed a little, pointing up and down at all our equipment and *TISK*ed three times. Without a translator, communication became a cross between sign language and charades. Dil did not give up instantly. He tapped his AK47 and then opened his IFAK. He showed a compression bandage from his bag saying, "soldier and doctor." Pointing toward the valley below and the advancing front, he said, "We need to go to the front, that's where we do our jobs." Dil was starting to get frustrated. I was sure the commanders knew what he was saying, but the man just kept insisting that we needed to go back to the hospital if we were doctors.

The conversation did not really seem to be going in the direction we wanted. I sipped my chai, feeling a little disconnected and still in culture shock. Why didn't they understand that we are a combat medic squad? What a strange world.

The man shook his head again, saying, "tisk tisk tisk." Then, out of nowhere, the air overhead shrieked... like a train suddenly skidding down the metal tracks, brakes locked up. It didn't end with a good sound either. It was a sound I knew all too well, a sound that was both exciting and terrifying.

SSSKKEEEEWW KAAA-BLAM! Soldiers below began scrambling for the cover of trees, as the air overhead screeched again, and another round came in, and then another. "Mortars!" Nothing about that sound is good. But then no attack came. Looking down the ridgeline, I saw nothing but a gentle slope dropping away from view. Behind us, three harmless, new smoking holes were scratched in the mountain's side. There were no casualties, just three new craters for some future traveler to wonder about.

Far below on the valley floor lay the village we would assault soon, but there was no sign of Daesh, just the sweet golden grass blowing gently in the wind. The idyllic day gave no indication of its sinister intent...

The mortars Daesh sent were to let us know: Daesh knows we are here, and they are waiting for us...

I called over to Dil and Chalak, who were also looking down range, but to my left, "You guys see anything?"

Dil answered, "Nah mate, we're fine." I rose from my knee and turned to see the commotion had started - into the trucks, gear and fighters quickly loaded. The forward observing element was being pulled back out of mortar range.

Dil was irritated and drawled out in his Kiwi accent, "Three little mortar rounds and they all get scared 'n run off!" He was looking around, shaking his head disgusted. Dil had a very dangerous temper.

Chalak just shook his head and also looked disgusted, exclaiming, "They don't even know what a combat medic is, man did you see the look on that asshole's face! Fuck!"

Another random mortar round came sailing overhead. We ignored it as it exploded against the hill and walked back to the truck, tasting defeat. The endless waiting... stupid fucking mortars. Again, we were being held back from where we needed to be, which was down in it - doing our jobs, patching holes and saving souls. Sometimes it felt like trying to get anywhere here was like trying to swim in quicksand.

Our flatbed truck, as if by magic, reappeared, going back the other way. The driver pulled over, smiling at us and motioning for us to get back in. "Ahh shit! The wrong way!" Chalak grumbled as we climbed back in and were taken to the rear about two klicks back. He left us on the side of the road in a big dirt parking lot. It was late in the day by now. The troops here were mostly local Syrian Democratic Fighters (SDF). It was a rear staging area of sorts. The SDF were very intrigued by us and we took lots of photos with them.

While we waited, I taught an impromptu class on battlefield tourniquets. About thirty SDF fighters attended. It was actually a lot of fun. But the fucking waiting sucked. We watched as the hevals left behind the fires they had been gathered around. They climbed onto Toyota 4x4 pickup trucks, up to twelve per truck, so many fighters on one I could barely distinguish the shape of the truck... only the front was not being clung onto. They headed down the road and into the darkness as the headlights wound away. I was angry. This was bullshit. Sitting in the dirt waiting.

Sometime later, the sound of automatic gunfire lifted up to us from the valley below, miles away. I kicked a rock out of the ground where I was going to sleep. There was just another one under it. A fresh wave of trucks arrived. Hevals spilled out of the trucks and rekindled the fires, making chai. Dil set out with Chalak to secure us a ride forward. I stayed with the gear, which was fine for me. Dil didn't find us a ride and after a time he and Chalak came back.

Then that night we slept in the dirt just off the side of the road. It was bitterly cold. I lay in my little sleeping bag on my blowup air mattress. I burrowed as deep as I could into my light bag, my breath making steam rise like cigar smoke.

The other two were really not happy about their predicament, i.e., no blanket, no ground pad. We had all been told that when we advanced, we would sleep in the abandoned houses and there were always blankets and sleeping pads. Now Dil, the big spoon, and Chalak, the little spoon, found some cardboard and made a ground cover. They used a box like a blanket, laughing and joking about who was going to be what spoon. Soon I was rolling with laughter at our predicament. We all lay there in the dirt, under the stars, on the side of the road in northern Syria, trying to hitchhike our way to a gunfight.

At some point in the night, one of the hevals, seeing Dil and Calak shivering together, laid a blanket over them and then another. We never saw who did it, but that was the way with YPG/SDF - sometimes they gave and sometimes they took. It was based more on community than anything I had ever experienced.

At the end of the night, who knows when, but later than late, I heard something, but I didn't know what. Sitting up, looking out into the predawn blackness, in the far distance, flickering through the mountain pass, a slow-going glow blinked on and then off and then the lights zoomed up near us and a commotion began.

Ambulance lights flicked on. What the? An ambulance?! I was confused. Dil and Chalak rose, grabbing their medic bags.

Hevals in bloody rags illuminated in headlights wrapped with bandages consisting of usually just a scarf or none at all appeared. Another ambulance showed up out of the night like a red and blue blinking unicorn. It was unreal. But what was really disturbing was the lack of any medical support in the back of the ambulances. The doctor in white and green scrubs in the back of the ambulance... turns out wasn't a doctor, wasn't a paramedic, wasn't an EMT. He was just a kind soul who rode in the back so the hevals could get water and not die alone.

I've never seen so many injured squeezed into one vehicle - loaded like sticks of wood into the back of the ambulance. There was nothing on the inside of the ambulances to make them medical transports: no blood pressure machine, no oxygen, no gurney, no defibrillator, no CPR mask, no gloves, most of all no medic, just a driver and the water giver.

Dil stepped forward, pushing past a crowd of hevals as their friends were loaded one by one. He told them, "Here you go, man. I am a medic. Let me attend to these casualties here in the back." But the driver just snapped at him, and I couldn't understand him. The others gently pushed Dil out of the way, slammed the door shut and the ambulance sped off.

Chalak frustratedly exclaimed, "What the actual FUCK?!"

I spoke up then, saying, "Did you see the back of that bus didn't even have a medic? What the hell?"

Chalak looked up and said, "My man Firat! He will help us. He speaks Kurdish, Arabic, Swedish and English. He is the man! We have to get him into our unit!"

Dil nodded, frustrated, "Fair enough mate, but not till after this operation, because who knows where he is now." Chalak nodded in agreement, turning to walk back toward our now all too familiar dirt patch.

Dil said, "OK for now. I say first light we go stand on the road with our thumbs out! Fuck this sleeping here shit! Someone will pick us up! Deal?" There was a mutual consensus among us.

We headed back to salvage what was left of the frigid night's sleep. Back in my bag, it started to warm up, but not enough. It was just too cold. Shaking slightly, I curled on my side and realized I had to piss. Fuck, it's always something... oh well, not getting up now, I'll hold it. I didn't want to be wandering around here at night near a bunch of untrained soldiers hopped up on Tiger energy drinks, armed with automatic rifles and itchy trigger fingers.

It's so much easier to only remember the glory of battle... to forget the shitty moments. War stories are always retold from the living to the surviving, the returned, and the never left, because the dead tell no tales. Someday, if we survive, we will re-tell stories, remember our fallen comrades and say stuff like, 'Sehid Namirin' or 'Rest in Power.' We remember lots of things, but not sleeping in the dirt, cold as fuck, waiting, and waiting for who knows how long. The tedium, monotony, and bullshit are the normal, not the other way around.

In the morning, with the cusp of the rising sun, Chalak walked down to the road. He stuck his thumb out and so began day two of the battle for Shaddadi. I sat there and watched him as the trucks coming through the high mountain pass would slow and stop next to him. Chalak would poke his head in the window, talk to the driver, and inevitably the truck would pull away again.

As the sun climbed in the sky past mid-morning, the SDF fighters brought back a dead ISIS fighter. By one foot, they dragged his lifeless body out of the back of the pickup truck he had caught his last ride in, allowing his body to fall with a loud thud onto the dirt and gravel. About thirty SDF fighters gathered around the lifeless form lying there. I looked at the dead man in his twenties. He had a scraggy beard, pasty skin, and blood in his teeth. His eyes were full of blood, so he was staring up at nothing that mattered to any of us. There was a celebration by some of those who had not already seen the true face of war, but there was also shock in the faces of some of them, as if perhaps looking down at their own selves dead on the ground. Indeed, many of our number would not live to see out the year.

There is a truth in war, that binds together all who participate in it.

Group of SDF

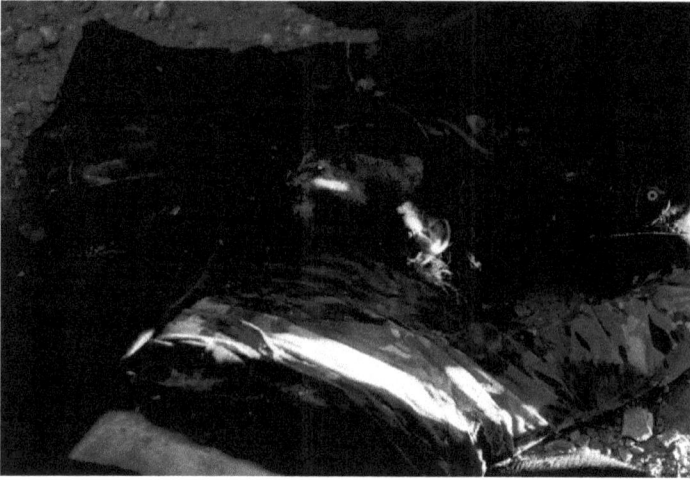

Dead ISIS fighter

I climbed a small rise and looked down at the valley below. There were plumes of black smoke rising like tendrils from the devil's hand. There were tire fires lit on purpose to mark the advancing front.

I felt despondent, as if we would never get a ride, but then I heard a commotion from down by the road. When I looked, I saw Chalak standing by a stopped truck. He was waving at me and Dil to come quickly.

Chalak had found us a ride to the fight. My heart raced with renewed excitement. It was a small taboor, and it only consisted of two pickup trucks. I didn't know who was sitting in the back seat, but they moved, and I was told to get in the truck, my AK propped out of the window.

My AK as we get a ride.

It felt so good, finally getting out of here!!! I thought for sure as eleven o'clock approached that we would spend another long cold night in the dirt, while the fight progressed further and further away from us. Ironically, what all normal people want to do with the war is get as far away from it as possible, as quickly as possible. We wanted the exact opposite and now was, at last, our chance. Maybe there was something wrong with us.

The driver shoved the truck into first gear and started down the mountain. Turning to me, he started talking to me in Arabic. He had a big smile on his face. I don't really know what he said - he spoke really fast… I just nodded and smiled and said what I always say, "Biji Rojava."

He laughed and repeated it with alacrity, "Biji Biji Rojava!!" and then turned on the radio. A YPG battle song started blasting on the truck speakers.

All the hevals clung to the back of the truck like ants on a cookie and started singing along and banging the roof in unison. I cracked the biggest smile on my face. We drove down the dirt road and then climbed onto the highway, gazing out as we passed little town after little town. Sometimes a town was not more than three or four buildings, but almost all of them were occupied by our forces… civilians just liberated were dancing in the streets cheering us on. I guessed we had climbed onto a truck that was headed to the tip of the spear. I asked Dil, "So how do they know when they've gone far enough?"

Still laughing, shaking his head, he cheerfully replied, "When bullet holes appear in the windows, mate! Welcome to YPG!"

We were joined by two other vehicles at a checkpoint. When we stopped, the hevals were excited. They were talking rapidly as they discussed the assault plans for the position we were supposed to take. I could feel the expectation building. I felt kind of trapped in the back seat.

I spoke up, saying, "Hey Dil, I think I'm gonna let one of those guys in the back trade with me." Dil shook his head, replying, "Suit yourself mate." I opened the door and climbed out. I went around to the back of the truck. The hevals all enthusiastically greeted me. I climbed up onto the tailgate of the truck and said, "Please, let another heval ride in the truck for a while."

This gesture seemed to please them very much and more room was made to accommodate me. There was not a lot of room to sit. I was actually held in the truck by the heval behind me. I only had one butt cheek on the tailgate, my heels clinging to the edge of the bumper. Then the truck ground into first gear and surged forward. Everything disappeared in a cloud of dust that swirled around me. "Ah God, this is awful." It was frigid cold in the sudden 30-mph wind as we accelerated.

All in all, it was the most uncomfortable position I've ever ridden in. It went from bad to worse as we pulled off the dirt road, and the truck hammered for miles across open fields. I was covered in dust, choking, ass splitting, heels hurting, calves shaking. At last, we stopped. I didn't know what happened to the other trucks, but I was happy to hop down. We were about fifty yards from a low squat farmhouse and yard. It was made of earth - a simple structure, but well lived in. A few hevals ran around the front of it, rifles up, but the place was empty.

In the distance you could hear the *POP! POP! POP!* of rifle fire... climbing a small berm in the distance, you could see another goond (small village). We waited, not really sure what was happening, then the radio crackled, and we all jumped back on the trucks.

I got the same real estate again, the tailgate, but now there was an excited feeling as we were getting close to the gunfight.

We waited our turn. The truck pulled back out onto the paved road, this time accelerating quickly.

We pulled up and stopped on a low rise overlooking a small goond. Not sure what to expect, we hung there momentarily, paused on the edge. The hevals jumped out of the back, so I followed suit. Then from the small village, two YPJ hevalas and a YPG heval emerged from the village and waved us in.

Walking around the truck and into the goond, Dil and Chalak started to set up a little triage spot. I pulled security.

The three of us waited near the first building in the courtyard. Then I heard shouting and a commotion from the other side of the village. Before long, the hevals brought a man to us who was in bad shape. His face was all busted up, his lips cracked and bleeding. He looked gaunt and half starved. Dil took the lead to treat him, getting an IV into him and washing his wounds. For my part, I sauntered thirty meters away or so and set up a rear security down the road. It didn't seem like the hevals were concerned that everything down that road was Daesh land, but I was at least going to keep an eye on it.

A little while later Chalak came over to my position, saying "Hey man, let me take over here for little bit. There's something you're gonna want to go see." I like Chalak. He's an American from Kentucky. I like Kentucky.

I nodded, replying, "Okay, what gives?"

He said, "Grab your camera."

I got up, grabbed my rifle and camera. I trotted around the outbuildings - seeing Dil, he waved me over to him.

When I got close, he said, "Ahh good, you're here. Let's go do a little family reunion, shall we!" I wasn't sure what he was talking about, but he had my curiosity piqued. Dil, I, and the now much cleaned up man walked back toward the other end of the village.

A heval waved to us, saying, "Doctors, over there." He pointed around some other small shed-like buildings to the side.

On the other side of the building we found five children and a lady who was crying. She was being consoled by a few YPJ hevalas. The kids saw the man first; they lost it, excitedly charging at the man, swarming all around him. The littlest started climbing into his arms. The lady was crying and lifting her hands, palms up, thanking God. She ran to him, hugging him. Then, pulling back, she looked at him, tears streaming down her face. All the kids started jumping up and down and yelling something. I didn't know what it was, but they were all so excited. It was as if they just won the lottery and could retire for life. Dil looked at me with an enormous smile. Then the woman did something very unexpected. She ripped off her black robes, and underneath she had on a colorful dress. She started stomping on the robes, now tumbled on the ground, rubbing her feet on them like a mud rug, yelling something about Daesh.

I've never seen more grateful people. I felt a surging sense of pride knowing how happy these people were because we came into town and ran off Daesh/ISIS.

After things had settled down a bit, I got the kids excited all over again. What can I say? I am a sucker for kids' laughter.

I held up my camera and asked, "Hey, can I take your picture?" They got much shyer, but their mom encouraged them, so the oldest one organized them all against the wall. I was sure I was the first American they had ever met, and I felt a deep sense of pride to represent America in this way to them. But what struck me the hardest was that, despite their fresh smiles, not far below the surface, I could see a deep sorrow and fear in their young, but not so innocent, faces.

Dil came up beside me, watching the mayhem unfold as the oldest girl tried to get the kids organized. She couldn't get the little one to cooperate, but finally bribed her with a Pepsi and a water a hevala produced for her with a knowing smile and wink.

Dil said to me, "From what I gather, the YPJ and the YPG hevals stormed the village. We were the blocking position, there down road." Dil pointed to where we had come from, and then continued, "When the hevals searched the village, seems they found the woman and the kids locked in the stable with the livestock. They found the man beat half to death and tied up in a closet on the other side of the village. I thought you would like to see the reunion mate, us being dads and all."

I smiled and said, "Yeah! That was rad! Thanks Dil. Super appreciated seeing that! These little ones here are why I came in the first place!"

The kids finished lining themselves up. Smiling at them, adjusting the focus and speed, I clicked the shutter button.

Sitting down, sending the image to my miniature printer, the kids gathered around excitedly. That's when Dil peeled off laughing at me and said, "Well, Tekoser looks like you got a fan club. Don't be long mate, I'll meet you back at the trucks! Five minutes."

The little thermal printer came to life with its *WWEEEBZZZZZZZ* sound and when the small color picture came out, that was it. That blew their little minds. The older girl with the sad eyes had waited quietly, staring at the little portable printer, her eyes never leaving it. So, when it finished pushing out and as it was developing, I handed the picture to her. The image appeared on the paper in front of her as if by magic. Bless her heart - for the first time I saw her really smile like a kid should, all the way to the eyeballs! She looked at the little picture as if it was a real, live, magic treasure. She stood there staring at it, completely spellbound, looking up at me as if not sure this magic was really hers to keep.

I smiled like my face would crack in half at her cuteness and said, "It's yours! You can keep it! For you!" I pointed at her. She excitedly turned and bolted to her mom and dad, holding up the picture, waving it back and forth. It was the sweetest thing. She was making the buzzing sounds like my little thermal printer and pointing at me excitedly while waving the picture around. Almost her entire life had been spent living under Daesh/ISIS thugs' rule. Commerce wasn't exactly flowing during their reign of terror. Kids' toys and portable printers were not exactly on the shopping lists of the Daesh/ISIS warlords.

Then the girl dragged her parents over to meet me. I finished stowing my gear and stood up as they came. The three approached me. "Salam malakim," I said as they drew near. I was sure they could tell by the way that I said it I didn't speak Arabic, but sometimes language barriers don't matter so much.

The man spoke first, a rich smooth voice that rolled out like water bubbling downstream. The woman added in her own blessing. Their voices wove a poem, or a prayer, or both around me. The man reached out, touching my cheek then his heart. He stepped close, kissing one cheek, then the other as is customary among those you respect here. He smelled like dried blood, urine, sweat, and fear.

The woman was still singing her beautiful Arabic prayer to me, its harmony rising up and down. Tears were rolling down her face, but in the near distance I could hear trucks starting. I knew I had to go. It didn't matter that I didn't know the words to her prayer. I understood it. I never felt like that before, you know. I smiled and waved goodbye to the family. Turning to go, I heard a truck honking in the distance, so I quickened my pace. We were leaving, now...

Back at the truck, Dil explained in more detail what he found out from Heval Aziz, our new commander. "So, it seems these two Daesh/ISIS scums came to the village about three weeks ago. They usually came once a month or so to take food, but then they would leave after a day. This last time, though, they stayed. Daesh had been taking so much, the families here were starting to go hungry.

"The villagers thought they were being punished for not giving enough. But then a big military truck came. I am guessing it was like an old seven-ton or something. Anyway, these fuckers loaded all the villagers, except this family, into the truck and took them away.

"The woman and the man didn't know where they took them. Two Daesh stayed behind. The family here was made to stay and work, irrigating the crops and what not.

"Then, four days ago, the two Daesh just started going crazy. They made all of them dig a big hole and told them they were digging their own grave. The kids had gotten scared, so the man had asked the Daesh fucks to let the little ones go. The scumbags didn't like that, I guess. So, they beat up the dad and dragged him off. His wife thought they had killed him because she had heard gunshots shortly afterwards. They came back and made her and the kids finish the hole. After that she had a hard time talking about it... she was talking to YPJ so... well, you know there are things women don't tell men."

I interjected angrily, "Like getting raped. The sick fucks!"

Dil nodded in agreement, also looking angry.

He continued, "So anyway, apparently the Daesh fucks thought they had beaten the poor bastard to death, but just to be sure, they had hogtied him and stuffed him into a broom closet in one of the abandoned houses. That was three or four days ago. He was still in there when they found him today. What a fucking mess! The fucking pigs raped the mom and the older girl for sure."

It made more sense to me then, and I said, "So that's why she really lost her bits when she saw her husband was alive!"

Dil nodded... "Hell of a day! Hell, of, a, Day!!"

Chalak, also shaking his head, asked, "Did Commander Aziz give you a BDA?" (battle damage assessment, i.e. how many were killed or what was destroyed).

Dil nodded, "Yeah, he said when we rolled up on the village the YPJ ladies killed the one fuck face, but apparently the other fucking rapist fuck ran off as soon as he saw chicks with guns."

"Fuckin' hell man! Who doesn't think chicks with guns are hot!" Chalak laughed.

I shook my head slowly from side to side, still thinking about what just unfolded here. "What a world man!! What a fucking world!"

But despite the bad part of thinking about what those sickos did to that woman and her family… especially the little girl with the sad eyes, despite the outrage at hearing what really went down there, I felt a little glow in my chest knowing we had all given them back something they would cherish forever: freedom.

PRESENT DAY: When I finally made it back home to the United States, I had the picture I took that day of the kids printed on canvas and I hung it on my wall. I look at it now to remember something important. I look at it to remember 'hope' because this picture represents everything all of us fought for, and are still fighting so hard for, in Rojava.

The kids' picture

Now, as I consider what it means to kill or die for someone else's freedom, I can see how drastically my life has been altered by this knowledge. The before and after of myself is like night is to day, opposite, but yet one does not exist without the other.

The "left behind" of war, for me, is mental illness. I am in a safe part of the world now, a place where war is only entertainment on TVs and video game consoles. Post-Traumatic Stress Disorder, or PTSD for short, is difficult to live with, but what is the alternative? Let ISIS have it? All the political blunders of the past led to today. Today we have a choice - do the right thing… or look away.

My decision to volunteer is nothing special. Sadly, this is just the price of freedom and that's why so many of us went. What I gave up personally does not matter in the scope of it all. It seems to me the real value is those kids having a chance to grow up. That's all… just a chance to grow up, to go to school… to become good people and grow old. The look on that woman's face after our YPJ women killed the Daesh/ISIS rapist that had been holding her and her family hostage… Women, Freed by Women, YPJ rolling into town slinging AK47s, Bixies and RPGs, Organic Middle Eastern Feminism. And this version comes dressed in camo and chanting, "Jin! Jiyan!! Azadi!!!" (Woman! Life! Freedom!)

Running through a minefield to get a casualty *in Shaddadi*

Heval Dil Sauz and Calak use the back of a truck to evacuate our injured heval. Unfortunately, our he fell sehid on the two-hour ride back to the hospital.

CHAPTER 12: The Grunt Medic

Last week I saw a picture of a friend of mine online that I hadn't seen in a long time. Looking at the picture, my eyes glazed over, and I stared off into space. I had a flashback then, transported by my brain and trauma to a place that is beyond space or time. So, if you see me like this, just standing there, looking vacant, or crouched next to my truck, it doesn't matter where you <u>think</u> I am. I am <u>not</u>, because right now, I am in a place called Manbij, Syria, or as I call it, "The Meat Grinder." I'll be back in a few moments. Please don't stare too long…

I was on the roof looking down the road. I hated our position; one car bomb and we were all dead. It was the end of my nobat (watch). I was handing it over to my heval so I could get two hours of sleep when all of a sudden *POPPA WW WOOO.POP.POP.POP WA.AA.AA CRACK! SNAP SNAP SNAP!* A gunfight erupted, the sound of automatic rifles crackling like pine in a hot fire.

From our position on the roof, we could see the tracer rounds arc back and forth through the blackness, almost slowly it seemed, until they abruptly disappeared into one of the windows. They didn't seem slow then.

Little detonations of sparks, smoke and debris exploded outward. A small fire glowed orange from inside the opposite building where the Daesh tracer rounds were coming from. The fight intensified as more and more supersonic explosive tipped bullets met wall, window, street, car, body, body, body. Sparks aren't sparks; they are molten bits of metal, seeking any flesh to burn their way into.

War. The big business of killing. Nasty, nasty stuff. From a new direction, but just out of our view, came another burst of gunfire. This was much closer to our position. Daesh was on the move. The front lines were changing again this night. I sighed, peering down the iron sights of my old AK at the still and empty road, knowing it was going to be busy here soon whether or not Daesh attacked our position on the line. Then, as suddenly as it started, there was a lull in the fighting. A pause, and the night seemed to sigh, but it was interrupted again. A different side a bit farther away. *SNAP! CRACK, SNAP SNAP SNAP CRACKA! CRACKA! BWAAAA!!!!* I saw tracer rounds tear straight up into the black sky like the dots on an old Pac-Man game… Daesh was pushing up the entire front. I wasn't getting any sleep tonight, that's for sure.

Down on the road, three figures were running, dipping in and out of buildings. They were trying to use the shadows to hide from the moonlight as they made their way back to their unit. There were no shadows on the open road, though and at some point, they had to cross it. Pausing, but out of options, it was time. The man in front says "Yek (One) Doe (Two) Sey (Three) ZOO! (Hurry)!" The first two figures start to dash across the street. The third man hesitates for some reason. Fear? Instinct?

It didn't matter the reason, it was the right call, from far away up the road, there were flashes, like a light bulb flickering, but never going out. One of the running figures grunted and staggered momentarily, but regained his footing and kept running, he made it across the road. The second runner, Kado, looks like he has tripped awkwardly, but after he fell, he couldn't get up, so he began to crawl. The light down the street kept flickering but it's not a light, it was gunfire. Sparks skipped off the ground all around Kado. The last man ran out, the angry bees came from the flickering light zipping past him. *ZZZZPPP ZZZZZIIIPP ZZZZZIIPINGG*!! Each one sounds a little different depending on how close it was. Somehow making it out to the middle unscathed, he grabbed his heval, dragging him all the way across to the other side. He fell, but they had made it to the safety of the shadows. The flickering light was still searching in the dark, probing for those soft parts that no one wanted it to find.

The last man across took out a radio, he keyed the mic "We have crossed back over but are injured. Send help or we will not make it back to base!" The radio crackled an acknowledgment.

Back on the roof overlooking the road, I could see it coming before it got to us. Lights flicker on, then off. From far away in the moonlight, a plume of dust rose. The light flickers on and off again: Kurdish night vision.

"Ah Jeez," I knew what was going to happen next. A truck zoomed up outside the makeshift casualty control checkpoint we call a CCP. Out in the street, a heval was calling "DR! DR!! ZOOO ZOOOO!! Bindar!" In Kurdish, this means one or many of our brothers or sisters were shot or blown up and we better hurry. And that was how my friend Kado, an American volunteer like me, arrived all shot up.

I helped load him out of the homemade armored truck. Inside it looked like a slaughterhouse floor, pools of blood had partially coagulated, dark matter was splattered on the bulkhead. More than one 50-caliber bullet hole let moonlight spill into the interior.

The armored truck driver gunned his engine impatiently as we got the rest of the casualties out. The truck would be cleaned later, cleaned by hevals who could only wash away blood but never stop it from flowing. Kado was covered in it, either his own or the others'. I guess it didn't matter at the moment. They were piled there together there like old sacks.

No sooner did we get them loaded out than the armored truck zoomed away; he was gone before I could even get the door fully shut. "FUCK YOU" I yelled after the BMB, but they couldn't hear me.

Kado was in shock, teetering on the edge of life. Always waiting in the darkness is the place where all warmth ends, where life stops. Shadowy figures lurk ever hungry here; because there is never enough blood to quench death and never enough fear to satisfy the devil.

"It's cold," Kado said, shivering, he smiled up at me weakly, almost apologetically, from the cot we were carrying him in on. I knew he was strong, but he didn't look too good… Shock from fear won't kill you, but hypovolemic shock will, and fast.

Kado was covered in blood and dirt from weeks of living like rats in and out of the rubble, sleeping in bombed-out houses. A dirty apocalyptic landscape stretched out as far as the eye could see. The smoldering rubble was all that remained of yesterday's dreams. Streets were littered with bodies the same color as the dust from the collapsed buildings; a body doesn't look like a body until later when it bloats and turns black. The flies are fucking horrendous. We had lost upwards of 1,000 hevals, as our forces battle house by house, block by block, to liberate this city from Daesh/ISIS.

Tonight, it was Kado's squad that paid for the real estate exchange. I guess to him, at that moment, it didn't matter because as soon as he saw me, he broke out into a guilty smile and said, "Doc Tekoser! Ahh shit! I'm sorry doc!" Anytime a casualty can smile, that is always encouraging.

I touched him on the arm, "Don't worry, we got you now heval!" trying to keep him calm. "You're gonna be just fine! Just fine," even though I didn't mean it.

Kado was not even close to fine. Every second right now counted. Once inside, I got him down on a discarded mattress. I worked quickly, getting my kit set up. The old man Pops poked his head in the room, so I told him to go find the DELTA medic because Kado is American.

Not thinking about how badly he was shot, Kado jokingly drawled, "Ahh shit! I'm sorry Doc, I broke my dang promise! I got myself shot up purdy dang good!"

I laughed, "Heval, it's not like a promise you can keep in a place like this! I'm just glad we got you here so we can patch you up!"

On the other side of the room, I could hear Doc Brusk working on the two less seriously injured hevals. I got Kado, the hard casualty, in exchange for Brusk's two easy. Fair trade.

ZIIIIIIPPPPPP the steel blades of my sheers sliced through any illusion of protection that clothing provides. I did take the time to take off his watch instead of cutting it off because it's not something you can replace here. I set it aside by my IV stuff.

Kado was one tough dude because he was shot the fuck up and was pretending it was all good - we all knew it was bad.

I lied and said, "Yup, just winged ya a few times heval, no big deal." My hands worked quickly, reducing his once neat uniform to a pile of bloody rags.

It's important to get casualties that are seriously injured engaged with you if possible, to keep them from thinking about how bad their injuries are. Also, you have to keep them awake because sleeping is really just dying, only they don't know that. You have to do all this while cutting off all their clothes to inspect for holes because holes kill. This is not the war that rages outside, this is inside, but the battle is no different, because it is for very life itself. I lose, you die.

I got a pulse on him; his heart rate was too fast. I knew I had to stick him with an IV as soon as possible. I didn't bother to take his blood pressure because it would just slow me down, and I was racing seconds, not minutes here.

Once a casualty loses consciousness or falls below a certain blood pressure line, that's it, they die. It's just that simple. I don't have blood to give and water don't carry air, IVs of water was all we had. As a combat medic, you have to prioritize the thing that will kill first and work backwards from there. Airway, bleeding, etc.…

Kado (Mathew) was a bleeder, so that was the number one priority. By the look of him, he was already on the verge of hypotension. There were only sixteen Americans in the whole YPG at this point, so we all knew each other and always looked out for each other like family. Kado was from the Midwest, and he was is lying on a dirty mattress at the edge of a place called Hell. This mattress that I had seen many others never rise from, this mattress that used to belong to a husband and wife, but was now just strewn on the floor of their bombed-out and looted house.

Doc Brusk, on the other side of the room, was finishing up his first casualty. We were working by red lights on our heads. Outside, high in the sky cutting at the darkness through the window, flares were shot up, and slowly, but never slowly enough, drifted back down as if pulled in by the darkness lurking below in the shadows. The changing light cast eerie shadows that jerkily danced from left to right, almost in tandem with our headlamps. Then they went out, and it was just dark.

Outside, the battle was like a storm that battered your shutters all night, but this storm was much more terrifying than any storm you've probably ever seen.

Kado was shot three times in the right leg and once through the dick - that round looked like it went on to strike his upper left thigh, just below the groin. There was no exit wound, which was very problematic. He was also shot through the left hand and upper arm.

I didn't want to be discouraged by the many holes in him or the dramatic loss of blood. He was straight blasted. They weren't all 7.62 either. The holes were too small. Most of his injuries came from American-made bullets now buried in his American body. Fucking 5.56 rounds are murder because the bullet is spinning so fast that as it hits the soft flesh, it changes trajectory. Once inside the body, if the bullet strikes bone, it can break apart even as it ricochets in different directions, still spinning. I have seen 5.56 rounds go in a leg and come out a neck and an arm. Nasty, nasty shit.

Deep red blood flowed out of Kado, seemingly from everywhere. I knew that somehow, up till now, it had miraculously missed his lifeline. And that's just how it works, the crazy randomness of war. Looking at the hole in his thigh, the bullet must have just barely missed his artery. Life or death here, the randomness of millimeters. "Fucking lucky bastard!"

The combat medic's dilemma? Inside your body, I am blind. I can't know where the bullet is. I have to go with the clues I see, and my gut. It's a tough situation when your gut gets your friend killed though. I didn't know if the bullet or fragment was pressed against the artery or not. Me packing the wound to stop the bleeding could rupture it, if that were the case. It was a chance I had to take, because he was leaking his life out more quickly than I could fill him back up.

I got after his right leg first as it was bleeding the worst. I proceeded to stuff cotton laced with CLOX, which cauterizes the flesh with a chemical agent into his wounds. The stuff sure burns like hell, but with pressure, it stops most bleeding in its tracks. He yelled at me "FUUUKKK!! IT BUUURRRNNNSSS!!!!"

Finishing his right leg, I went to work on his left groin. I was still hoping there wasn't a bullet lodged against his artery, but I didn't have a choice; there was no more time for hesitation or second guessing. My decision already made, my fingers worked deftly as I wrapped two fingers with the gauze which I held in my other hand and, like a sewing machine, over and over I stuffed it inside him; my fingers disappeared into the large hole in his leg until the last of the CLOX bandage was piled on top and wrapped with a pressure bandage. Winding the bandage tight, I went to work on his arm and hand.

I kept repeating, "don't worry, you're gonna be fine." Waiting to see blood... waiting... to see if it started squirting out the bandage, or worse, to see his leg start to swell. When you bleed under the skin eventually it gets so saturated, it's like a water balloon, only it's not water... and you're not a balloon.

Out here on the front, arterial or severe internal bleeding means you're already dead. Even if you didn't know it yet, I would.

I hit him with ketamine and diazepam. He smiled as the drugs went to work. The boss, Heval Baz, had a no main-line policy, but I broke the rules this time and hit Kado in the vein. He started to relax and giggle a little.

I tried to laugh along with Kado, who was now high as hell and the best kind of casualty, not scared, just relaxed and letting me work without fighting me. Kado started cracking jokes about getting shot six times as if it was no big deal, like he just fell off a skateboard and skinned his knee or something.

I prepared the IV. I watched his vitals closely. His heart rate was still too fast, but not increasing; not yet at least. A steady heartbeat offers a glimmer of hope, because it means I have at least arrested the hemorrhaging. If his heart rate kept increasing, it was a sure sign he was dying because that would mean he had internal bleeding and that I couldn't stop. I was still worried about where that last 5.56 round had gone, but that would have to wait till he got to Kobani.

I stuck Kado with the IV, squeezing the bag of saltwater into him faster, in order to increase his blood volume, a hyper fill. He needed it fast!

Heval Kado was laughing, and I knew we had turned a corner. On to the small stuff... the bag three quarters into him, I put it on full drip and hung it on the wall.

I hadn't told him about his dick being shot because some guys will really freak out about that; I mean, to the point where you have to sedate them and I couldn't sedate Kado because he didn't have the blood pressure to sedate. Looking down at his dick, the last remaining patch to do, he said, "Is it bad Doc?"

I shook my head. "Nay, they just winged it!" I told him, "Maybe they will give you the Dirk Diggler upgrade at the hospital."

Kado laughed, "Yeah good thing I am a grower, not a shower! That Daesh fuck would have done more than winged it!" I cracked up.

Doc Brusk came over, having finished. "Just in time," I told him jokingly.

"What?" Doc Brusk said. I pointed at Kado's bloody dick.

Doc Brusk said quickly, "You, your patient, your patch," as he tried to turn away. Kado, for his part, half joking, half serious, whined, "Come on, one of you has to touch it for me!... Look, I promise I won't tell!"

We all started laughing at that. In the end, we both had to touch it, which only made it funnier as around and around I wrapped it while Doc Brusk held it aloft. I made sure to leave him a little pee hole at the top.

All wrapped up in a warm blanket, the IV was really working its magic. I grabbed another bag and swapped out the IV, slowing the drip down. Kado's heart rate had really started to come back down, and I hit him with another sixty of Ketamine and Diazepam. He started laughing and singing, "Take me out to the ball game!" The lead DELTA medic, Alex, checked in with us, two of his guys milling around the room. Kado started giving them some good-natured digs. He said, "You guys know how I got here?"

They looked at him, shaking their heads. "No, how did you get here?" asked one of the DELTA dudes, going for the bait.

Kado laughed and said, "I was in the Army, you know! Have my Ranger tab and all, but when I applied for special forces you guys said, noPe!" He said it with a pop at the end, like chewing bubble gum. Laughing, he waved around the dingy room, saying, "Now look who got to have all the fun while you DELTA boys who were too good for me had to sit back and watch! Hahaaaaahaaa I got into a gunfight every fukkkinnn daaayyyyiieee nnaaww Immj ee ss J o k inng haahahaaa."

The ketamine really had Kado spun. The DELTA medic, Alex, laughed along with him. Turning to me, he commended, "Shit man, you guys did good!" He patted me on the shoulder. Looking back at Kado, he said, "One tough bastard right there!"

I said to Alex, "Listen, we are gonna be transporting him to Kobani. But the same round that clipped his dick, hit his inner thigh. I think it spun up and in. No way to tell, really. I just know there's not an exit wound."

Alex nodded at me and Doc Brusk, saying, "All right, we can't take him right now, but if it gets worse, we got a field hospital being set up on the other side of the front. We can get him transferred there in a few days. See what they say in Kobani."

I nodded, "Okay will do." The ambulance driver, Heval Adnan, arrived to take the casualties off the front. Heval Adnan resembled a Kurdish George Michael. And I'm not even kidding. Looks aside, he was one of the bravest, most dedicated and loyal friends the TMU had in Manbij. We loaded Heval Kado and our other two hevals into the back of the ambulance. It was just past 0200.

Sliding Kado in on the gurney, I patted him on the shoulder, saying, "Take care, buddy! OK! Nothin' but a peanut right, brother!" He smiled easily at me. "Sheeeiiiitttt you see the look on those DELTA boys' faces. Haaaaaaa Hee-Hee, man that felt good to say. Hee-hee-hee. They were so jealous."

I laughed with him. "Yeah you sure told them!" I patted him on his good shoulder. "Look, we'll check in on you in a few days OK! Just rest up now, here." He gave me a big smile and a thumbs up.

Doc Brusk climbed in and I shut the door, maybe a tad too hard. *WHOOMP!* It closed with authority and the lights flicked instantly out. It is a three-hour drive to Kobani, three hours across some of the most treacherous land one could drive through at night alone. But, despite this impossibility, somehow, we always made it there and back…. maybe with a few new bullet holes in our ride to show for it, but what the hell, that was the least of our issues.

Standing there in a dark cloud of dust, listening to the retreating sound of the diesel ambulance speed away, the night growing quieter, I thought, "Damn it! I forgot to give him back his watch!"

I wondered if he would make it. I wondered if any of us would make it. I turned and went into our bombed-out house. I fell over and passed out. I didn't care where I was at this point. Sleep didn't care, either, but in the end, I didn't get much of it. It seemed that just as my head hit my arm on the floor, I hit recycle and repeat. "Doc Tekoser. We got casualties coming," someone called out. "ZOOOOOO!! ZOOOOO!" My eyes red and blurry, back to my feet, I went back outside to get another friend out of the back of another dusty, bullet pockmarked, homemade armored truck.

TODAY: Some volunteers made it home, many did not. I am back now in this strange place they call "the real world." The real world is a place where I don't fit in anymore. PTSD? The doctors say I am "fully saturated, a byproduct of trauma experienced during war."

So, if that car door shuts too hard? And you see me jerk or duck, or you just see me standing there staring off into space? I am not here right now. Maybe I am watching my friend Kado speed off into the unknown darkness again.

Then my dog pushes against my leg, I am standing there again in the parking lot, confused for that second.

You know this is the random stuff; things outside of my control that are now exceptionally difficult for me to deal with on the daily. But that's not the point, this is… I saw a picture of Heval Kado yesterday - it was on his social media page. He was alive and well, standing between his two brothers. They were all smiling and looked really happy.

I picked up the phone and called him; it was an old number, so I took a chance. But a familiar voice answered the phone answered, "Hello?"

We talked for hours…. He plans to come for a visit so I can meet his wife, introduce him to my partner and… I can finally give him his watch back!

He said he still had some health issues from being shot up so bad, but he sounded happy and that was more payment than I could have ever asked for.

So, I got up this morning and, without complaint, picked up my PTSD rucksack and shouldered it up, because I am a grunt medic and that's what grunts do. Seeing that picture in the long run won't take this pack away, but it sure helps give me some pride to carry it.

Kado in the middle, with his two brothers

CHAPTER 13: Airstrike Baptism

We were getting slaughtered. I mean, that's just the best way to describe it. It took me by surprise. It took all of us by surprise, except the commanders; they knew, they always knew.

Hiding in a bombed-out house, Daesh attacking our position, I thought about all the choices that got me here. How many bad choices does one get to make before there are no more chances left?

What is the purpose of all this killing and dying, all these tears and all this blood? Why in this modern world would such barbarisms become the norm?

In the end what could I really do? Save the whole world? I, just one man, just an ant, one teeny tiny ego carrying only a small leaf. Only one of millions of leaves on the forest floor, thinking I, the ant, am actually carrying the whole world on my back. Silly, silly little ant and so naive of me to believe I could really change the world. I would likely die here, and no one would even know.

In the distance, the shelling had started again, *BOOOOOOMMMM*! The walls rattled. Fucking Daesh had a 155-artillery piece and knew how to use it.

I could hear the devil laughing at me for making the choice to come here. My naivete had led me to my own undoing.

I moved across the room, lifting my AK47. I let out a burst on whoever was shooting at us from the building across the street. I couldn't tell where my bullets went. Some of my rounds hit low because I saw the dust puffs where they hit the building's wall.

BLINNGGGBLEWWWW! a bullet just missed my head by inches. Fucker missed again, though, didn't he! I repeated my move to the window. I popped up from a different corner, firing my AK fully automatic. The rifle bucked in my hands, just a short burst. The dark window and tattered curtains were all I could see from here. In all my time here in Manbij fighting, I had never saw the Daesh attacking me; I had never seen more than a distant running figure. I definitely didn't see the fucker shooting at me now. Daesh, the faceless monsters. Upstairs on the roof, I heard our bixie open fire and then *WHACKSHAKKKE*!! Another round ripped through the wall a few feet away from me. FUCK! That was close. However, it also gave away the position of the sniper in the building opposite me, a hole pointing right to him.

I rarely got to shoot back. I wanted to make it count. My pay-back time for all the friends we lost to these fucking murderers. My heart hammering away in my chest, the line between fun and not had definitely been crossed. I shifted to the right a few feet.

BLEWWWINNGGGG! Another bullet ripped through the wall where I might have been standing before… Fuckin' hell! Maybe he has a thermal scope? Another close one! I was showered with dust and debris again. The Daesh shitbag had a 50 caliber, and my number. I slapped a new mag into my AK47. I took a gamble, sitting as deep as possible in the room while still maintaining a shot at Daesh's most likely position; I laid out an automatic burst. *BLA.A.A.MBL.A.A.MA.A.M*!

Despite the fear of getting shot in the face, it's actually a great feeling to let out a good burst in full-auto. Like riding a motorcycle across woop-de-woops… I could see the dust hits, as my rounds tore through the cheap cinderblock walls. *BLA.A.A.MBL.A.A.A.M.M*!

I didn't give a shit. Battle stressed to the max, gone crazy probably, I yelled out, "Fuck YOU!!!" This was my payback. Daesh scum! I continued to fire. OUT - my gun clicked empty. I rolled out of the window and scooted quickly back into the room by the doorway to the hall.

I half expected an RPG round to hit me next. I was crying from fear, anger or excitement, probably all three. It was all the same by this point. But no bullets came back at me, no RPG plowed through the window.

I swapped my mag out and waited, my heart hammering away, feeling a euphoria I can't really describe. There was still nothing on my side. Was Daesh creeping upstairs to my location?

I eased off to the side a bit more, so my back was not completely to the door behind me. I tucked into the wall so if someone entered, I had a dead shot on them. My feet crunched on the concrete rubble underfoot, sounding weirdly loud to my ringing ears. Still nothing… fear was all I felt in the room with me. Who knows what happened? Daesh left? Were wounded? Killed?

Then suddenly, out of nowhere, came a terrible shriek. *KKKWWWEEEEEWWWW*!!! The sound of twin jets ripped open the sky and almost simultaneously the ground heaved and bucked. Dust and debris, a horizontal rain of concrete bits and chunks of metal, blasted through the windows and what was left of the tattered curtain hanging there. The building we had been firing on down the street was vaporized.

A muffled, eerie, sunless glow instantly bathed everything around us in an asbestos-tinged fog. It had a weird, brown-orange glow to it and little bits of what looked like metallic glitter were floating everywhere.

Rolling over, I didn't even realize I had lain down; sitting up, I tied my chafe (scarf) around my face. I guess Daesh got the full point of that exercise. The assault was over as fast as it started.

I could feel the building shifting; I scrambled to my feet and dashed for the door. I felt like I was moving through mud. I thought of my daughters sadly, "I am so sorry I let you down! I failed to change anything, and now my one real gift has been wasted; I will never be able to say I love you again."

Out in the hallway, I ran, building debris falling all around me, as I tried desperately to get out before it came down on top of me. I dashed through an apartment and past a hole in the floor that opened up to the level below.

"I, River Rainbow O'Mahoney Hagg/Tekoser Azad, just a name only; a shadow who never honestly looked at myself. Never knew myself and so I died alone and ignorant. Buried alive in Manbij, Syria, like so many before me, and so many more to come. Why now? Please?" There was a deep and penetrating sadness in realizing I had wasted my whole life, not getting to <u>know</u> me before there <u>was</u> no me. Too late! A deep and penetrating sadness of all I had wasted, thinking I had all the time in the world, when I did not. So, like an idiot, I danced right up to the edge of the end without ever even knowing it.

To my surprise, though, I emerged from the apartment building unscathed. Once outside, I joined with my other hevals, who had also run out of the building. There was a great feeling of relief that clung to us all, like the very dust we were coated with.

Later, back behind the line, still trying to calm down, I heard the familiar call, "Doctor, embichem binadar!" One of my friends is hurt and needs me. I got up and trotted across the empty courtyard and out onto the street to go find my injured comrade.

The back building that almost collapsed

CHAPTER 14: PTSD Flashbacks Suck

Nowadays, they have all these so-called experimental treatments for PTSD. Things like M.D.M.A, mushrooms, ketamine, psychotropics, off-track weird shit like gabapentin. The list goes on and on, but you can't take back or drug away some things. You can't ever fully un-train your mind from the savagery of war once it has been experienced.

The realization that this IS the end, is different from thinking about it. Even when it somehow turns out NOT to be the end, in so many ways, it is. After coming home, after that kind of experience, I can tell you as a fact: relationships, career, mental health… whatever they were before are going to be vastly different upon return.

So, take it from me… if you're going to go to war? Go to be helpful, go to aid those in need. If you're going to destroy your soul, then do it for something just and noble. Do it for equal rights, in defense of the sick or the weak. But don't waste this beautiful life you're given, because there are no takebacks.

So, if I am looking at you again but not, and you wonder why this time, maybe it's because a jet just flew overhead too low, or perhaps you're holding some orange tic-tacs in your hand... there may be a front loader across the street, or a car outside honking… it could be the smell of dirt or fresh-plowed fields, the sound of hail falling, popcorn in the microwave, booms, bangs, helicopters, women screaming or yelling, kids shrieking in laughter; all sound just like screams of pain.

The stupid list goes on and on and maybe I repeat myself, but so do the sounds. There are so many triggers. I don't pick the moments. No combat veteran does. But one or more of them will happen every day; it's random and can range from uncomfortable to downright terrifying, and since I <u>didn't die</u> there that day, this is just a part of life now, and you know what? I am OK with that trade. I am not OK, not warning you about it as best I can, so you don't think war is cool or fun. War is like cutting your heart out with a dull spoon and doing it every day, over and over.

CHAPTER 15: 'The 'Monster'

I remember the first living ISIS/Daesh fighter I saw. We were back off the front after Shaddadi fell. We had been holed up at the hospital in Al Hasaka for about a week.

I was upstairs when they brought him in. I heard a great commotion taking place down below. Heval Firat poked his head out the door.

"Yo Tekoser, they brought in an injured Daesh prisoner, let's go take a look." It had been otherwise a very boring day and the prospect of seeing a real monster in person was intriguing.

We were staying on the roof of the hospital in a small addition. Initially, it had been meant for visiting doctors and doctoral staff that stayed overnight. But when we showed up, they put us there.

The hospital was a large three-story building on the edge of the city. From my perch on the roof, there was a commanding view. One could see out for several miles over fields of garbage.

When the wind blew hard, it would lift great tornadoes of plastic trash bags into the sky. They would fly like odd-shaped birds. Random bags would float thousands of feet up, lifted from the debacle of uncollected trash to fly freely from one part of the great field to the other. In the end, it didn't matter how high they could soar. There was no escape from here, so they always came back down to earth.

There are a lot of things people don't consider about war, and the blow-back from it - for example, there are no trash collectors, dumps or sanitation departments. Just day after day, year after year of trash pilling up... until now... until this…

Firat interrupted my thoughts, poking his head back out the door. "Come on heval, let's go," he said impatiently. I got up and went in.

Together, we headed down the large, wide staircase to the first floor, where we made our way to the ER.

In Hasakah, we were fortunate because there were actual doctors at the hospital. Dr. Mohmand ran the hospital, which was no small feat considering the situation. The nurses, doctors, orderlies, and clinicians all lived at the hospital; such was the need for them. Their living situation was a true testament to their dedication.

Down in the ER, the medical staff were quietly and somberly moving around, getting suction going and the Daesh's clothes cut off. Fancy 511 tan pants and Merrill boots hit the floor, discarded. Unlike with a heval, though, there was not an immediacy to their work. It was as though they were patching a hole in the wall or something.

I moved around the room so I could get a better view of the Daesh scumbag. He was shot in the head, but he was wide awake, his eyes wide with fear. I will never forget it, this Daesh fighter looking around terrified. They strapped him down so he wouldn't thrash about; they unwrapped his skull.

I had come downstairs to see a captured 'monster,' but it was not the monster I expected. Instead, what I saw was a fifteen-year-old child fighter. I looked over at Heval Firat. His face seemed pale. I had never seen his face with that expression as he looked at the young Daesh/ISIS conscript. The ER was pretty busy, though, so Firat and I quickly stepped back out to avoid being in the way.

Outside of the ER, we sat down in some orange plastic waiting room seats against the hallway under fluorescent lights and the courtyard window with the cracked and broken fountain in the middle. I looked at my heval and he didn't look so good.

I asked him, "Hey man, you feel okay?"

He shook his head and looked down at the tile floor, where the blood spots dotted a line from the entrance down the hall to the end of opportunities. A fly landed at the edge of one blood spot to feast.

From the other room, you could hear some medical orders drift out as they sedated the Daesh kid. And then it grew much, much quieter and I could hear the fluorescent lights overhead and see the fly stick out his little tube to get a fresh sample of Daesh blood on the floor.

Firat spoke, "No bro! I'm not okay! I'm so fucking angry at these fuckers!"

I nodded, and I said, "Yeah I get it," but I didn't really get it, not yet.

Firat spoke, I was still staring at the floor and the fly, "You know bro, when I look at that kid in there, I get so fucking mad because he's just a kid you know! What the fuck! You know he could be my cousin or something! Shit, he could almost be my son!" He paused there, looking pained. "You know this is my country! These are my people! All of them, I am Syrian Kurd not just Kurdish Swiss and those Daesh pieces of shits with all their fuckin' lies put this kid out there to die! While they are all back safe in a bunker or some shit! The fucking cowards! I mean, look at him, bro... he's just a kid... he can't even shave! He doesn't even have a mustache! Bro, it makes me so fucking mad!! Makes want to murder those fucking Daesh fucks sooo bad, bro!!"

I shook my head. I didn't know what to say to that, but I knew exactly what he was saying, so I didn't say anything for a few minutes. I just sat there and looked at the fly at the edge of the pool of blood with my heval. "I am sorry, heval." I reached out and put a hand on his shoulder.

He nodded, "It's OK, Heval Tekoser. It's not your fault, you don't have to apologize." He looked at me and smiled, "We are all in this together, my brother!"

You know, that perspective he shared with me made me understand something very important about the power and danger of ideology. That's the first time I've ever looked at an enemy combatant and not seen the enemy lying in there, but rather a victim. He is a victim because he is a Daesh/ISIS conscript, his shit luck of when and where he was born, the sick ideology he was taught by adults, and the terrible crimes he committed were all due to exploitation. Now I saw only a scared, injured fifteen-year-old kid, no 'monster' here... not anymore, anyway...

A short time later, they wheeled the Daesh conscript kid out and down the hall to a room by himself with a guard at the door. We left; I went back upstairs. Firat said he was going to take a walk.

A few hours later, I heard yelling coming from downstairs. Angry yelling; angry yelling was not common here. It's one of the rudest things you can do in the middle east. The yelling got louder and then quieted down. A few moments later, up the stairs and onto the roof, appeared Chalak and Firat. They were both furious. I got up as they approached.

"Hey... What's going on?" I asked.

Firat just looked irate, paused for a moment as if he wanted to yell, but then didn't. Taking a deep breath and steadying himself, "I need a minute!" he said and stalked off.

Chalak, pretty pissed off himself, says, "So, Firat there goes by to look in on our little Daesh murderer and he sees the guard down there poking him in the fucking brains, man! Anyway, this little guy's leg jerks every time this fuck-nut pokes it! The sick bastard is laughing about it and poking it over and over! Firat came unglued when he looked in and saw that shit! Anyway, I figured I would pull Firat off the fucking loser before shooting started. Good thing I was down there helping in the ER!"

I shook my head astounded. "Oh Damn! What the fuck! The guard was poking him in the brain. That's fucked up!"

Calak nodded. "Yeah, no kidding! The sick fuck! Anyway, I got Firat back up here and Dr. Muhamad said he was going to discipline the guard. I doubt the little Daesh bastard is gonna make it through the night. But what a disgrace either way... really!!"

I was still slowly shaking my head back and forth, letting out a low whistle. "Damn!" was all I could really say to that.

Calak turned to go back down to the ER and left.

I saw Firat at lunch, but he still looked pissed, so I just left him alone. It wasn't long after lunch that a van arrived with a bunch of injured hevals, and then another and another. The hospital buzzed with activity. I tried to stay out of the way; I was not a hospital medic. We needed to get out of here and back to the front. It was time to get out where we did our thing, especially with casualties coming in.

The next morning Calak, Firat, Dil and I decided we had had it with being here, so we packed our newly acquired van and told Dr. Mahammad we were going to head back to the Shaddadi front. He thanked us warmly, but he had a surgery to perform, so he hurried away.

I had to piss; I walked around the back side of the building to relieve myself. Lying there, wrapped in an old blanket against the wall, was the dead child Daesh fighter, wrapped up like a carpet and left out back to be taken later with the trash and dumped in the field.

I stopped there, looking down at him. I wish I could have hated him. It would have made it all so much easier. How could I hate this nameless victim of war profiteering? The dead child lay there now, used up and cast aside. He was already replaced by those who teach this disgusting ideology for their own power and profit. Fucking Daesh Fucks!!! So, to all who think war is cool or heroic: This is all you get when you buy war.

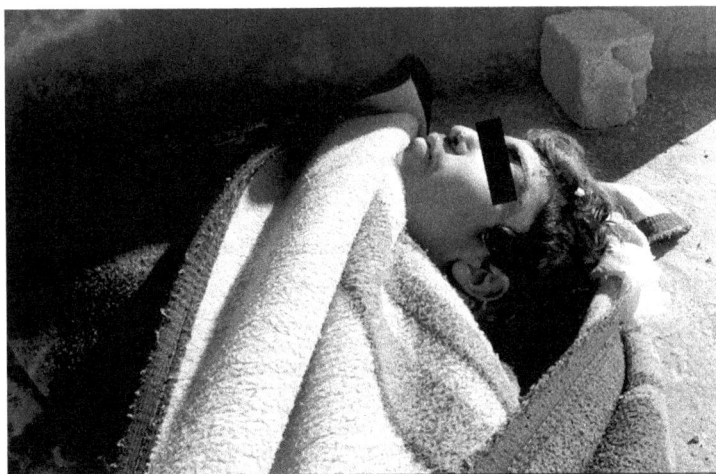

(*The deceased ISIS/Daesh child conscript left behind the building*)

CHAPTER 16: The Front Loader Ambulance

The homemade armored truck zoomed up to our casualty control point (CCP) honking. The driver hurriedly got out, dust still swirling around the truck from its hasty arrival. I was in the back of the small box truck we used as our main ambulance. I was rigging my kit. I had already gone out twice that day and had depleted a lot of my supplies.

I was tired; it was hot. The sun was getting low in the sky now. Rojava has the most beautiful sunsets.

There was a pause in the fighting, a brief moment of tranquility… Daesh prayed. We prayed, though for very different reasons… The sunset's golden-speared, cobalt-rimmed perfection was proof that even here, there was potential for peace, even if it was just for this moment. A commercial airliner's twin contrail drifted high up in the heavens, disappearing into the coming blackness and the dystopia that lay below.

I imagined people currently lounging around at the gate of the airport I left all those months ago. The businesspeople still stressed out and rushing toward their gate, worried about some big deal they wouldn't remember in a week.

I gazed with melancholy at the rust belted sky; I could have been back home looking out across the central valley somewhere near Sacramento under the Sierras. I took a deep breath to pretend I was, but pretend doesn't last, because it's make-believe… and this wasn't SacTown. This was Rojava… and we weren't anywhere near peaceful sunsets yet.

Out of the darkness, trucks arrived one after another as they amassed to push deeper into the city. While the hevals waited to advance, Kurdish music was put on and they danced in the headlights of trucks meant to take them in, but not necessarily back out. They danced for a victory that cold eyes may never see, for a hope that only others would ever know. The words "Sehid Namirin" (heroes never die, heroes are never forgotten) carried a much deeper meaning here at the demarcation line.

Watching the spectacle, I couldn't help but think sadly to myself that we danced at the edge of nothing.

It was only when I looked out at the rim of the world, spinning us backward into darkness, that I was able to see home. When I could see that sunrise in this set, in that moment, that's when I could pretend to talk to my daughters, pretend to be away from here; I could be anywhere other than here, here where I had chosen to be.

Baz came to the to the back of the truck/ambulance looking for me, tearing me away from my imaginary world.

"Tekoser, the panzer driver is here. He will take you to the front now. He is insisting on you. Are you up for it?" He asked this as if hoping I would say no, which I never did. Baz waited as if the question was not rhetorical. The German worried too much about me. I was the only dad in our unit, and I knew that had something to do with it. Baz, looking to give me an excuse to not return to the front, said, "I know you have been out twice already today, jah."

I nodded at him and before he could continue, I replied, "Yeah, I am up for it." I started grabbing my gear.

Baz said, "Are you sure? Because I could send one of the others."

Shaking my head, stuffing my medic run bag, two IVs, cannulas, giving sets, I responded, "No, you know me Baz! I always like to get out. The more the better."

Smiling at me, he conceded, "OK then, I thought you would say that...." He paused, looking worried like your dad does before he gives you the car keys for the first time. "OK, well hurry then. It seems he is very impatient."

I grunted under the weight as I shouldered up. I could hear the driver gunning the panzer even as I hastily grabbed the last of my kit and my AK47.

A short ride later, the panzer stopped. I was ushered out and told there were casualties in a house I couldn't see, on the other side of the berm, in the middle of a field. That was it.

It is pitch black; I scrambled over the dirt and earthen berm and ran through the darkness. It felt like a cross between floating and falling. There was a sound like popcorn in the microwave on full pop in the near distance. Up in front of me were some flashes, a chaotic mosaic of white, yellow, orange, silhouetting square shapes and circles against more blackness. Maybe that's the farmhouse?

Fuck! It was dark. I stumbled over the uneven ground, plow rows, and holes that couldn't be seen. Tripping, falling, I landed awkwardly; I smelled onions on the ground here. I scrambled back up, running again.

There were orange tic-tacs glowing... floating suspended in the air. A dotted line, arcing across the sky, was slowly moving closer. They seemed so innocent. Tripping and falling again, the orange tic-tacs went from dots to streaks... ripping just over my head. I could feel the tug and hear the snap of each bullet as it tore past me across the darkened night, seeking to bury itself in my flesh.

ZIP ZIPZPAPzipzip-PLAPP! I heard the sound of bullets striking soft dirt. "FUUUCCKK!!!" Bits of dirt and debris covered me. I rolled hard three times to the left, up to my feet, running, lungs burning, heart pounding. I hit the dirt again, now on scraped knees and bruised elbows.

"Ouch!" It hurt. I couldn't stay here. I had to go. Back up, scrambling on all fours at first, with bleeding dirty hands, I was running again. I stumbled and fell, landing hard, grunting, smashing down to the dark earth, getting back up, I ran. Everything seemed to rattle. My lungs burned; it was hard to breathe. Fucking Arden cigarettes!

Orange tic-tacs from suspended dots were hanging there... again ripping past me *ziipzaaZAPSPP!* I hit the ground hard again. I cringed, waiting for the rounds to penetrate me... but they didn't. My head screamed at me! "MOVE! MOVE! MOVE!" Back up running, almost there! The sound of our PKM (Soviet belt fed machine gun) firing stood out against the popcorn noise of the AK47s. Then, from somewhere farther behind me, *CHUNK!weeeeezzzzzz! CHUNK!weeeeeeeezzzzzzzzzzzz!* 32mm shells came whistling sickly just over my head, fired from our Duska truck. They have this sound to them, like a whiffle ball going 4,000 feet per second... a good sound when it's your hevals on the trigger.

There was a small ditch to the left, a darker cut on the dark ground. Sliding down into the cover it provided, I belly crawled along it; I got into the cover of the building that was now looming up in front of me.

I called out loudly so I didn't get shot by my own crew, "Heval! HEVAL!! DOCTOR!! HEYYA!" Jumping over a low wall into the courtyard behind the building, a heval appeared out of the shadows. I knew him; it was Heval Demhat. He was on the base in Til Tamer with us.

He hugged me and kissed my cheek, as is customary for friends here. Demhat says, "Doctor, it is good you have come, please quickly! Azadi is bad, we can't move her." He motioned me to follow him. Heval Demhat led me around a low wall into the hallway of the now destroyed farmhouse. The roof had been blown off, so it was just rubble, walls and stairs.

Hevala Azadi was there on the ground, writhing in pain. She was lying on her side in the shadows. Just looking at the dark figure there, I knew she was bad off. I could hear her quiet, desperate groaning. This was the sound someone makes when they are dying and don't want to. 'Want' and 'will' were two different things here.

Putting down my bag and rifle. I placed my hand on her shoulder, saying, "Hevala." I touched my chest and said, "I am a doctor, nava min Heval Tekoser. I got you now, OK? You're gonna be fine. OK?"

I could feel her nod at me in the pitch blackness and it felt like a bit of tension was released. Hevala Azadi was definitely in a bad way. She had a low rattle in her chest and shallow, quick panting breaths.

Heval Demhat said, "She is shot badly. We were scared to move her. As you saw, it was difficult to reach this house, yes?" I nodded 'yes' to him, grunting, but only half listening to him. My mind was already reaching for the chest seal.

Heval Demhat was still standing there as if waiting for my answer, so I did what I always do when someone is probably not going to make it. I lied. "Don't worry heval, she will be fine! We'll get her patched up and we can move her together. I will need your help to carry her and we will definitely need some covering fire."

As I was saying this, something exploded against the front wall. *KAABOOOMMMM!* The whole structure shook; dirt and chunks of building were blown over the top of it, pelting us with debris.

Heval Demhat said in Kurdish to me, "Yes-yes, tell me when Doctor."

I nodded OK to him, getting out the bandages I would need. I talked to Hevala Azadi in English as I started to work on her.

"So, I come from California and Hawaii, in America. Now I am YPG in Rojava, Biji Rojava!" I did a quick sweep of her for injuries. "You like the ocean? I bet you would love the ocean in Hawaii, it's so warm and blue, someday you will have to come see it for yourself." I kept talking calmly to her, easing her down as much as I could. It didn't matter so much what I said, more just that I sounded calm and relaxed. My casualty then also felt more relaxed. It can make the difference. I didn't feel calm or relaxed inside, so I did my best to keep my voice smooth and even.

She was shot in the abdomen and right leg. I hit her with a preloaded ketamine shot to take the edge off. Her breathing was labored, but first I had to stop her bleeding. The copper smell of blood, gun smoke and fear filled the small hallway. Godamn! It was dark as fuck.

I wiped my hands on my pants to clean her blood off. Opening the hemostatic bandage I stuffed it into the hole in her leg where she was bleeding the worst. I talked calmly to her as I did so, saying "O'l Doc Tekosers got-chyou now, Hevala Azadi, don't you worry about a thing. Kafemka? (understand)"

Hevala Azadi whimpered in pain. Finishing her leg, I wrapped a pressure bandage, wound it tight, *BOOOOMMM!* Something big exploded again, rocking the already destroyed house. The hevals in front of me returned a furious fire at Daesh.

I needed to get her patched and moved soon. "Fuck!" Fumbling, my stupid hands wouldn't stop shaking; more shit kept spilling out of my bag. You can't use lights on a battlefield at night, red, green, white or infrared. No fucking way, no how! Hevala Azadi was now steadily crying, piteously low, with a little choke and wheeze to it.

I whispered to her, "SHHHSSSShh... Now... it's gonna be OK, hevala, I got something is gonna fix you right up. All the way from America."

In the flashing light of gunfire, I saw her look up at me with trust but also real fear. She looked pale, even in the flickering light of the yellow muzzle flashes. Her color, her rough breath, I had to act and act immediately because she was fading and fast.

Tearing open the chest seal with my teeth and one hand, my other hand already started to open her camo blouse top one button at a time. I had to cut her tee-shirt open, *ZZZiiiippppp*; the black carbon scissors made quick work of it.

Azadi's bra, once lacy and a light blue perhaps, was now just a bloody rag. I cut it off. It doesn't matter when you're shot, all modesty goes out the window. I don't see gender. I see injuries, bleeding or not, and how to fix them. In this case, if I did not seal up her chest, she would be dead in ten minutes or less.

Even in the blackness, I could see the angry little black hole. I slapped the chest seal on it. She might be lucky because the hole was past her mid-clavicular line and high up, so, not a big hole in her lungs, a slow leaker. The chest seal was sticky and sealed up nicely; it was one of my good ones. I didn't have many, but she needed it right away and she needed it to last. The latter is the most important part of the equation.

I needed to find the exit wound. My dirty hands, sticky with Azadi's blood, searched under her body. I didn't find one, which was good and bad. It meant one less hole in her, but it also meant a bullet still in her.

I said to her calmly, as if I really meant it, "Don't worry Azadi, it's gonna be OK, I've seen way worse." It was true, I had seen way worse, but most of them had died. You know, kids her age back home in America were getting ready for the Senior Prom or college entrance exams; yelling at Mom or Dad because they didn't get them a new Land Rover or an upgrade on their cell phone to a XXGOLD+.

Hevala Azadi was just a kid, seventeen or eighteen years old, tops. She probably wouldn't live through the night. Her privilege in her short life? Defending her home, her parents, community, and the idea of a freedom she had never known. I shoved the unfairness of it all out of my mind.

The ketamine flowing through her now, she was calming down. The pain was easing and with it the fear of death. I had to act fast.

"So sorry Hevala Azadi, I have to do this." She just looked up at me with big scared eyes and nodded trustingly, almost unable to talk. Taking my hand and feeling her collar bone, then two ribs down, steadying my shaking hand, I pushed a huge needle straight down into her skin, slowly going deeper and deeper until I felt it pop. I heard air whistle out for a few seconds. She immediately started breathing better. I put an abdominal bandage over the chest seal, clumsily wrapping it in the blood and the dirt.

We didn't have much time; she needed a ride out of here right away. Quickly, I tossed her bloody shirt aside and buttoned up her camo top.

Azadi smiled at me. My hands shaking, she put her hand on mine, saying, "Spas Doc Tekoser/Thank you."

I shook my head. "Don't thank me yet little sister, we still have to get you out of here."

BOOOOOMMMM!!! Another huge explosion. Holy fuck! I covered her with my body as debris rained down on us again. I heard the hevals yelling at Daesh and firing back. I rolled her onto her side with the chest seal, so it was easier for her to breathe. She groaned but didn't have the strength to really scream.

"Water," Azadi croaked out through dry, chapped lips.

"I can't." I said, pushing her bloody hair off her face. "The best I can do is this," I took out a bit of a sponge from my side BDU pocket and I got it wet. I let her suck on it but didn't let her drink from the canteen.

I called out to the hevals fighting back, "HEVAL, WE'RE READY!"

Azadi wanted the canteen, was reaching out weakly for it. "Please" she cried.

"No!" I barked and briskly pulled it away. It broke my damn heart to hear her beg and cry for just one little sip.

"Please! Please!" she said, "I am dying!!! Just one sip - just one sip of water for me before I die!! PLEEEASEE... I am soo.ho.oo.ho.oo thirsty." Azadi begged piteously, reaching up weakly with her hand. I gently but firmly put her hand down. "Goddammit!" But what could I do? She couldn't drink water with unknown internal damage. Sometimes I fucking hated my job! I had to wait until she was evacuated to the other side of the berm, then I could give her an IV. Poor kid. Finishing up, I repacked my bag.

I told her, "Don't worry. OK? We're gonna get you out of here now," patting her on her shoulder. A moment later, Heval Demhat appeared around the corner.

"Yes, Doctor. We go now."

I nodded at him, "Slav/yes." I motioned to him to move around the side and help her get up. "We must go quickly! She is not well."

Hevala Azadi groaned slightly but did not scream. Half supporting her and half sliding her, we moved her around and over the rubble, trying not to fall. She let out little squeaks each time she was jolted in pain. She was a tough kid, man. A tough fucking kid!

There was a pause in the gunfight; we knew we had to get her out of here right away. Now was our best chance. Demhat and I got Hevala Azadi out of the hole in the back of the house and started back toward the berm. It was just a few shots every second or two as the two sides had begun the deadly chess game that's not a game at all - it's called night combat, a treacherous place where the only rule is to kill or be killed, flank or be flanked. Trench to trench, night to night, the game is played out, always with the same two results; either quick, or dead.

I looked at Heval Demhat and nodded to him, "OK let's go!" And with that we spring up, draping Hevala Azadi between us by the arms. Out across the farm field, toward the berm, we ran. Her feet skipped off the ground; she was crying in pain. Just a steady crying, not too loud, but loud enough to get right down into my heart.

I couldn't stop being angry. "Just kids! They're all just fucking KIDS!" Even though I should have been scared, I was not. We went in what seemed like slow motion, tripping and cursing, but somehow always staying afoot. My heart racing, lungs raw and burning, again I was cursing those fucking cigarettes!

Clumsily, I struggled to balance my medic bag, rifle, and Hevala Azadi. The rifle had slid awkwardly around so it was hanging in front of me and banging painfully against my leg. My head felt dizzy from the lack of oxygen, but just as I thought I couldn't make it any farther, I saw the familiar shadow of the berm drawing near.

Heval Demhat and I dragged our now semi-conscious Hevala Azadi up over the top and slid down over the other side... to what we only hoped was safety.

The earth mover had filled in this side of the ditch as a breaching point, trench warfare at its finest. The panzer was still there, idling. I could hear the radio crackling as the commanders directed their troops from the rooftops, up and down the front.

Getting Hevala Azadi down, I said to Heval Demhat, "Please tell the Panzer driver she needs to go straight to the hospital!" Nodding OK to me, he ran over to get the panzer.

Taking a chance, because I was behind the earth berm, I used a small red light to set up an IV for Azadi. She had lost too much blood and was getting close to hypovolemic shock. I had to get fluids into her or she would be lost. After all that hell we just went through, I would not let that happen. Not today.

I wrapped her arm with a scarf for a tourniquet and felt her vein pop up. I went for it and my needle found purchase with the first stick. "Good to be lucky sometimes," I said as I started delivering the lifesaving fluid to her.

The panzer pulled up, squealing to a stop. The door slammed open and we loaded Hevala Azadi in. I started to climb in after her; there was a new flash of gunfire from the other side of the berm like so many twigs breaking, and the panzer driver said, "No, no doctor! You stay." The gunner in the back of the panzer closed the door and I watched the homemade armored truck speed off in a cloud of dust that quickly blended into the darkness.

It was fine with me. I belonged out here, not like I would get any sleep at the casualty control point on a night like this anyway. I scrambled after Heval Demhat, back over the berm, because the devil didn't have enough blood to drink this night.

Heval Demhat and I ran back toward the house. But then he wasn't at my side anymore. I dove into the dirt and I heard him call out from behind me in Kurdish,

"I'm hit!"

We were much closer to the house than the earthen berm. I crawled back over to him, calling to the hevals in the house, "Hevals! Hevals! I need cover!!" Was I seeing shadows? Or was my imagination running in the field? I fired from the prone with my AK.

BLA>A>A>A>AMMM!

Firing was not the best idea I ever had, as I gave away our position. The rain of God came back at us. I could feel the rounds impacting all around me. I rolled over, dragging him with me.

"FUCK!!! I DIDN'T WANT TO DIE!! NOT HERE!" My whole stupid life, and it was not going any further.

The hevals in the house returned fire and Daesh quit shooting at me for the moment.

"FUCK THIS PLACE!" I scrambled on three, clutching Heval Demhat by the back of his rig, my AK47 banging the shit out of me again. Whatever! Dragging him back toward the house three feet at a time, I could hear the rounds like angry bees zipping around us. Ours or those of Daesh, who knew? I got us to where the low shallow ditch was; dropping down into it, lying perfectly flat, we were even with the ground. The only problem here was my bag poking up like the hump on a camel. I worried that they would shoot it and blow up my last IV. I grabbed my bag straps and pulled it over my head to the side, rolling on my back so I could access it.

I asked Demhat, "Heval, where are you shot?"

He grunted with considerable pain, "My stomach." He groaned again, "It HURTS!"

"OK! OK. I got you. Don't worry." I yelled to the house again as loudly as I could, "HEVAL! BINADAR! EMBICHEM ZOO!!"

Opening my medic bag, I started to unwrap a bandage. Bullets randomly zipped just overhead; a reminder, Daesh knew we were still here. The pressure was off though, as long as we didn't move.

Then from the house a solo figure came running up. He had an M16 with a thermal scope. I could see its faint glow as he ran. He made it to us, taking a knee, cool as ice. He started peering through the scope, saying "DAESH!!!" He fired over us in semi-auto.

BLAM.BLAM.BLAM!!! Fuck it was loud! I doubled down to get the dressing on Heval Demhat.

The heval with the M16 kept firing. He was calling out his hits on the flanking enemy. Now it was their turn to be caught off guard with no cover, caught, pants down in the middle of the field, trying to flank the house. For our heval with that thermal scope, it was like shooting ducks in a barrel.

BLAM.BLAM.BLAM! He fired another three shots in quick succession. He was happily calling out his hits. "SEA, CHAR, PENCH!" Goddamn, he was smoking them. He yelled then, like some sort of pre-human wild animal, the pure cry of endless grief, hate and love all in one desperate lonely howl.

In the dark, I struggled to finish and not lose too much gear as I worked by the light of my heval's muzzle flashes; death is sent to protect life. The hevals in the house joined in, their bullets tearing the night to shreds.

It was a real struggle in the darkness and chaos, dropping shit on the ground, stuff never to be found again, whatever. Fuck it! My heval, with the M16, dropped down to change mags. I was almost ready.

Daesh was caught pants down, their trap busted accidently by Heval Demhat and me. My heval with the M16was back on his feet and began shooting again, yelling a Kurdish version of "GET SOME, FUCKING SCUMBAGS!"

BLAM.BLAM.BLAM! Muzzle flashes and tracer rounds from both sides burned like laser beams on my retinas. The glowing orange phosphorus rounds arced out and were returned like they were being bounced back and forth in a game of glow-in-the-dark table tennis. My heval saw a whole different world though, through that thermal scope of his, and he had not stopped shooting. Each shot seemed like it had a purpose. Not looking at me, but in between shots, he said, "Doctor, this is not a good place! You go now! YES?"

Grabbing my bag, slinging my AK47, I grunted under the weight of my heval as I put him in a fireman carry.

"Yes," I said, hoping I hadn't lost anything too important. If I had, it was too late now. I got myself and Heval Demhat safely to the building without falling or getting shot.

Then the hevals in the house began to cheer. Suddenly they took off running across the field that we had just been fighting over.

Only sporadic shots were coming from Daesh's side. The hevals yelled wildly and charged across the field to take the next batch of structures. There was a halfhearted attempt of a lone Daesh to act like many. The hevals didn't buy it, swarmed across the field and killed him. They took the now abandoned and smoldering village with ease.

The battle continued to get farther away from us as the hevals pushed toward the next small goond. Not wanting to get left too far behind or forgotten, I helped Heval Demhat up. We hobbled across the field after the hevals, occasionally walking past the crumpled body of a dead Daesh fighter. Heval Demhats' arm over me, I was half walking, half dragging him as we followed after the dying gun battle.

Suddenly, a figure came running up to us out of the dark. "Doctor, come this way!" It was one of the hevals from the house; he motioned to me to fallow him.

"I need help!" I grunted.

He took Heval Demhats' other arm and much like Hevala Azadi, we carried him between us as we made our way to the outskirts of the village. Once in the little town square, it seemed eerily quiet. The running gun battle got farther and farther away. Victory on this night was all but secured.

Pointing to the side of a building, my heval said, "Doctor, please wait here, they are finding you a ride." Turning, he ran off alone into the darkness.

It was just Demhat and me. "Fuck." I didn't like being alone in a village that had literally, twenty minutes before, been completely overrun by Daesh.

I flipped the safety off my AK47, we waited. The moon had begun to rise. Her silver light brought relief to the spotted dots inside my eyeballs and gently filled in the blackness.

I heard what I thought was a tank. I dragged Heval Demhat around the shadow side of the building. I knew Daesh had tanks, so I wasn't going to take any chances. My heart was hammering away in my chest. We waited there . When I could finally make out what was making the sound, it wasn't a tank; it was a Caterpillar front-loader. Its lights flicked on for a moment and then off, YPG night vision. The big bucket was lifted three quarters of the way up. It drove up to the center of town and stopped. The lights stayed on this time.

I helped Heval Demhat out toward the big yellow front loader and the bright halogen lights. It felt like we were walking toward the lights of the mother ship.

The driver emerged from behind the bright lights and waved at us. "Doctor! I will take you now! Please get in. We must hurry; it is not safe here." He pointed at the bucket. He jumped back up and into his cab, alone.

"Now I've seen it all," I thought, "a front loader ambulance! Only in the YPG!" I laughed. I didn't care what it was at this point. I liked the idea of getting the fuck out of here by any means necessary, and the sooner the better. So, like a ride at the county fair, down the bucket came. I turned to face Heval Demhat, so I could lift him gently into the bucket. As I turned back to load him in, lo and behold… there were two women and four small kids in the bucket already.

"Holy crap!" I was startled and surprised. The civilians looked terrified. I felt bad; I didn't mean to startle them, but I didn't expect this. I said in English, "Wow! Would you look at this! Hey, Heval Demhat, we got us a little family here." He grunted in pain.

At first, the two women pulled back in fear at the sight of the big American standing in front of them, covered in blood, holding an AK47 and a sagging comrade. Heval Demhat said something in Arabic to them. I think he told them, "It's OK, he's not the devil but YPG and really a doctor."

I smiled in the bright lights of the front loader and said, "Nice to meet y'all. I am Doc Tekoser Amerki and me and Heval Demhat here needs us a ride outta' Dodge, so what do you kids say? Can we share your bucket with you?"

The two older girls giggled. Taking that as a yes, getting Heval Demhat into the bucket over the large metal teeth was not an easy task. He almost passed out from the pain of it, but at last I got him in and turned in a comfortable position.

I smiled at the kids, trying to put them at ease. "Boy, that is some scary night, huh? Well, don't worry, cuz where we're headed is safe. OK?" I used my hands to point and demonstrate us leaving. As the bucket lifted, the kids were startled but also excited. I patted my chest, "Me, Amerki YPG Doctor! Don't worry, you are safe now. OK?"

The two women spoke rapidly in Arabic to the kids, and both flashed reassuring smiles at me. The kids, I am sure, had never met an American before. I lifted my AK, scanning the tree line at the edge of the village. My rifle scared the kids, who started crying at the sight of it. My heval was now in too much pain to talk to them. There was no way I was lowering my AK47, but trying to ease their fear, I said to them, "It's OK! It's Ok! The AK is for Daesh, boom boom for Daesh! Daesh mafi (finished)."

One of them, a little girl shrouded in darkness, asked somewhat in disbelief, "Daesh Mafi?"

I told her, "Yeah, that's right. We kicked their fuckin' asses tonight!"

The kids laughed right away when I cursed, probably because it was actually the only English they knew. I felt bad; I shouldn't curse so much, but fuck it, right? Not like I know I will be alive tomorrow anyway; let the bad habits die with me.

The Cat front loader cut through an orchard and across a moonlit road. The whole time I was in battle mode, swinging my rifle left and right. I peered down my iron sights at what I hoped would continue to be nothing. Who knows where Daesh is? He is definitely out here.

Slowly we made our way back to safety. To cut the unbelievable tension and make driving through Daesh lands seem less scary to the kids, I started singing a Bob Marley song.

"Rise up this morning, smile with the rising sun….

Three little birds sit by my doorstep….

Singing sweet songs of melodies pure and true, saying this is my message to you ooo oooo

So don't worry… about a thing

Cuz every little thing is gonna be all right…"

My voice rose and fell to the unheard beat in my mind as we rolled through ISIS territory back toward the comparative safety of the CCP.

The kids looked at me, giggling. I no longer seemed so dangerous. They never heard a Daesh bastard sing… ever! Poor kids, their first music after four years of Daesh/ISIS rule was my out of key ass.

The moms smiled outright at me now. The lights of the front loader flicked on and off as if in beat with my song. The kids laughed openly at me, the big goofy American who cursed and couldn't sing in tune. That was my job, though, and that was why I was good at it. I made them feel safe, when we were as unsafe as you could be. The two women had smiles that you could have bought the world with.

Almost over. Almost through this night. Just a few more miles. After what seemed like forever, we pulled back up to the CCP. I was still singing; I was on Brooks and Dunn's "Neon Moon" as we rolled in.

We were unseen from the height of the lofted bucket. Most of the tactical medical unit (TMU) were there, though, and maybe it was the Mormon who said, "Hey, is that Tekoser singing?"

I started to laugh from the bucket.

Someone else said, "What the HELL?"

I called out to the TMU and a few of the DELTA guys who were also there helping out, "I got a serious casualty here."

The bucket lowered. Setting down with a thud, I climbed out first to help the others.

The dudes couldn't believe their eyes! I handed off Heval Demhat first. Razon and the DELTA medic Alex carried him off for triage. Then the little family climbed out. The little kids were smiling at me and waving as they were led away to an area where refugees were gathering to make the long walk to wherever refugees here go.

As Heval Demhat was being carried away, I watched. I didn't feel like I won anything this night. Just thinking about those women, their kids and Hevala Azadi, I was left feeling tired and sad.

Just as I was coming down off the adrenaline high, starting to feel blue, Heval Baz, very relieved to see me, came over and slapped me on the shoulder. "Job well done, Tekoser," he said, still chuckling. "Only you come back with a refugee family and a casualty in a Cat front loader. Only you!" He made me smile, too.

"You're right, Baz, only me." I chuckled.

Baz said, as he was turning to go, "You know I always wanted to ride in one of those things. I always thought it looked fun... We could have done without the dramatics, Tekoser, but we're glad you're back safe!"

I laughed, "Yeah, well it was crazy out there tonight, boss."

He nodded, "Yes, we were very busy here as well, but when the panzer came back without you, I got worried."

"It was fine, Baz, I just had one more casualty I had to get out, that's all. I was never alone or in any danger." I didn't want to admit to Baz how close I had come to getting it tonight because fear is the enemy of action. So instead, I just said, "Nothin' doin Baz... Nothin' but a peanut...." I turned and walked off to get some shut-eye before going back out and doing it again in a few hours.

TODAY: It was one of the days that make the hard days of fighting worth it, and also, it was one of the days that make some days hard. I have never hugged dirt closer and I have never seen the world smaller or felt smaller in it.

So please, next time you're in a jet, zipping across the night sky, could you look down and wonder what's happening below you? Just remember that maybe, just maybe, your troubles are nothing compared to those you fly over.

I often wonder about Heval Demhat and Hevala Azadi from that night. I never knew what became of either of them after Sarin field hospital. Did they heal? Did they survive the war? Or the following Turkish invasion and genocide? I will never know. I guess it's not for the combat medic to know these things. We just patch them up and keep moving forward.

So, I chalked it off to a win. In the end, there are so many things I will never know and not just on this day, but so many like it as well. So, I tell myself they are both alive and happy all these years later.

Perhaps, when I am stronger, I will go back to Rojava and walk through the same fields I once lay in, terrified, fighting for life - my hands over my head, momentarily frozen in fear, covered in the blood of my friends. And someday, when I make it back to Rojava to walk through this land, where so much of me has been left behind, and there is peace, then perhaps I will feel I have lived a life worthy of dying.

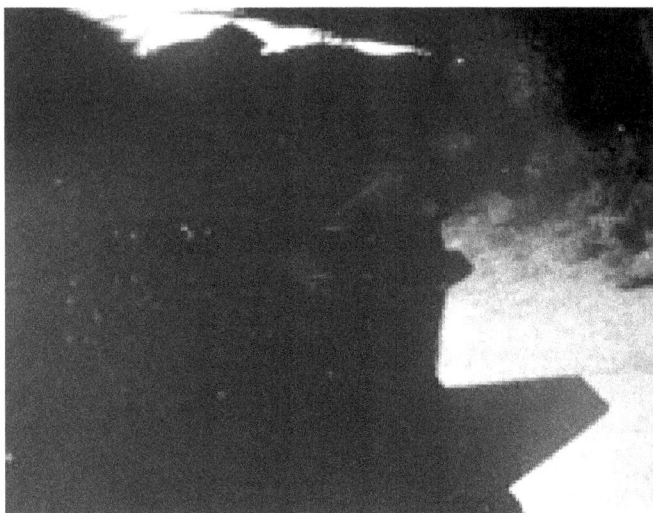

Selfie from the bucket that night. You can see the top of my hat on the left and the teeth of the bucket on the bottom right.

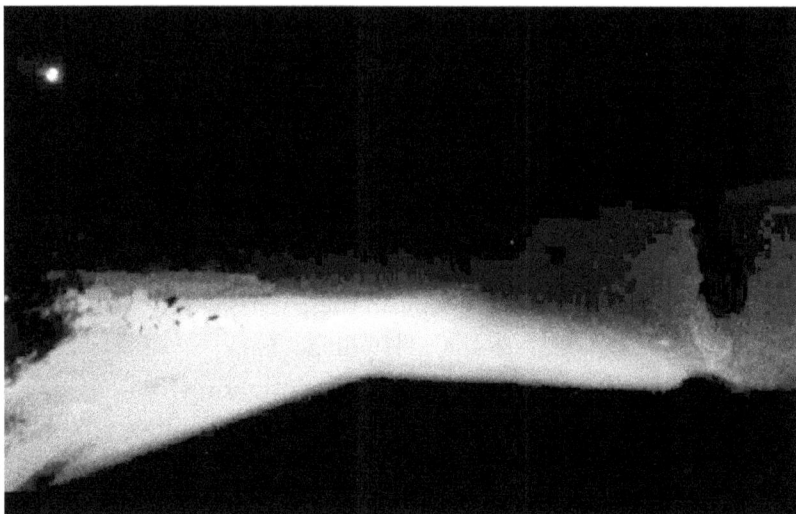

Through the darkness, our view from the bucket

Front loader we rode in that night

CHAPTER 17: Refugees

It was hot and dusty; a big white-hot spot you couldn't look at hung suspended in the sky… Everything, the ground, us, our trucks, our guns, everything matched… brown.

A thin dark line, like a layer inside a cake, lay on the horizon from the burning tires, which were the sentinels leading the way forward, their smoke like skinny black fingers twining toward the heavens, ominously proclaiming, "This way if you dare!"

Droves of people moved worriedly away from the tire fires and their homes. They walked heads down, carrying all they could on their backs as they walked out into the fields. This time, three hundred people were fleeing the killing, but not necessarily the dying. Groups comprised of young and old alike moved past our position just off the road with nowhere to go. Life here was hard. An old man and a young man carried a dead child between them. I looked down at my scuffed and blood-stained boots. We were in the field too; we didn't take roads. Roads have mines; mines blow you up. No one wants this.

The people looked worriedly over their shoulders, intermittently, as if escaping some kind of monster that defies description, but is always following behind them, waiting to eat the stragglers.

These people they call refugees… I really loathe that term by the way, as if they would find a place or state of safety anywhere near here. Their refuge? A dirt field, hot road, heartbreak, no home and the oncoming, wet cold winter. There was nothing left here but death and tears. People just like you and me, fathers, mothers, kids, grandparents; their only fault was being born here.

There was a sad irony to be found here under the angry hot sun. An irony that the poor and the wealthy were now reduced only to being alive. A utopian society, as it were, created out of the equality of despair. In the field, class was finally meaningless. Heartbreak was the glue that bound them all together now as they moved slowly in the same direction… nowhere.

Lost and confused, these poor souls struggled under burdens seen and unseen. Their backs were bent, dragging suitcases and carrying everything they could carry, because anything they could not had already been dropped or left behind.

What is important in the end? What would you take if you had to fit your whole life into just one bag?

Sadness dwelled in my heart as I envisioned myself and my sick mother trudging down the sweltering hot road, trying to keep up but falling farther and farther behind.

The heat waves rose between us and the passing people like vapor snakes. It seemed like an atmospheric magnifying glass… a view to cry for.

I took another drag off my cigarette, exclaiming, "Fuck, it's hot!" The tip glowed red, the only other prevalent color today. I exhaled the mini meditation; it didn't matter if I smoked a pack an hour now. I knew where we were going, right to where there was a good goddamn chance, we would all get killed. I mean fuck it, though, right? That's what we had all wanted when we left our home countries and volunteered here, isn't it? Getting to the front and into the fight. It's what we all had fought so hard for, gave up so much for. The dying part? Yeah, that too… well, one had to know, that goes with it - part and parcel. Before I came to the battle of Manbij, I had always pictured myself living, but after having gone through so much and being so far away from leaving, I knew deep down the real truth of war. It didn't matter how good I was… killing and dying here were as random as we were.

I thought about my own kids and my previous life of privilege. I saw so many people here with no homes or places left to go. I felt the privilege now that I left behind. My real privilege was to choose to do so, to help others in great need. Even if that seems naive to you, to me it was worth it. If and when I died here, I hoped my kids would know that Daddy helped people that needed help. Also… if my death could be quick… and if I didn't have to know I was dying… even better! It was a lot to ask, I knew.

Why is it on the edge of death, and the end of it all, that life is so vivid?

SCCCCcchhhaaaaaaa…BOOOMMM! In the distance there was a loud explosion. I watched as the refugees reacted, flinching or jerking as if jabbed with a fork in the neck, even though the explosion was almost a mile away. It was a collective reaction, each independent from the other, but all at the same time, as one. And as they fled for their lives from the battle, we advanced into it, because that is why we are called "The People's Protection Units."

Civilians fleeing the city as we advanced

This little girl had no parents. She stuck around for three days in the field and then I never saw her again. I tried to help her, but she would just run away every time I got too close.

CHAPTER 18: They Call Me Doc

In the distance, gunfire erupted, it shattered any semblance of peace. It wasn't the good kind of gunfire; it was three or four automatic rifles talking back and forth. I looked up, back at the road. You can hear the battle coming.... I stomped my cigarette butt out on the ground, grinding it in with my heel.

BAAAPPBAAAWWWAAAA!! More automatic gun fire.

The radio crackled to life, time to roll. The Aussie was driving that day. I hopped in the back, swinging the door shut as I did. Reaching up and flipping a small black nob to 'max,' I cranked on the AC unit. We could only run it when we were driving, but the cold air licked at my sweaty skin and wet shirt under my body armor. I held on as the vehicle lurched forward.

In the back of our 4x4 box-truck ambulance, blood spots were splattered on the floor and walls, blood from our many friends who had lain here bleeding and injured, day after day, week after week.

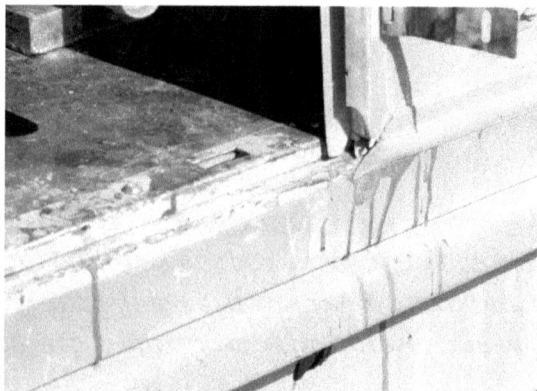

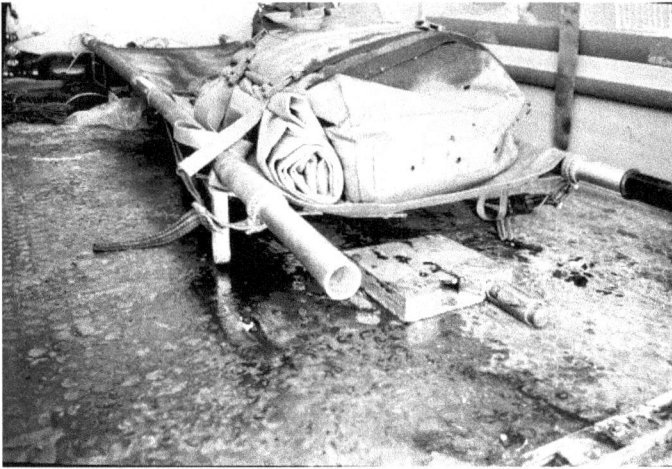

The back of our box truck ambulance,

It builds up, you know, living with the smell of death all around you. I was lying on a putrid mattress. It was a faded, orange, rubber-coated thing terminally cracked by age and use. For sure the rubber leaked; over time, blood and other bodily fluids had saturated the interior foam. There was a rotten smell to it that no amount of washing would clear away - as if I could find water to wash it. What a huge problem. I started thinking about the swampy water we had been drinking from the water truck, which was just drawing it straight out of the Euphrates River. The cool, green water would quench your thirst and then steal it back, all at the same time, with the runs. I had heval after heval come to me in pain from intestinal issues. What could I do? I didn't have the right antibiotics to give them. So, I gave them Pepto chewable tablets that we had scavenged from the Daesh rats. They didn't need them anymore, as they now lay black and bloating in the hot summer sun, dragged off to the side, not fit for burial. My hevals would look so happy with me at the little pink chewables that wouldn't actually help much. The fact they didn't help much didn't matter to them; it was that we cared that counted.

I loved how my hevals and hevala jin loved us medics. I never knew such kindness in anyone. They would come up to me with such belief and innocence, as if I was a real doctor and I could heal any ailment, not just a hack, a combat medic.

During the quiet times between fights, we opened up the back of the ambulance and held clinic. We treated everything you can treat when there are only four medics for a whole army.

Oftentimes we put our collective heads together to try to find the right solution, a patchwork of guesses that usually came out right. The easy part was in the field, getting shot at; there the job was straightforward. "Stop the bleeding and keep 'em breathing."

The hevals or the civilians we helped here, they thought we were like the best doctors in the country. It broke my heart in the end, those I couldn't keep here. "I am sorry...................... I am so sorry," I would say as I closed their eyes; you had to hold them like that for a bit if you wanted them to stay shut. You know they deserved better than me as a second-rate medic with no hospital to send them to closer than a three-hour drive across Daesh lands... Well anyway... Another time wishing, I was better, had more and didn't let them down. I would lie all the way to the end, calmly uttering, "Shhhhhhhhhh now, you're gonna be fine, you're gonna be just fine." Somehow, my English transcended continents and languages: Arabic, Kurdish, English, German, French, Aussie, didn't matter. There was a camaraderie in the field, a friend holding your hand one last time, for one last breath, as their fingers twitch and spasm in yours.

I started CPR. We never once quit on a casualty even when they were gone. We fought because they deserved it, each and every one of them.

Back of the ambulance clinic. Heval Adnan, on the left

CHAPTER 19: Binadar Heval Ashti

The ambulance slammed to a stop. The Aussie, Bagok, yelled out the back window to me, "Weaa he'ay!"

The back doors swung open. It was Baz. "Tekoser, you take up a position there." He pointed toward a low wall by an earthen building. The Mormon, Razon, was already by a corner, his AK leveled down the road. He was calm, just sitting over his rifle's iron sights, watching and waiting. In the distance, the echo of gunfire rang out.

BAAAAPPPAAA! *BAAAAPPPAAA*!! Baz was confused; were there no casualties here? In fact, we were alone here, just the six of us.

I called over to the Aussie, "Yup, brought us right to it, Bagok! Good job mate," half sarcastic, half not.

I knelt down on one knee, near an earthen barn stall. I could smell manure mixed with old hay; whatever had lived here had only recently left. I could hear the sound of automatic gunfire again.

BAAAAPPPAAA! *BAAAAPPPAAA*! It echoed from two different sides. I panned my AK slowly as I looked out across a low road and long line of buildings; there was no movement.

I looked the opposite way, at our other flank. The Mormon, Razon, was still calmly kneeling and waiting. He was an Army veteran from Utah, so he had plenty of grit. He was like a pure white snowflake, and I don't mean that in a bad way. We were engaged in the bloodiest conflict of the century, and he didn't drink, smoke, curse or tell dirty jokes. The Mormon wouldn't talk about sex, never had coffee, but he wasn't weird. He was actually, in a weird way, the most normal person you ever met.

Behind the Mormon, I saw Baz in the background arguing with the interpreter. Farzad was not a soldier, but rather an intellectual. He was thrilled when they told him he was going to be the terp for a western medical unit. I am sure he envisioned himself safely in the rear, but I guess old Farzad didn't realize we were a combat medic unit. We fought on a line until we needed to do our real job, 'patching holes and saving souls.'

I think because he was scared, Farzad was always sandbagging us to try to keep us as far in the rear as he could. He made communicating with the commanders a huge ordeal. Times like this, his misdirection put us over the edge of danger and into lost.

Thank God, the Aussie was a like homing pigeon. I think this was because he used to be a sea captain before the war. He would get us pointed straight, I hoped.

Baz, making a whirly with his arm, finger pointed skyward, said, "Ja, we are moving! Come on. Let's go!" Baz had a smooth, German accent. When you imagine Baz talking, picture a young Armin Mueller-Stahl.

I hustled back to the back of the box truck ambulance. Inside, with the door shut, we hurled to God knows where; it was a weird, suspended feeling. I couldn't see where we were, or where we were going, from the back. Inside we had shelves, gurney, and a bench. There were two small windows on the back doors we blacked out so light could be used inside at night. During the day, like now, the front sliding window was open, but it was too hard to look out the window and keep myself wedged in for more than a few moments at a time.

Bagok not only talked like he was from the outback; he drove like it too. Everyone knew he was the best driver in the unit, but his foot never found a brake pedal... ever.

It was hard to know what was happening; at one point I heard Bagok yell back to me, "We're taking fire here!!! I see the rounds impacting the road in front of us!" I gripped on as hard as I could, as he punched it full throttle, hoping none of the bullets being shot at us went through me. Everything slammed around, including my eyeballs in my skull as - up airborne - we sailed and then crashed haphazardly back down again. The ambulance skidded around corners and zoomed down abandoned streets.

Just as fast and crazy as it all started... it was over. We came to a stop. For a second it was quiet.

"Am I here? Did Bagok get shot?"

BANG! The back doors flew open. Out I came, AK up. I took a second, looking around. I saw the Mormon a little farther away; I trotted over to him. Calmly, I dropped to a knee next to him, asking, "What's going on?"

He just shrugged; I could hear automatic rifle fire from the next row of buildings.

BAAAAPPPAAA! BAAAAPPPAAA!!

"Sounds like they are fucking getting it now! Jeezzous!" I said, looking down my rifle's iron sights. Though I could hear fighting close, I couldn't see anything but a long row of cinder block houses across an empty field.

The Mormon said "Well, I guess we got attacked on two sides. This side here," he motioned to our left, "is no-man's-land... that is where the new interpreter's directions first took us."

I was pissed. "What the hell, man! That fucker is going to get us all killed."

The Mormon spoke in a calm voice, even though there was near constant gunfire drawing closer by the minute, "Yeah, we were well past the front. No damage though; I guess we got lucky!"

I shook my head, "Fuck!! That guy's incompetence is gonna get us all in orange jumpsuits on the nightly news back home!" I was still peering down my AK47 back the way we had come. There was no movement.

The Mormon said, "Last I heard on the radio was, we have a casualty, or casualties on the way. Not sure?"

Shaking my head, I was still fuming at what I had learned. "Six of us driving around Daesh-land lost! That's just fuckin' stupid!"

It would have been a double paradise for the Daesh fucker that captured or killed all of us. I, for one, was not going to be captured though. I had a hand-grenade just for the maximum, final moment. *KaBOOOM!* I had seen up close what a hand grenade would do to a human. It was the worst way to die, but one nasty, nasty way to kill. God, I sure hoped I never had to use it. I shuddered at the thought.

You know, that was the kind of war we were in, though. For YPG/YPJ/SDF, there was no surrender option. If we surrendered, we would end up beheaded, burned alive, drowned in cages, and that's just the start.

On the other hand, when Daesh scumbags would surrender to the hevals, sometimes they were injured. We would be called up to treat them; numerous times we did this. We had a unit policy we all adhered to: we treated these murdering, sex slave dealing, rapist, fascist fucks as we would any other casualty, because while we might have hated them, we were not them.

A gun truck zoomed up and at the same time the Mormon called out, "I got two hevals on the fence line coming in!"

I looked back at the gun truck and two hevala jin got out. One had her hat on backwards.

"What a badass," I thought as she trotted off, the AK47 almost as big as her. Whatever she lacked in height; she did not lack in attitude. She and the other hevala jin both looked like stone-cold killers. The commander got out of the truck and directed the two hevals that had just showed up to set up security on the road.

The hevala jin got the gun truck turned and repositioned so it was looking laterally across the field and our position. The gunfire was drawing ever closer.

BAAAAPPPAAA! *BAAAAPPPAAA*!! Hevals kept showing up as Daesh pushed the line back. Six became ten and ten became twenty. That was when the first two casualties showed up and so did the rounds, cracking overhead. The two hevals who had run up began intermittently shooting back. The once distant sound of gunfire was again close at hand. We heard the sound of pine logs in the fire, random *pops* and *popopopopopsss* followed by a *crack snap* and *whhhhiinnnnggggggg*, a ricochet whining its way somewhere close by me.

I wished I could fight back; it made me feel so angry getting shot at. The first casualty was a hevala jin; she had been hit by the blowback of an RPG and had shredded her hand.

Fuck! She was screaming in pain. Baz told Brusk and Razon to treat her. I was still in a flank guarding position. Another truck came zooming up, and there was a heval on the back. They got him off and I was put into play. "Well, it looks like I ain't gonna get to shoot me one of those pieces of shits today," I thought. The rounds were cracking overhead almost constantly. I hoped we didn't get cut off because it really sounded like Daesh was on the move around our position.

I moved my casualty to the alleyway between two buildings. He was shot in the shin. It was a nasty wound made by a large caliber round. Cutting his pants to work quickly, I felt him all over, looking for any other injuries. He would probably lose his leg, goddammit!

I mean, back home, you know they would have been able to save it, but out here? Ahh shit, well anyway, I treated it like he would keep it. I got a tourniquet on him right away and gave him a small shot of ketamine. It was nothing, but I didn't have much and I had to conserve. I stuffed his shin with cotton and got a bandage around it. Using two sticks, I wrapped his leg, so it was immobile. The whole time, that tough bastard never so much as groaned.

My heval was ready for transport to the hospital. There was another eruption of gunfire and some yelling. I ran back out to see what just happened. Our duska gun truck had been hit hard. It skidded to a stop just outside the row of buildings. The hevala jin with the hat on backward had been shot in the neck. Two hevals helped get her down to me with a blanket, but it didn't matter because she was already dead. I knew right away by looking down at her face splattered in blood, her once golden tan skin now just a pasty pale color. Her eyes were half open - a look of surprise on her face, her backward hat now smashed below her face in the blood-saturated blanket she was wrapped in. Her comrade stood over me - a look of shock on her face.

I knelt down to take her pulse, knowing I wouldn't find one. I looked up at her friend, shaking my head, muttering, "I am sorry hevala, she is sehid." I looked back down at her half open, milky eyes. I closed them the rest of the way. It broke my heart. The best surgeon in the world couldn't have brought her back, though. She died there in that hot dusty field, protecting others. She was shot by some random bullet, no one ever saw who shot it. It just sounded like sticks breaking.

I wanted to cry, but there was no place for that here. We were all just one moment away from joining her.

The fallen hevala jin's friend returned with her AK from the gun truck. She ran out into the middle of the field of fire, yelling in Kurdish, "I AM JIN YOU HEAR ME!! JIN!!! YOU HEAR ME!! DAESH!! I KILL YOU!!! JIN YOU ARE DEAD BY JIN!!!" She fired her AK at the low-lying houses until it was empty, the barrel smoldering; only then did she run back to cover.

I breathed a sigh of relief that she was not shot. I looked back at my charge, quiet now for eternity; I covered her back up in the colorful blanket. Her commander helped me carry her over to a truck that would take her back after the fighting was done. There were no words to say. By the end of the day, she would not be the only comrade we had lying in the back of that truck. All our martyrs were there together, staring up at the sky through the same empty eyes.

I was on my way back to the wall to see if I could shoot one of these Daesh fuckers. I really wanted to kill one of those cockroaches now, even more than ever. I passed Baz and Brusk, who were working fervently on their casualty. I might add, he looked mostly dead.

I halfheartedly offered to the German, "You need me?"

He said without looking up, "No, you're on deck!"

Relieved I didn't have to have another heval die in my hands, I hit the wall and watched for anything to shoot. No sooner did I settle in on my rifle than Baz called over to me, "OK, Tekoser! He is ready to go!"

"Well, shit! There went that plan!" I peeled off the wall and trotted back over to help. At the box-truck ambulance, Baz said, "Tekoser, I need you and Razon to ride in the ambulance! This heval is in critical condition! He is shot in the neck; we don't know where the exit wound is. You have to keep him on his side, or he will drown in his own blood."

Baz and Brusk had already put their casualty in the back of the ambulance. Razon was there holding his head to the side. Also, in the back was our hevala jin with the injured hand. She was in a lot of pain. My first casualty had already been taken by his own hevals.

Baz told the Aussie something up front. It sounded like "blaaablaabllaaaa, shooting at you, just don't stop! Jah!"

The Aussie called back to us, "It's gonna be a bit bumpy at first fellas." We were still trying to get situated; he punched it. The only reason I didn't get ejected straight out the back was because the Mormon reached out and caught my body armor as I fell out, yanking me back in just as we smashed through a ditch. Clanging, the door slammed shut. The truck hit the back side of the ditch, causing us all to go airborne. Weightless for a split second before slamming back down to the metal deck, our injured hevala jin screamed in pain as she came back down on her hand.

I yelled, "FUCK!" Getting tossed around in the back was like riding a mechanical bull blindfolded. I screamed again as I flew back into the air. Our heval, shot in the neck, fared the worst as he bounced hard on the floor where he was lying. Our hevala was clutching on with her one good hand as we slammed up and down again and again. Razon held our heval's head, flying up and landing on his knees, over and over, never letting go. He was able to keep him from choking on his blood, which was freely flowing out of the side of his mouth onto the deck.

Bagok was yelling something about taking fire. I couldn't really hear him over the noise of the engine, wind and the wall separating the front of the truck from us. *WOOOOSSHHH>>>KAAABLAMMM!* Feeling momentarily weightless, floating there for what seemed an unnaturally long time, we slammed back to earth, all four tons of truck and us.

I heard the Aussie clearly this time, as he yelled, "THEY JUST SHOT AN RPG AT US!! STAY THE FUCK DOWN!!"

I gripped the hevala as best as I could, trying to keep her from flying up again. She was crying as we slammed around the back. Tears were streaming down her face, which was contorted in pain. My eyeballs were bouncing around, and with each smash up and down I saw stars.

Bagok yelled, "STAY DOWN! STAY DOWN! THEY'RE STILL SHOOTING AT US!! WE'RE ALMOST CLEAR!!"

As fast as it went to shit, we hit pavement, turning down the blacktop. The ride suddenly felt so smooth, like a silk carpet. It was finally smooth enough to help the poor hevala jin. I took out a syringe and gave her morphine. As it kicked in, I almost felt her pain subside. She finally looked less tortured; her face relaxed some. There is not a drug in the world that can make a blown-up hand, shredded to a pulp, not hurt worse than life itself. Out of all the injuries, a blown-up hand has to be the worst. Not one finger, but all five peeled, like a banana.

After a while, Razon looked over at me and said, "Hey Tekoser, you see this Kurd has a confederate flag tattooed on his arm?" I was perplexed for a moment, but then I realized that our heval was not Kurdish, but an American volunteer named Francisco. His code name was Heval Ashti.

We all knew him; he was from unit 223. That's how messed up your friends can look when they get shot, unrecognizable.

Razon said, "There's an entry wound in his neck just missing his jugular and the bullet disappeared into his head somewhere."

Sometimes, as a combat medic under-trained and overworked, it was like being in a black cave walking on a single plank over a 1,000-foot drop. One wrong step and that's it. There was no way to know when you lift your foot up to take that step if there will be a plank or air under it. It was hard to see what direction to go in the blackness, but you would make that walk with me and that's how it felt in the back of the ambulance. We were the one long shot at hope, fighting for life, slamming over dirt fields, across ever-shifting Daesh lands toward Sarin field station and the only chance they had left.

I got an IV in Heval Ashti and about half the bag into him before we dipped off the road and back across fields. The IV was yanked out by a particularly big smash. The Mormon still faithfully held Ashti, injury side down.

We tried to put in an NPA, but it was also next to impossible in the violent jarring of the interior. So, what else could we do? We just held him for the almost two-hour ride, occasionally rolling him on his stomach so he could drain out the pooled blood. He wasn't losing too much, about a pint I guess, but that still looked like a lot of blood on the floor.

Razon and I debated other options, but as long as we kept him in the recovery position, he didn't choke on his blood, so it just came down to holding a thirty-pound head for a few hours. The Mormon never wavered - never once dropped Heval Ashti's head, even as he himself was battered and bruised to do so. I had the easier job, keeping his body immobile and taking care of our hevala jin. My heart really went out to her. She was going to lose her right hand for sure. It had soaked through her bandage, so I had to reapply her tourniquet. She cried piteously as I wound it down tight. Ahh shit, it broke my damn heart, but I didn't have any choice.

After what seemed like forever, we pulled up to Sarin field station. The lights glowed brightly; it felt strange to step out into it. The staff at the field hospital wheeled our two casualties out of the back. A real ambulance bound for Kobani, another ninety minutes away, was loading up. My first casualty with the leg wound was getting wheeled into it. Seeing me, he waved happily with all the love in the world. He called out, "Heval Tekoser! Doctor Hello! Galic Spas!" (Many Thanks!) He waved. I waved back and smiled, seeing him stable and out of pain. He was on the way to a real doctor and the best chance he had of not losing his leg.

I followed my two charges into the ER, holding Heval Ashti on his side to keep him from choking on his blood. The two orderlies set Heval Ashti's stretcher on the ground. I knelt down next to him so he would not roll over. Heval Razon explained to the hospital staff about the two injuries and instructions for care, like keeping Heval Ashti on his side.

The only doctor there, Dr. Mohammad, gently patted me on the shoulder. "Heval Tekoser, I will take care of him now. Please, we have some food for you to eat. If you go out to the table, the nurses will bring it to you."

Just before I stood up, touching Heval Ashti on the shoulder, I said, "Heval, don't worry. I'll let 223 know you're OK. You got this 100%!" Ashti couldn't talk, but he gave me a thumbs up and flashed me his best attempt at a smile.

I stepped outside under the orange glow of the sodium vapor lights. I lit a cigarette and sat down, suddenly feeling like a thousand pounds. A nurse came out with her million-dollar smile and gave us some hot food and fresh tea.

God, it felt good to just sit there like a human for a few minutes. None of us said a word. We just crammed our faces with eggplant and ground lamb.

Bagok said, in his thick Aussie accent, pushing back from the table, "Well, I hate to be the bad guy here, but we gotta get back to the front. We're the only ambulance there." As he rose to go, we both got up and begrudgingly followed him. Waving goodbye to the hospital staff, we climbed into the ambulance for the long ride back to the front.

When we did get to the front, Baz was worried. Razon shared the good news with him that Ashti had made it in stable and good condition. There was a big cheer all around. Baz said, "Oh thank God! He was dead when we first got him, drowned in his own blood, almost too far gone to get back." Baz and Brusk had acted quickly, though, getting Ashti's airway cleared and his breathing resuscitated.

The Aussie had to drive us across the open field because the rocket-propelled grenade had only missed us by feet as we left. It hit the wall next to the ambulance. The problem was that the field was wide open, so Daesh had a clear line of fire on us the whole time. It was a fricking miracle we didn't get shot. A round passed right through the Ambulance, barely missing the oxygen tank that was just behind where Razon was sitting. Had he or I been where we usually sit on the bench by the forward bulkhead, we would have been shot for sure. It was pure luck that we were on the floor near the back between the two casualties.

At the moment, it didn't seem like a big deal, but it felt good. We don't always get wins that close to the edge of death. It's easy to forget the wins in the endless sea of losses. The meat grinder chews us up and spits what's left out a piece at a time.

TODAY: Heval Ashti survived his injuries. He returned to Arizona, where he took medical classes and then went to Jordan as a humanitarian aid worker in the refugee camps. From Jordan, Heval Ashti returned to Rojava in 2017, where he led a highly effective combat unit for the final days of the war with ISIS in Raqqa. He is currently home in America.

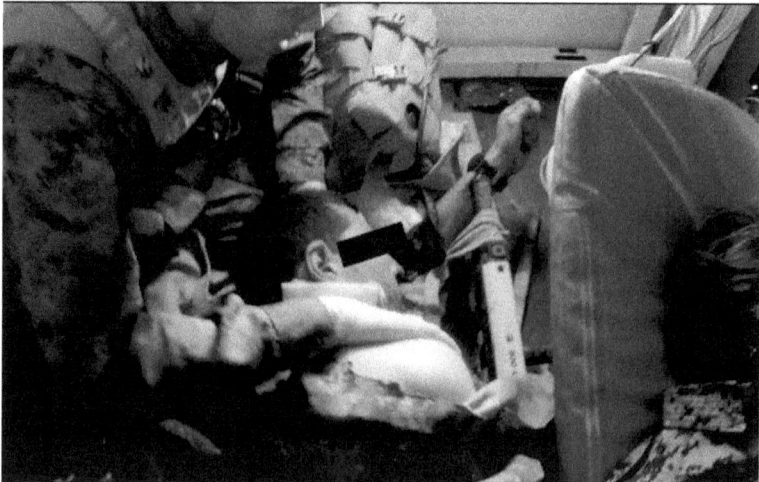

Heval Ashti being held by Heval Razon.

Our hevala jin, who fell sehid, being carried by her friends to me

Sticks for a splint

CHAPTER 20: PTSD and THE DMV

The line stretches around the building. Inside the truck, I feel my heart rate quicken as I see it. It's 0823 - DMV opens at 0900. "So much for being early," I say under my breath. The DMV is a low squat building pulled slightly back off a palm-lined street with a sad looking, half watered lawn. I flip my blinker on *Tic.. Tac.. Tic.. Tac.. Tic.* I turn in, hand over hand. Pulling into the lot, looking at the neat lines of cars already parked…. I find a parking spot near the back. The lot is already ¾ full. I take a deep breath in… holding it a moment, I breathe it out. Pulling into the spot, I look around me, checking the cars and my mirror for anything out of place. I look toward the long line. "Fuck!" I hate being in large groups of people.

The building? I've seen so many like it before overseas - they didn't look so neat by the time we rolled through though. I imagine the DMV crumbled as I look for would-be fighting positions to assault the building from. There are none because it's just the DMV and the line is the only thing to fight here.

It's eerie being in a city with no one alive except a few people still lurking about that really want to kill you, having no way to know at any given moment when that will happen. One is left never feeling safe, for months at a time on edge. From Shaddadi, Manbij to searching goonds (small villages), land mines, drones and snipers, it didn't matter. Death was always close by. The tempo of fear beat a rhythm into my heart for too long. The thing is, after feeling fear for too long, it's like leprosy from within. A cold worm twists and turns its way into your soul, which gnarls like an old, deformed tree to its cold, slimy touch.

My service dog, Doc Stella, whines next to me. She can tell I am here, but not. I snap out of whatever the fuck you call that moment, realizing I've been off somewhere else.

Doc wags her tail slowly as if asking a question, "Are we here?" Getting my paperwork together, opening the glove box, I take out the documents. I start to get upset with myself because my fucking hands are shaking. "Fuck!" Doc whines again and pushes into me. She is rad that way. Still looking at me, slowly waging her tail... once, twice, she puts her paw on my leg. She wants out. "OK," I tell her, and I get out her service vest. After seeing the familiar gesture of reaching back behind the seat to get the vest, she becomes ultra-happy, her tail now whacking the window, the seat, the dash. Her happiness makes me laugh. "OK! OK! Silly dog. Let's do this!"

Deep breath in.... out.... opening the door to get out, I turn around and look at Doc Stella. She waits patiently on the driver's seat, now serious but also eagerly looking at me for the sign to exit the truck. Her tail sways slowly again in anticipation. She makes me smile again. I point out the door - silently she hops down. She walks at my heel toward the building. She is happy to be here, and I am sure she is the only one. Silly dog... it's the DMV...

Doc Stella, my service dog

CHAPTER 21: Rocket Panzer

Pulling up in a cloud of dust and diesel exhaust, a BMB arrived. A moment later, Baz yelled out, "Tekoser! Brusk!" Running up he said, "Shit, dudes, one of the American volunteers was hit by a sniper. You are up. Hurry! Let's go!"

I jumped up, "Oh Fuck! Which one?" I called back.

Baz just said, "Hurry!"

Grabbing my kit, I ran over to the BMB; black smoke poured out of its twin stacks like an armored train on wheels. I squeezed myself and my gear in, through the small hatch, Brusk following close behind.

Inside was dark, the door shut behind us. I couldn't see out of the front and there were no windows in the back. Brusk sat opposite me; the BMB was shoved into drive. When it took off, there was a weird floating sensation inside, not unlike our ambulance, but this thing rode like floating on a pillow.

My eyes adjusted to the dim interior. There were four low benches that ran the length, separated by netting in the middle of the two. I didn't want to sit with my back to the bulkhead, as if that would make a difference if the BMB got shot by a 50-caliber. The large round would ping off the walls, like being on a racquetball court... but it wasn't balls, it was bullets bouncing around inside. The object of this game, though, was for it not to touch you because if it did, parts of you would come off and you would probably die.

I tried not to think about the 'impossible to not think about,' so I rechecked my rifle for the 100th time. I mentally went over my Unit One-bag again, had I forgotten anything? The truck zoomed down the road, gliding over bumps and divots that would have killed us in the ambulance.

The deep irony of war: All the money was spent on the killing shit, not the medics or our broken ass ambulances.

The driver, passenger, gunner and Brusk were all smoking, so I didn't have to. The thick smoke wove through the interior, drawn up and out. Shafts of light spilled in through the turret hole around the top gunner, like a disco club. I never envied the top gunner in an armored vehicle. Everything around the gunner is hard steel, except for the gunner. The gunner is soft… and exposed.

We stopped; I could hear the BMB driver, he sounded angry. It was hard to hear what he said, just the frustrated tone of it. Sitting there, leaning against my body armor, I had no clue where we were. I just knew that we were in-bound to somewhere. We turned around again and took off back the way we came. I was fairly sure we were lost.

A short time later, the armored truck screeched to halt again; there was rapid talking between the driver and people outside.

Brusk looked over at me. "Hey, you think we're here?"

I shook my head. "There is no way to know."

My heart picked up tempo. I half prepared to exit the vehicle. The back doors opened, and bright light spilled in, blinding me. Hevals reached in, through the overexposed, bright white of my dilated eyes. They passed in sacks of food and ammunition. The three of us in the back stacked them against the back of the driver's seat wall.

The BMB was loaded up, just like Santa's sleigh, only we weren't bringing candy canes and gift-wrapped surprises. Our camo-painted sled only had stale bread, canned beans, water, and mostly munitions. There were no stockings with candy surprises at this year's festivities and the bombs weren't gift wrapped. Instead we handed out rocket tubes, mortar rounds, grenades and belts of ammunition. We handed them out to overly excited hevals who couldn't have cared less that there was no colorful paper, ribbons or bows. 'Welcome to BOOM TOWN BABY!' The two back doors slammed shut and we pulled back out onto the road.

I laughed sarcastically and said, "Us, and 5,000 pounds of explosives all locked up together in a rolling target! Fun ride."

Brusk, for his part, looked pained at my bad attempt at humor. The gunner was propped, one knee on the supplies. The BMB was shoved back into drive. I felt it turn around and go the other direction again. We zoomed down the road, and I could tell we were on the blacktop. The large aggressive tires sounded like I was in a Ford 250 back home, on my way to go mudding.

We turned hard to the right exiting the pavement, an unceremonious departure. After a few minutes clanking down the dirt road, climbing over another smooth blacktop, back down onto the dirt, we stopped. Again, I heard rapid speaking from the front; it still sounded angry.

"Man, this driver sure is a dick," Brusk laughed.

I nodded grimly at Brusk, "Yeah, well think about his job bro. I mean fuck, it has got to be the worst job on the front! Driving around just waiting to get burned alive by a rocket or plugged by a duska round. Fuck that! I want out of this thing as soon as possible!"

Stopping again, the back door opened. The bright light streamed in and smoke spilled out. The gunner motioned for me to hand out a bag of logistics and ammunition. I knew the hevala who grabbed the bag from me, it was Hevala Berxwedana. I was surprised and excited to see her.

The TMU had helped give her unit medic training classes. Hevala Berxwedana and I had become friends during my IV class; she had the knack for it. Not very many people have a knack for getting the needle in a vein; it's a touch you either have or don't. An IV on the front for an injured person was worth its weight in gold.

The taboors nocta was a giant house that looked like a castle. The house was on top of a rise, cut into the base of the Del Zor mountains. It was on the edge of a large planted pine forest. The mansion felt like it should have been in another time and place; its grand opulence was backed by rugged snowcapped mountains that reached up behind it toward very heaven itself.

The hevals were very curious about America. For most of them, we were the only Americans they had ever met. They all wanted to know more about life back home. I told them about growing up in California and Hawaii, surfing and filming rocket fish.

Some of the hevals would inevitably do their favorite movie impressions like "Go ahead… Make my day." We would laugh, joking with each other because this is the way hevals are. I loved it. I felt almost like an ambassador. I was representing what makes America so great: not a high-fallootin' rich jerk, just a blue-collar guy, teaching his hevals how to save each other, while fighting for freedom. Don't get more American than that!

When Berxwedana saw it was me handing out supplies, she got a big smile.

"Hello Doc Hollywood," she said, looking surprised to see me.

I smiled at my young friend. "Hey, Hevala Berxwedana! Good to see you." Handing out the bag of logistics to her, I asked, "How have you been?"

Her friend took the bag from her and I started to hand out the ammo cans and rockets.

Berxwedana smiled brightly, saying, "Yes, we are good Doctor! We kill many Daesh!" She leaned out and the hatch was slammed shut with a *CLANG*!! I heard her call out "Biji BIJI YPJ!!"

I waved goodbye to the closed hatch, "Take care." The BMB was crammed into drive and lurched forward.

"What the actual fuck!" Brusk said. "I mean, we're supposed to be getting a casualty, not playing UPS driver!" Brusk was known for his temper.

I just shook my head, irritated. "Heval, how the hell am I supposed to know?"

The BMB lurched forward and turned around. It felt like we went back down the road we had just come up. We climbed over a curb, down another dirt-washed homemade road, and the process repeated.

The back doors were shoved open and bright light spilled in; smoke spilled out and with it another bag of logistics and ammunition was handed out.

The hevals gave such genuine smiles for a bag of stale, moldy bread and a sack of ammo. The door closed. The BMB was shoved back into drive. Even I was upset by now! I mean we were supposed to be getting a casualty, not stopping at every nocta on the front, handing out a week's supplies. When minutes count, this shit was taking hours.

"What the hell's going ON?" Brusk openly fumed again. "This is complete and **total** BULLSHIT! What the fuck!" Brusk leaned past the gunner's legs. He yelled at the driver, "HEY!"

I thought, "Gol'dangit it! Brusk and his temper!" I grabbed him by the shoulder and interrupted him before his "HEY" could be misinterpreted as more than just trying to be heard over the loud interior noise. I violently motioned for him to sit back and shut up. Fortunately, he did. Instead of the driver, though, he leveled his complaint at me. The armored truck stopped again.

There was loud talking outside - the back door was opened. I handed out the last bag of logistics and ammunition. The door shut and the driver spoke to someone, asking for directions again.

Brusk looked at me. He said, "Yo, you hear what I hear?"

I nodded. "Yeah, it sounds like our driver doesn't know where we're going but we're going into the city; he's asking for directions."

Brusk shook his head, a gleam in his eye. "Yeah, we're going in to get our casualty! About fuckin TIME!" He racked his rifle, grinning like a kid at Christmas. "Locked and loaded!"

I laughed and shook my head, saying, "Hey take it easy there cowboy."

"Yeah, don't worry old man," he said, as he kissed his rifle.

Laughing. I replied, "You're too much, little buddy!"

After so many stops and turns, I was beyond confused about direction or where we were. The road went from dirt to smooth city asphalt. The driver and the gunner were arguing about directions again. Then the BMB stopped, backed up, went forward, backed up, and then forward, doing a tight U-turn on the tiny city street. The driver and the gunner angrily yelled at each other about whether we were supposed to turn chep (left) or rost (right).

I had that sick feeling in my gut, you know the one. The one that has us lost in a city full of Daesh/ISIS, all itching to kill us. The BMB made another hard left. I heard some yelling in Kurdish from outside and the sound of a gate. We pulled forward, about thirty feet or so, and stopped. The back doors opened; we were ushered outside.

We were in a part of the city I had never been to before. The base was a large house that obviously used to belong to someone of high stature.

This is a theme here, not just because mansions are fancy, but because they are strategic and large enough to accommodate a taboor or two.

Inside the mansion, my casualty was a YPJ commander who had gotten gashed across her hand. She needed stitches. She had done her best to keep it as clean as possible, even though actual cleanliness was not possible. I gave her a shot of antibiotics near the edge of the cut. She didn't pull away, but she grunted and flashed me an angry look. The look didn't stick, but a shot like that hurts like hell.

I asked her, "Are you OK?" She nodded.

While I took care of the YPJ commander, Heval Brusk had set up shop and was doing health and wellness visits for the taboor. A Canadian volunteer, Servan, Alex Moreau (RIP) had made up about 200 health and wellness kits. He had brought them to us just a few days before. Brusk was also handing these out. They had simple stuff that made a big difference, things like hand lotion, aspirins, talcum powder, toothbrushes, small band-aids, and a few small hard candies that were the biggest hit in the end.

Outside, not too far away, you could hear the chatter of automatic rifle fire pick up its tempo. I had scavenged some lidocaine the last time we were in Kobani. It wasn't much, but I used it now to numb the sore looking tattered edges of the commander's cut. As I stitched her up, I noticed her slender smooth hands. Too bad, this was definitely going to leave a scar. It's a shame, as my stitching skills leave a lot to be desired. I mean hey, I am proficient, but let's face it, I was never going to be a plastic surgeon.

She was a handsome woman. Perhaps in some other world, some other land or time, she was the kind of woman I would have asked out for a cup of coffee to get to know better. I pushed the thought from my mind. Finishing up the last stitch of eight, I carefully bandaged her hand. There was a strength and sorrow in that hand, the hand of combat platoon leader.

I smiled at her. "Tomorrow change the bandage. OK?"

She nodded and I handed her an extra 4x4 bandage, gauze, tape and some expired little antibiotic ointment packets. She smiled at me, a real genuine smile that lit up the room, a smile I could tell was loved by many.

"Spas, Heval Tekoser." she said.

Then, from outside the building on the back corner of our position, automatic rifle fire opened up. This was not wild, like during an assault, but leveraged with intent.

BWAAAA WAAAA! Shots were outgoing and incoming; Daesh was probing our position. A heval came running in. "Doctors, we must go!" He motioned for us to follow him out.

There was no time for niceties, like tea. Brusk and I went out the door, back toward where the BMB was parked before, but the big armored truck was gone. Confused, I stopped on the back porch.

The heval saw me stop. He said, "No, no! follow me Doctor, you have a new driver!"

"That's just fine with me," Brusk said.

We hurried around the building and there was a smaller armored truck/panzer parked there waiting for us.

"What the hell, let's do this!" Brusk said, over-amped, climbing in.

The gate of the compound was wheeled open and we zoomed out; a hard left, the big tires squealed and then it sounded like someone hitting a metal plate with a jackhammer. *TAKting!TAKting!TAKting!* Instead of the gunner opening up with the topside machine gun, he dropped inside and hid from the incoming bullets.

The driver took another hard left, tires squealing; the sound of fighting grew instantly quieter. The gunner, smiling somewhat sheepishly, gave us a thumbs up and he stood back up.

We didn't go far, perhaps half a mile. The armored truck stopped again. The gunner popped down. "We wait here." he said.

The back door opened. I stepped out. It was surreal. We were in the middle of the city, in a tidy blue-collar neighborhood. The street was fairly narrow here, no sidewalk, just tall earthen walls on either side of the street.

Behind the seven-foot-tall walls, the houses had yards with a few thirsty looking trees, a small dead garden and a shop or shed. The lots were probably 10,000 square feet, total. One wall of the house shared the street. The wooden doors that led out were all beautifully painted. The arched wall over them was inlaid with tile and stone in intricate patterns. You could see the personality of the houses here.

You could also hear the automatic machine gun fire in the near distance picking up tempo; the sound of gunshots and explosions ripped out across the city, like beating a metal drum. I felt my skin crawl knowing Daesh/ISIS was so close.

Brusk and I stepped through a partially open door into the courtyard of one of the houses. We went very slowly and carefully, because there is always the thought that every step here could be your last. IEDs and landmines were everywhere here. The walls, floors, windows, hell, Daesh had even put remote detonation IEDs on chickens.

Slowly, we inched our way through the door, looking for any sign of booby traps. It looked clean. I breathed a little sigh of relief once I was safely inside.

Standing there for a moment, taking it in, I was left feeling like an intruder in someone else's life, wondering where they went. Inside the wall of the miniature compound was an oasis. The neat little house was colorfully painted, decorated with pottery, and filled with long-dead houseplants. A beautifully beaded curtain hung limply in the open door to the house. It was dulled because it was covered in dust, suggesting to me the people who lived here had left months ago, if not longer. I could hear the haunting song of an old wind chime; it softly gonged its sweet melodic melancholy to no one but us and the ghosts.

I was sitting against the wall in the shade, not really wanting to explore more than that. I felt like we were the last two humans on earth and we just got caught out after dark in zombie land.

Brusk and I sat quietly as we listened to the raging gun battle while we waited. I had no idea about the 223 heval who got shot. I figured he was dead by now unless it was minor.

Baz had said that he got shot with a 50-caliber round; not much survives getting shot by one of those. It has been known to fling a person fifteen feet or more into the air on a direct hit. Think about it like this; a 50-cal round has 13,000-foot pounds of kinetic energy – kind of excessive for killing people. It's like using a sledgehammer on an ant.

I had given up hope for whoever was shot. We had been out now for some four or five hours already, and we were no closer to finding our injured heval than when we started.

I wasn't sure where the driver and gunner went. I hoped to hell that ISIS didn't find us because I didn't want to blow myself up, not today. It was a pretty valid fear since there were literally thousands of Daesh/ISIS fighters in the city. They also had tunnels big enough to drive trucks in, connecting every part of the city. Fittingly, Daesh moved subterranean, like the cockroaches they were, appearing at random in swarms. Who knows? The next yard over could be an exit for them, maybe even the shed in our backyard here. I kept my rifle handy.

We waited for some time, like two ghosts in a town devoid of people. Then the armored truck driver poked his head in our gate, looking even more pissed than the last driver. He motioned for us to follow him.

Brusk and I trotted back out the door. I was glad he didn't leave us. Back into the armored truck, it was shoved into gear and started careening wildly through the streets of Manbij. Suddenly I heard two loud slaps.

BA WANK!... BA WANK! The armored truck driver yelled and punched it again. We bounced around inside like the rattles inside a spray-paint can. The gunner stayed up but didn't shoot. We careened left and then right, we braked hard and abruptly squealed left… then he punched it. That's the way it went for a while.

I felt like I was on a ride back home at the county fair, but this wasn't the mixer and there were no BBQ-corn-on-the-cob stands, monster trucks or daisy dukes clinging to hot buns on warm summer nights. Nah, this ride was poison, and the only way off it was all the way through it.

Finally, slowing and then stopping, we were at a position on a small rise just on the outskirts of the city.

The gunner popped down, saying, "Ok, we wait here." He and Brusk got out, but I hesitated - I didn't know why.

My door opened; it was Brusk, "Come on, this place is tits!"

I started to grab my bag.

Brusk said, "Hey, just leave your bag in here. We're not gonna be here long."

I still went to grab my bag.

Looking irritated, he repeated, "Leave it!" Turning, he went inside.

I let him go without me; I would not leave my medic bag, camera or laptop. I took my bag with me everywhere because I had already seen Baz lose his medic bag. He had left it in a truck of hevals, the bag never to be seen again. That was one full Unit One Pack gone and gone in a place you couldn't replace it. A combat medic without a bag was like a gun with no bullets. Well anyway, I wasn't going to repeat that mistake, that's for sure.

I stepped out of the armored truck/panzer with my bag and all I heard was…

WoosshHHKAAAABAAM!!!

I was flung off my feet by the blast. I rolled to the side. A heval ran past me, yelling, "Rockets!"

Getting to my feet, I scrambled toward the door of the structure directly in front of me.

"WHAT THE HOLY FUCK!" Turning, spinning, I saw the armored truck behind me had burst into flames!

Brusk yelled at me, "TEKOSER, GET OUT OF THERE! THEY HAVE ROCKETS!!" I ran toward the backyard, where there was a YPJ Duska truck and those women were hammering away on the thirty-mm, at whatever they saw. Whatever they saw, it really pissed them off. And believe you, me, hell hath no fury like a hevala jin armed with an automatic thirty-mm cannon.

If Daesh had planned an attack, that sure turned them around, at least for the moment, anyway. I had never been so happy to have a five-foot-tall hevala jin save my ass.

Brusk started yelling furiously about the flaming armored truck. "My FUCKING BAG WAS IN THERE!!"

The armored truck driver looked at his panzer; as flames shot out of it, the rounds had begun to cook off and explode. The driver smiled because he was not also in it burning. It was as close to happy as I ever saw a panzer driver.

Brusk lost his temper because he had screwed up and he knew it. He was so pissed he flexed at the wall like he was going to hit it. Taking his rifle, he slammed it through a window, but it didn't bring his bag back or change the fact that we were stranded there.

The YPJ Duska truck, though, got another mission and zoomed away. "What the hell!"

About five minutes later, another homemade panzer pulled up to get us out. We all squeezed in the back: the old driver, gunner, Brusk, and me, all sitting on each other's laps.

The gunner on top of the truck started yelling. I couldn't tell why, just that he was yelling. The driver panicked, drove wildly backwards, and then smashed into a tree. Jamming it into drive, the heavy, armored panzer was bogged down and stuck in a ditch. We were like a mouse on glue paper with a cat in the room.

"Fuck!" We were definitely stuck.

I no longer felt the armor around me provided any more protection than a wet shirt against the cold. I now understood the terse looks on the drivers' faces and the feeling of dread because rockets don't give a SHIT. And that's all the warning you got before you were burned alive. The panzer driver would never have crashed had he not been scared shitless to be exploded by the next rocket.

Not fifty yards away, I could see clear as day the other panzer with flames still shooting out of it. The smoke created a huge black finger, pointing to the sky, saying to Daesh, "We're here, we're alone now, and we're stuck!"

CRUNCH…. WEEEEERRRRRRR! The panzer tires spun uselessly. The gunner hopped out and opened our door. We all scrambled out and began to walk across the open field away from the smoldering rubble, away from ISIS and from any hope of actually finding the American volunteer we had set out, so long ago, to rescue.

Heval Brusk looked angrily at the flaming panzer, still in disbelief that he was a medic without a bag... and then.

Crack..SWWEIINGG! Crack..SWWEIINGG! The sound of incoming rounds passed overhead. We began to run. I was loaded down with my full medic bag, body armor, water, rifle, ammo and my two cameras, roughly 100 extra pounds. It was about as easy as it sounds. I was the last one. My body armor slammed up and down, bouncing my eyes in my skull with each step, sweat dripping down into them. making me half blind. My breath was ragged, my legs burned, my side split like a knife stuffed in my ribs. We were about 150 meters up the dirt road, all our backs exposed, as we all ran for our lives. I should have paced myself better from the start, but fear is a hell of a motivator.

In the distance, a lone cloud of dust could be seen just over the rise. It was coming at us fast. I didn't know… Should I keep running toward it? Or run back? Running back was not in the plan. I could barely run now anyway. By this point I was reduced to a methodical, painful, grinding half-run-half-walk pace. It was my best effort to escape a beheading, being burned alive, dipped in hot oil, or drowned slowly over and over in a cage.

My body had found its failure point, and it was not only from smoking, but also from a mixed bag of malnutrition, mild dysentery, and lack of sleep. Not the most winning combo.

The dust cloud turned into our van; inside our van, sitting alone with an AK propped by his lap, was the Aussie Bagok. The van skidded up to us like a trophy truck in the Baja 1,000.

The passenger window automatically rolled down, and the Aussie said, "I erd-yaa might be needin' a lift?" He grinned, with his easy down-under smile. "Well, jump-on-in mates, this taxi is in a hurry!"

And he didn't have to repeat himself either as we all scrambled in.

On the way out, Bagok did one full doughnut, sending rocks and dirt spinning out in a great cloud of dust before he straightened out, fishtailed and headed toward home.

Our dust cloud was a middle finger in the eye of the Daesh fuckers who were, even now, swarming over our last position. We didn't care. Not on this day anyway. Maybe tomorrow we would care, when we had to take it back.

There was great joy in the van as we sped away that day, almost the happiest I have ever been in my life.

Bagok, 'the Aussie,' was driving a van alone through ISIS-held territory. He came straight toward an oncoming Daesh assault to rescue us because he heard on the radio we were in trouble.

He did not know where we were at first. He followed the smoke plume from our exploded armored truck for miles; across fields and past empty hamlets, he sped blindly forward, looking for us. When he found us, we were almost all done in. Daesh was no more than 300 meters behind us.

Postscript note* I wish there was an international medal to give out for those hevals who demonstrated such extraordinary heroism, going way above and beyond the call of duty. If this medal existed, then I would nominate the Aussie Heval Bagok, because that day, he not only risked his life and being captured, but also, he saved all of our asses. Bagok never really mentioned it again. That was his way, you know. He just downplayed it, like it was no big deal.

The hevals retook that position a few days later but the panzers were not recoverable. The panzers were dragged off the side of the road and left there. In the future when they are seen by passersby, they will imagine the occupants exploded, dead or burned to a crisp. In this case, their imagination would be wrong. In this case, we all lived without a scratch on us. This time we got lucky. But here on the front…there is always a next time.

The panzer I was in that was hit by the rocket.
My still open back passenger door.

CHAPTER 22: PTSD and The Balloon

Doc Stella and I are in the produce section of the supermarket.

BANGG! A loud explosion goes off just behind me. Spinning, I drop to the ground, not sure where the shot came from. I am preparing to move to contact, waiting for the next shot… there is no next shot. It was a balloon popping. That's all just a damned balloon!

I know where I am… home, kneeling on the floor, in the produce section by the flower stand. I rationalize it, "It's OK bro. We're just in the store! Nothing is happening." But that doesn't change how I feel inside. The chemicals my brain instantly produces in response to the sound don't just go away.

I am the only person on the ground. My service dog, Doc Stella, is licking my face. My heart is racing and I'm thinking, "Stupid fucking me!" People are looking at me weird… I hug Doc Stella for a second. I take a few deep, even breaths in and out.

"It's OK to look stupid," I tell myself. I earned the right, so they didn't have to.

I get to my feet, embarrassed, but there's always my hat to hide my face under and the ground to look at.

I want out of here. I leave in a hurry. I don't even check out. Maybe for you it's just a balloon popping; for me, it will mess up the rest of my day. That's the shit part about PTSD; I never know what will set it off, where I will be, or when it will happen.

The cost of war no one wants to talk about… the long-term mental damage inflicted is as significant as an amputation, but not visible or physically manifested. The invisible suffering of the inner soul can't be seen, only felt.

CHAPTER 23: Tal Nasri

In the upper Khabur Valley of Jazira in northeastern Syria, there is a small town named Tal Nasri. It lays just off the highway, down a half mile of single-track road. The town is surrounded by yellow and gold wheat fields that dance in unison under the breath of a gentle breeze. In the distance, on the low rolling hills, little dots that make up herds of sheep and goats grazing are visible. The sky has those little puffy clouds, shaped like animal crackers, floating peacefully; it's about as close to heaven as you can get here.

It was before Manbij, but we all knew it was coming. To prepare for the big fight, Baz had meticulously worked with Chalak (Kentucky) and Firat (Sweden/Rojava) to translate the US Army's Tactical Combat Casualty Care Handbook (TCCC), into Kurdish. After it was complete, we taught it to as many different taboors as we could in the canton.

Today I had taught my lessons on hemorrhage control and stabilizing broken bones. I was free for now but later I had a small group of hevals for IV training. I looked at my arm and grimaced slightly, "Sorry arm."

The nocta we set up to teach the class in was just outside of the ghost town. It had a little manger and an earthen wall that connected it to the house. In the back courtyard was a large pomegranate and a few peach trees. By the house were some empty garden beds that had once held tomatoes, maybe eggplant and some green squashes.

Since arriving here, the hevals had started watering the fruit trees. They were happy to be irrigated again. In a matter of days, they seemed to have sprung back to life, but the planters remained empty and dead. The hevals had had enough of farming; now was the time to fight.

From the vantage point of our nocta, I could see there was heavy battle damage to the small village. Bullet scars pockmarked the walls. The streets had weeds growing in the middle from lack of use. The town looked post-apocalyptic.

Walking down to the village on the now unused road, I contemplated what had happened here. I thought to myself, "Who knows if one survives this kind of hell? How can you see enough combat and not get hit?" I couldn't take the fear of dying away because down on the front, we all knew the real truth of war was... "it's not a matter of if... but when." I pushed the dark thoughts from my mind.

The first building on the edge of the town used to be a shop of some kind. The back had a concrete garage facing the road; it was blown all to hell. At the base of the concrete wall was a murder hole just a few inches above the ground. The small, blackened orifice was pockmarked from countless rounds impacting it. I studied the field of fire; it was an impressive position. It covered the road all the way to the highway: a heavy machine gun position, for sure!

I went back through the destroyed gate; the backyard was all dug up. In the ground running from the house to the garage was a six-foot-deep trench, sandbags on either side. The defender of this position could go from the garage to the house completely subterranean. It was a simple but effective design to keep freedom of movement, even when getting shelled or hit from the air.

I followed the trench inside the garage; it ran into a fortified fighting hole. Shell casings littered the ground against the back wall. In the fighting position, on the wall, graffiti was written in Turkish, Arabic, English, German, French, Chechen. Who knows? A hell of a lot more languages than I wrote, that's for sure.

A medium-sized, hand painted Daesh flag stood over religious quotes the maniacs had used to convince themselves what they were doing was holy. It was weird to look at them now, just stupid doodles made by bored soldiers on watch.

Next to the fighting position, on the wall to the left, were listed a bunch of firing ranges. There were bullet marks stitched in a pattern against the wall. The bullets had been fired from the doorway behind me.

It would have been impossible to take this town without taking this position. Daesh not only had the whole road covered but they also had a near perfect fighting position. I whistled softly to myself. The smell of gun smoke was long gone, but in my mind, it still lingered. Looking around, I imagined what happened here in this room the day this position finally fell.

Turning, I climbed out of the fighting position and walked back to the doorway. At the doorway, I pretended, I was going to clear this space. Looking down my AK, I could see again the automatic pattern to the bullet impacts on the walls and floor over Daesh's foxhole.

"Pssswwheeew," I quietly whistled to myself. From my position at the door with my AK still up, I imagined the gun team inside hammering away. The smoke must have been thick in here. I could see my imaginary foes more by their silhouettes cut out of the muzzle flashes as they pounded at our YPG roadside positions. In my mind, having a hard time seeing through the smoke, I squeezed off a burst where I thought their heads were. I guess I was high because the two of them scrambled to the left. I would have opened up on full auto in the small room; the sound would have been deafening. Two Daesh, lying on the floor. Dead. I walked over and emptied my clip into them before grabbing the machine gun and running out. Take no chances.

That's how it played out in my mind, anyway. The floor had two large stains where the blood had pooled and dried, then rotted away. Kicking some empty shell casings with my foot, I picked one up. It was 7.62x54 from a heavy machine gun. Daesh was trained, equipped and ready for us to come. Still, though, despite all this, my hevals had snuck around back and murdered them anyway. Gutsy bastards. That's what I loved about my hevals... they would hang it all on the line for their comrades. Rojava and freedom!

Stepping back out of the garage and the grisly scene inside, I walked through the disheveled house. I felt like an intruder to its grief and silence as my feet crunched loudly on broken glass and other debris scattered on the floor. The front door had been blown open and there were dried blood splatters on the walls and bullet casings everywhere. The spent rounds were mostly 7.62, but there were also some bigger 50-cal. casings on the ground. At one point a sniper had been shooting here as well. I looked across the room. The side widow had a clear line of fire straight down the road into town. The window had what was left of a tattered curtain now partly clinging to the corner. From the back of the room looking out, if the curtain were up, it would have given a good fallback position for a sniper's over-watch.

I walked up to the window with the curtain; in the distance, I could see a solitary man. He was slowly pushing a cart down the middle of the road. Every once in a while, he stopped and stooped down; he picked something up and tossed it into his cart before beginning to push it again.

The cart had an old axle and with every turn, it squeaked. It was big enough to put a considerable amount of stuff in. The man pushing it looked down. His shoulders were stooped, he walked with melancholy in his step. I watched curiously from my vantage point. I eased slowly out through the door and propped myself against the wall and waited.

I stood against the wall motionless; I could feel the sun start to heat up my cheap uniform. I didn't blame the YPG for the cheap material. The thing would ignite like a gas rag if touched by flame. It didn't matter that the uniform was not finished on the inside either. I was a heval, and hevals didn't usually live that long. All in all, it was not so bad, considering the circumstances. The uniforms were made in the basement of a bombed-out factory building in Kobani. Rojava was sealed off from the outside world with an unjust embargo by Turkey, Assad, Iran and Iraq. There were no supplies getting in and no way out. Still, despite all these obstacles, we were winning.

What did I know anyway? I had expected to be fighting in blue jeans and t-shirts so to get a uniform was a genuine surprise to me. It made me feel like I was a heval... and that mattered a lot to me as a volunteer. The fact that we were treated as hevals and included was the greatest honor.

The man drew slowly closer and I stepped away from the wall as to not startle him. Upon seeing me, he waved, saying "DemBas heval (good day)."

I waved back and walked out to him.

The man was Assyrian; he spoke a beautiful sounding Arabic and introduced himself. Like water, it bubbled out of him, and though I couldn't understand his words, I am sure I understood his meaning.

I tapped my chest and greeted him in return,

"Nava min Heval Tekoser. Amerki-YPG."

The man made me feel like I was the president himself standing there. In one swift motion he stepped up. Hugging me, he kissed my cheeks, blessing America, Obama and the YPG, touching his forehead and heart. It was humbling and surprising to be greeted so warmly.

The man was in his late fifties, perhaps; he smiled at me. Growing quiet and somber, he touched his heart with his right hand and bowed his head slightly before he started talking to me. He was telling me a story. I couldn't understand him at all, not a word, but sometimes words don't need translating.

The man pointed down the road at a house and then another, talking faster as the grief welled up in him. He looked up at the sky, both his hands held low, extended slightly outward and palms up. He paused for one shuddering breath before pointing to a church steeple that had been toppled. Turning back to me, tears in his eyes, he pointed to his cart, still talking. There were bits of broken everything in it, from chunks of concrete, old furniture and smashed porcelain dishes.

The only words he said that I know were the words 'YePiGay,' 'Daesh' and 'ochotyella' (Jet). I wanted to comfort him, so I put my hand on his shoulder.

"I understand. I am sorry!" I dropped my hand. Tapping my AK, I said, "Biji YePiGa! Serkiftin!" I did not really know what else to say. I wished I had better language skills.

In the distance, I heard my name, Tekoser, called, tugging me back to my responsibilities. I pointed toward our nocta.

"I have to go." I said to the man.

The man gave me a hug and three kisses on my cheeks, like his son. Singing me a prayer of some sort, he took my hand and placed a small cross in it. Speaking still, he pointed toward the crumbled steeple again, tears in his eyes. He folded my hand around the little cross, patting it closed, and he said, "Biji Heval Tekoser Amerki. Biji Biji YePiGay!"

With that, he turned back to his cart in the middle of the road and continued on his way, stooping down here and there to pull a weed or pick up a piece of trash and put it in his cart.

I headed back to the nocta we were teaching in. I walked quickly through the waist high grass of an empty lot. I wondered what happened to all the people in this town. What was that old man with the cart trying to tell me? I looked down at the simple cross attached to a chain in my hand. I felt some great tragedy had unfolded here.

I stepped into the classroom just as Razon was finishing his class. Baz looked irritated. I am sure he was thinking that I wasn't going to be back in time, but as soon as he saw me, he smiled and then stepped out. Firat had the worst of it because he had to translate all of it, day after day, over and over. The three of us only taught certain segments so we always got breaks in between. Firat never complained about it though.

After we finished class, Baz and the Mormon wanted to go to Til Tamir for supplies. Firat and I were supposed to take the ambulance back to our nocta. As we were finishing packing our teaching supplies into the back, I asked, "Hey Firat, what happened in this place?" He looked at me silently for a moment before he said, "Yeah bro, what happened here is really sad."

I put the last practice bandages in the back, closing the door, rubbing my sore arm from one too many students practicing IV training.

Heval Firat motioned to me, "Come on man, I'll show you the church."

That reminded me of the small cross and chain the man had given me. I had put it in the chest compartment of my body armor. Reaching in, I held it in my hand, not saying anything about it or the old man with the cart.

Grabbing our rifles, we walked a different way into the village than I had taken before. Just over a hill and around a corner was the church, totally destroyed. Everything was blown out of it and scattered on the ground. Most of the roof had collapsed but not all of it. The steeple had been blown over and lay cockeyed and detached. Rubble lay strewn everywhere and tangled in it were bits of tapestry cloth and shredded paper that had been emulsified by the sun and rain. Tile and wood pews were nothing more than broken shards, all the ornate carvings that would go inside a beautiful church, violated. A beheaded statue of Mother Mary lay on her side. The church must have been very beautiful before. It was not very big or grandiose, but when you stood inside the front, the stained-glass windows would have faced east; the sun in the morning would have shone through them, igniting the interior in an angelic glow of peace and love.

Now there was no stained glass left in the windows, only fine bits that lay crumbled on the ground like so many broken dreams, brightly colored and scattered under my feet.

A deep feeling of sadness permeated me. I asked Firat, "Heval, what happened here to this place?"

He paused momentarily. Looking at me, he said, "This town...." Shaking his head slowly side to side, he continued, "Daesh came through here in the middle of the night. No one knew they were coming; they captured the whole town all at once. This was a Christian town, Tal Nazrin. You know Daesh, heval... They separated out all the young women. Took all the able-bodied men and then put everybody else, including the children, into this church here." He waved around at the decimation and said, "And then they blew the church up with them all inside!"

I shook my head, feeling ill. "What the fuck?!" I said, wishing I could have heard something different from my heval.

He continued, "They took all the rest to Raqqa as slaves and what-not, no one has ever heard of them since. There's only one man left from this village. He had been away visiting his family in Qamishli." Firat shook his head sadly from side to side. Turning, he said, "Come on, let's look around a little more."

We walked out toward the church's community hall. Firat said, "Daesh had this village until about six months ago. It took over 120 Sehids to kick ISIS out of here. Bro, they had a tank in this town that they hid in a building and would roll out and back in so you would never know where the tank was. Heavy, heavy fighting here, heval!"

I whistled softly. My heart was heavy at the scale of this tragedy, the wrongness of it all. Of all the sick backward shit, this took the cake! I walked around now, looking at the church in ruins. I scanned the empty town with tumbleweeds blowing through the empty streets, thinking of the lone survivor there, day after day cleaning his village in hopes someday the others would return. I didn't know what to say because there isn't really anything you can say. We walked around the village together, in and out of houses, in silence.

I imagined that night, how terrifying it must have been to be dragged out of your bed scared, half-naked, hearing gunshots and screams as girls were raped and their fathers murdered. The bearded, scary men armed with machine guns and machetes swept through the entire town before anyone could escape, indiscriminately and randomly killing people. By morning, everybody was collected in the community center next to the church, only now separated by fate.

When I walked into the hall, the destruction inside was total. All the ceiling tiles were crumbled on the floor; the sky had become the celling now. As in the church, broken chairs, shredded hymnals and bibles lay smashed and torn on the floor. Against the back wall of the stage was a giant mural of the Garden of Eden. The mural's message was brought sharply home by the grotesque bullet scars gashed across and through it.

Pointing at the mural and a tight group of bullet holes, Firat said, "You can see this is where they executed some of the people before they put the others in the church."

The sick irony was not lost on me. I looked around the large hall, imagining the 300-plus residents of this town all huddled together, terrified, as one by one they were tortured and murdered. Thinking of children ripped from parents' arms, husbands from wives, I had tears in my eyes.

Turning to Firat, I asked, "Who does this?... What the HELL!!"

He shook his head, looking even more sad. "I know bro… that's why we have to KILL 'em all!"

I nodded now with a new understanding of the genocide taking place here.

My heart was heavy for the old man I met earlier who gave me the cross. He was still heroically clinging to hope, as day after day, he worked to restore what was left of his town. Hope in the face of absolute loss and grief is the greatest tragedy of love. His was a lonely life shared only with the memories of the past. I shook my head, feeling sadder than I have ever been, and wishing that these things that were, were not. Unfortunately, wishing only works in fairy tales and movies. There was no happy ending here, no justice to be had, no valuable lesson learned. All that was left here was the crime scene and the ghosts of the murdered.

Firat looked at me, imploring, "Heval, let us leave this place, it makes me too angry and sad."

I nodded somberly at him. "Yes, let's leave. My heart is breaking, heval."

We walked back to the ambulance in silence, each with our own thoughts. Every house that we walked by had battle scars, as street by street, our friends had fought and died to get this town back from the army of the black flags... Daesh.

The cross the old man gave me

The Church ISIS/Daesh blew up with all the people in it

A beheaded Mother Marry statue in town.

The bullet-scarred walls of the ghost town, Tal Nazrin.

CHAPTER 24: The Storm Inside

Peace is like the calm water in the eye of a hurricane.

Floating suspended in idealism, weightless.

Putting out of mind just for a time the horror we just went through or the back side of the storm that's drawing ever closer.

The intentional destruction of humanity and my willing participation in a violence so raw that it has a taste. A fear so deep my eyeballs jiggle, like dice in a cup.

There is a great pressure in the air where every breath is someone's last.

The edge of destruction approaches.

The end of peace.

I should run, but I can't… because it's already too late for me.

I am already broken beyond repair.

Fixated with the end, as even now it descends upon me.

So, off the edge of the world all hope is shoved and flung backwards into darkness.

Falling… into the endless abyss.

Why is it we live this life?

What is its purpose?

Living as if we have no death? As if there is no end, even as the clock is continuously counting down.

Living like there is plenty when there is none.

Perhaps this life is not even a billionth of a second in the endless line of time.

Why would one assume that <u>ONE</u> is so great? That one ego is so much better than the other? So much better, in fact, that it is entitled to take and kill with impunity?

And why the hell do we feel so much love, if life is so cruel?

If you're expecting an answer here, go get a self-help book.

Maybe there is a better world somewhere out there in the stars.

Maybe this world we are born into is a purgatory?

Maybe it's a hell?

It definitely can't be heaven. Can it?

The pendulum swings.

Good/Bad, Bad/Good.

Peace, war, killing, peace.

Hope deceived by greed, greed consumed by death, death consumed by life and life goes on until some asshole pushes the nuke button and all the lights go out.

The sky is a surreal glow. The disappearing orange orb licking the last of the horizon. I look at it sadly.

The ground drinks hope here like water, and it is always the thirstiest after dark. Now the smoldering city lays crumbled before us, the burnt offerings of war and the desperate struggle for survival.

The residents left in the city couldn't flee.

Those that tried lay slaughtered in the streets where they were gunned down by Daesh.

Packs of starving dogs eat the faces off of the newly slain, ISIS, hevals or civilians, makes no difference here where hunger is tinged with madness.

The living now, not the left-behinds of war. Their eyes once wide in fear and alive with tragedy now just blankly staring up at nothing. Their last moments here? Are all our last moments… and only the foolish can deny that.

Dead ISIS/Daesh fighter my heval killed.
The dogs ate only his face off.

CHAPTER 25: Hard Target

It is hard to say if I ever murdered another man; if I didn't, it wasn't for lack of trying, as bad as that may sound to you. When the ideology of war is put aside, that's the raw truth of it. War is murder.

You know, I wish we lived in a world where hate was not sold as a religion to all sides, where killing wasn't the most profitable business on earth. A world where there was peace, love and equality all around us... but we don't live in that world, and until there is a real evolution in humanity's empathy, we won't. Until that hopeful day, know these pages describe an infinitesimal portion of the ongoing cost for this abject ignorance of hate profiteering.

Please, try not to judge me, lest you end up looking at yourself too closely in the mirror. Good or bad, the enemies we fight, and kill are all already a part of us. We are not a separate race; black, white or brown, we are one race… the human race. The death of one of us is surely the death of all of us. I do not hate my enemy on the battlefield; I hate those who sell hate off the battlefield.

Combat? Yeah, it's good... until it's not. When it's bad, you know. It's not like on the video games where you get to see who you're shooting at in slow motion. Life is not a digital pixel that ends with the game restart button if you fuck up or are unlucky, nor are there more lives, limbs or med packs to instantly heal. It's not a movie that cuts to a shot of the bad guy still on his smoking gun so you can place a well-aimed shot and see his head explode in super slow motion. The reality is, when you're in a gunfight in the city, it's hard to say who killed the dead bastards lying behind the window we were all shooting into.

Sometimes, it's not the enemy lying there... maybe it's a woman and a kid that were just hiding scared and trapped, maybe there's a car full of civilians trying to escape and not a car bomb. How do you know?

Combat is not so neat or clean and it's almost always confusing. Maybe today whoever is shooting at you is deep behind a murder hole, so bullets appear as if by magic, 200 meters away; there isn't any clear direction... just one of your own falls over, blood suddenly seeping out through a new hole. Someone else starts to yell. Then gunfire erupts down your line, shooting back at the unseen, but there's no guarantee your heval even saw anything to shoot back at. So maybe you shoot back? Maybe you wait? And then another one of your friends is shot and now you know it's coming from the left flank... not at all where you thought.

There are a million windows and crumbled walls, corners and debris-littered streets full of half-burned cars and downed trees. Now you know the only way to see that fucker who is shooting at you is to go and poke your own fool head out and look yourself... and wait.... and hope... you don't get shot in the face... but sometimes you do. That's just some shit luck though; you won't know it because bullets go faster than sound! I am not saying that this is how it is all the time. Lots of guys had different experiences. This was just mine.

It's the parts we don't like to remember that are likely the hardest to swallow, like the waiting and the frustration of not being able to do our jobs while our friends are being hurt and killed, the pain of seeing little kids blown up, grieving mommas wailing over dead children. The end of hope and innocence dropped my false pretense of heroic anything. You want war? This is war.

...

There was a buzz of activity. Suddenly, people were running everywhere. We didn't know what is coming, just that something was coming. A murmur went through the line; you could hear the fear in it.

"Car Bomb!"

Everyone was edgy because car bombs are scary as fuck. They are hard to escape because they are so massive when they go off. Also, the car is being driven by someone hell-bent on dying... and, it's being driven at us.

Lying there, I was the furthest out. I was looking down my rifle, waiting. There was no sign of the car bomb. Maybe it was a hoax.

It was hot; the land had heat waves rising off it. I should have taken a position back by the trees, in the shade, but that position lacked a clear line of fire. There was a lot of dust in the sky, creating a brownish blue visage. The air was still and heavy. Something was tickling the back of my neck. Was it a bug or sweat? I felt it slowly roll down my back, concluded it was sweat. I adjusted my kaffie/scarf so I was under its shade more. I waited.

Far off in the distance, there was a honking sound, barely audible. *Beeeeeep..... beeep.beeep.* Once, long and slow, then twice in quick succession. Hard to say, maybe it was just my mind playing tricks on me. Then it went again and in the distance a car appeared through the heat waves. I watched it get closer.

"Goddamn it!" There was no way to know what it was. Life depended on the right decision here. My gun bucked in my hands, *BANG!* I fired a warning shot. A tracer round went out in front of the car, skipping off the ground in front of it. I was almost surprised I had squeezed the trigger.

The car began to speed up, heading toward our position and now began honking in earnest! *BEEP! BEEEP BEEEP!* Car bombers honk just before they blow themselves up, so everyone comes out to see what is happening. I fired again, now with serious intent. The car came lurching to a halt.

There was a small earthen berm the sabotage unithad hastily dug across the road only a few hours before. The heavily armored car bomb stuck to it as it tried to go over it. The berm was not that big, just a few feet tall. The car bomb was like a cockroach stuck on a trap.

I fired at the stalled car again. *BANG.BANG.BANG!* I saw my tracer round hit the car dead center. It was definitely a car bomb, no doubt about it now. There was not much hope an AK round would do shit to a car bomb but at least it created harassing fire. It couldn't feel good to hear bullets hitting your rolling bomb, whether they made it detonate or not.

BANG. BANG. BANG! I watched the tracer rounds' orange phosphorus trail, a glowing firefly arching up. up. up... and then slowly down like an arrow across the sky and into the car.

I gave it three more rounds: *BANG. BANG. BANG!* My aim was spot on. I wasn't really expecting any reaction, but car bombs have driver's slits in the front. There was a small chance that one of my rounds could go in through it... like one in a million...

Car bombs are fricken scary because they are so hard to stop. You can shoot them all you want, but unless you have a heavy machine gun on it or a rocket, it's going to keep coming at you. *BANG.BANG.BANG!* I didn't want them getting too comfortable in their ride to hell.

Without warning, the passenger door opened; someone got out and bolted up the ridge line. It surprised me. I didn't expect a passenger. I swung my rifle after the fleeing figure, but I was too slow and I didn't get a bead on him before he disappeared over the side.

I swung my rifle back down toward the car just as the driver's door opened and the driver emerged, running after the passenger and right into my sights. *BANG.BANG.BANG!* I ripped off three quick shots at the fleeing figure, my tracer round impacting just a tad behind him.

I shifted my rifle right two degrees, then I let him have it. *BANG.BANG. BANG.BANG!* This time he ran into my fire.

I watched my tracer heading toward the running man. One-one-thousand, two/ it looked like the little running man and my tracer intersected. I could see him go down suddenly. "Did he trip? Did I hit him?" He got back up. Scrambling a short distance, he disappeared over the far side of the ridgeline. Lucky bastard! They both got away. "Well SheeeeIT! I guess I only winged him!"

Their escape was disappointing, as they would attack us again another day no doubt. When a fucker drives a car bomb at us, I definitely don't feel bad about trying to drill him.

It turned out both their minutes were numbered because some hevals from the far side of the road flanked back to where the driver and the passenger of the car bomb had disappeared. A short time later I heard a brief automatic rifle burst. *BAAAA WAAAAAAAAA!*

The radio, just behind my position, squawked and I could hear the heval's voice came over the box, exclaiming, "Daesh mafi." The hevals around me cheered. The 30mm gun truck arrived and started shooting at the car bomb. *CHUNKwweeeezzzz... CHUNKwweeezzzz... KAAAABOOOMMMM!!* The car bomb detonated.

Daesh was good at packing cars with thousands of pounds of high explosives, enough to literally take out a small city block. I had never seen anything so massive explode that close. I could feel the air suck in a little and then, like water in a pool, the shock wave passed over me. For almost a minute afterward I could hear metal bits falling from the sky.

Tink….tink.tink….. clunk…. Clang. The car came back to earth like hot metal confetti, raining down from the closest to heaven I would probably ever get. But luckily nothing landed on anyone. The road, minus a giant crater, was now again clear for traffic to resume, which it did almost immediately after.

...

Sometimes now I wonder about that day, about those two in that car driving it. What were they thinking in those miles they drove toward their useless impending deaths? Did they contemplate whether they were wrong? What if the raping and head chopping weren't in the name of God? Did they contemplate that? I am sure they did, that's why Daesh had started using two suicide bombers, to make sure they both carried it out. One drives, one detonates. Did they have on prayer music as they drove? Boy, talk about some grim conversations! Did they think they were going to heaven by killing themselves? That's some fucking blind faith man, to believe so much, to believe in something so evil it calls you to willingly detonate yourself in a final twisted act of stupidity and self-flagellation.

There is the internet and all the world's knowledge available at our fingertips, quantum physics, missions to Mars, and yet these idiots still believe that if they blow themselves up, they're going to heaven and getting seventy-two virgins? Who wants virgins anyway? I want me an experienced woman who knows how to love her man.

Do you want to know how I know that Daesh doesn't really believe in God or heaven. It's because I saw the rape house they had in Shaddadi, the one with the ripped-up porn mags on the floors and the spent needles next to empty bottles of morphine, ketamine and diazepam. I saw chains bolted to the walls and beds. If their perverse prophesy of paradise were true, then they would have waited for it there and not needed to rape little girls here.

You can say whatever you want, but the basis of ISIS, or any other religious extremist group, is rape, slavery, drugs and fascism. ISIS/Daesh promised a so-called caliphate but instead they delivered hell. Once the poor people were sucked in or trapped, there was no escape, and the people were preyed upon. Their hope was eaten like the Daesh corpses that later fed the starving dogs.

It gets me so mad just thinking about it. I want to say I shot a Daesh fuck because it doesn't sound as good to say, well, maybe I got him. Maybe I shot a stupid, misguided human, taught to hate, rape and kill. When you break it down and remove the ideology, that's exactly what happened. There were no heroics in it; it was just killing and dying. Either way, on this day, both those fuckers got their wish. They were killed by the hevals. Whether I hit one or not, I guess I'll never know. I do know both Daesh were killed running away from their failed attempt to kill us. In the end all they accomplished was ongoing warfare, barely even noticing.

Car bomb I was shooting at, exploding

CHAPTER 26: The White House

The white house was not finished. It was like somebody had stopped time here. When the war started, all construction stopped. Tools were laying at the job site where the workers had left them that last day. The house was now our opulent base. Its grandeur stood in obscene contrast to the poverty of the surrounding countryside.

In a countryside dotted with small villages, farms, and herders, the mansion seemed more like one of the king's castles. The giant skeleton now empty, it felt like a half-built sarcophagus to greed and the dreams of the rich and corrupt.

The house's grandeur stopped at the unfinished walls, open doors, and glassless windows. The house stood as an abject symbol of repression and revolution, all wrapped up in one. Now, instead of the dictator's third cousin, the house belonged to us, the army of maids, cooks, nannies, gardeners, ex-soldiers, expatriates, dreamers, artists, teachers, and tire changers. Despite our varied backgrounds, we all had a commonality; no matter what individually drew us here, our common goal was the same: to end ISIS.

We encountered the smell of hope and a future that hung unseen in the air. Rojava is a place where no one must live like a non-person, a slave, or in fear of ethnic identity. It is a place where women are also the leaders, scholars and generals - side by side and equal with men.

On the other side of Rojava and the hevals are ISIS/Daesh and Erdogan, the Turkish dictator who is backing them. They are depraved lunatics who want to completely annihilate Rojava and the People's Protection Units, YPG/YPJ and SDF.

Rojava is a place that some rich asshole couldn't run our lives like a factory floor. So, today the house was ours ...... tomorrow?... who knows? Should it matter? Can freedom be measured that way? I don't know. I am not a college-educated man, but it doesn't take a degree to see how freedom is paid for, or what its real value is.

Over the last week, the white house had been attacked every day. Mostly it was a harassing fire, but it was sent with deadly intent. Every few shots or so would get a lot closer than I would ever like.

The sniper shooting at us could see me easily through his scope, but it's hard to hit somebody at 300 meters. Still it was unnerving knowing someone was always watching, trying to kill you.

I kept a non-predictable pattern to movement: walk a few steps, stop... take two or three quick steps to the left or right. Never stand still for more than the count of 'one, one thousand.'

You know, it's crazy the things you can get used to on the front. Over time, we had grown nonchalant about Daesh trying to kill us. When you live with that much tension and random moments of terror for so long, it becomes the norm. It's like putting a lobster in cold water and turning the heat up slowly, tricking the mind into thinking the boiling water is balmy.

It was early afternoon; Razon and Baz were hanging out near the van. I trotted up in a zigzag. Baz laughed at me but offered to scoot over, sharing the shade from the fruit trees. I was standing off to the side; I wasn't staying long. I had found a little shady spot and I was headed there to curl up for a nap.

I had just leaned against the van when *SNAPPWwinggg*!! A round whipped just over my head.

Baz laughed, "Damn Tekoser. I bet that poor sniper is so pissed he missed you again!!"

Quickly squatting down, I laughingly joked, "Sniper-obits.. keeps ya movin'."

Razon the Mormon said, "I almost feel bad for the guy. I mean, think about it, every day for a week he shoots at us... over... and over... and he can never hit a thing!"

Baz cracked up. "Maybe he should start bigger."

I laughed. "Yeah, slightly bigger - like the side of a barn bigger! Build up his confidence, you know."

The Mormon joked., "Yeah, maybe he is vision impaired."

Baz laughed! "Jah.. The world's worst sniper! The Elmer Daesh Fud of snipers!"

After all this suffering and loss, laughing felt so good, as if the sniper could hear our conversation, *SNAPPWwinggg*! Another round cracked overhead. He was getting way too close for comfort.

To our east, across a small orchard that dropped away to an open field, was a large factory building. It had a variety of adjoining buildings next to it and was surrounded by a tall concrete wall. To our north was another set of buildings, a small farming hamlet. To the northeast was a large barn. The orchard was the line, and everything over it belonged to Daesh.

Today the Daesh sniper was shooting at us with a 5.56 round, which is American made. I knew it was a 5.56 because earlier I had a hole suddenly appear, as if by magic, in the door of a truck I was standing next to. The bullet went *zip.TINK...CRACK*! Did you know sound lags behind bullets?

I wondered if the person back home who made that gun, or that round, gave a crap that it was in the hands of a psycho maniac army of killers trying to stamp out freedom and democracy, that Daesh was lining people up in ditches and massacring them with it. 'American Made.' It is big business, selling our guns to Turkey. Stamped below the corporate logo, the motto of the weapon's manufacturing plant back home in America reads: "In God We Trust." I wonder what god that asshole is talking about.

I looked down at my own busted up AK47 from 1973; it had a homemade combat sling and some brown spray paint on it for camo. I wished I had the same well-made new shit to fight these assholes back with. Equal rights, feminism, peace and self-determination… that don't sell guns! So, in this fight, the bad guys get the Gucci 511 tactile gear and backdoor corporate sponsorships. Daesh was sponsored like professional athletes as they swept across the land like a plague of death and terror.

Later, when the sun was behind us, the YPJ commander sent out an assault after the sniper in the barn. Like ghosts, my comrades snuck through the trees toward the structure and then across the open field.

A YPJ Duska truck started cranking out 30mm explosive rounds into the distant barn. Fear was sent back the other way as the tables turned on the would-be hunter, to the now would-be prey.

The hevals ran towards the barn firing their AKs. There was a small flurry of activity from inside, another burst of automatic fire, and then it was quiet.

The hevals reappeared out of the barn a few moments later, holding aloft a new M-4 with scope. The commander's radio crackled upstairs. I heard the hevals around the white house cheering, an easy victory.

The brief struggle to end one man's life was over as fast as it started. I thought about that, but I didn't feel anything. "Fuck Daesh!" It was nice to walk around almost normally.

The next day, there was another sniper. This sniper was better. Several rounds cracked by so close I could feel the pressure difference as they passed. It felt like an invisible tug and the sound of a whip or bee. Sometimes not unlike an old spaghetti western, the bullet would ricochet, whining off, to wherever bullets go.

The Mormon had been texting off some poached sim card and a two bar Turkcel signal because we were close to the Turkish border. I was surprised, but the Mormon Razon had the knack to get tech shit working. He laughed at my surprised reaction to his communication ability. As I was standing there, a round narrowly missed me. It went *BAA WWEEEENNNGGGG* just past my head. I dropped to a knee.

The Mormon said, half joking, "Well, maybe I'll put my phone away now."

I laughed at him, still impressed he was texting from here, on the edge of no-man's-land. I poked around, starting to look for the new sniper's position.

I asked the Mormon, "I wonder if they told him the guy he replaced today… we zapped yesterday?"

The Mormon said, "Probably was his pal!"

I grunted, "Hope so! That way we can kill him too."

I leaned up against our minivan. We had painted it brown with old brooms, a bucket of water and dirt, mixing the dirt into a thick mud paste any eight-year-old would be jealous of. It was a frugal attempt to blend the shiny white paint into the brown landscape, to become less obvious, as if four western medics, one with a giant camera, didn't already stand out more than a mud paint job.

It was hot. Summer had begun in earnest now. It was the kind of hot day where you can hear crickets sing and flies buzzing around. There was no breeze to speak of... and then, out of nowhere, everything erupted.

The sound of automatic rifle fire and bullets ripped past us, *FUUWAP. WAP. WAPWAP!* You could hear incoming rounds separately, but all on top of each other. I had taken my bullet-proof vest off for a brief reprise from its oppressive weight. "God damnit! Of all times," I swore as I quickly scrambled back into my armor, rolling over now like a fat Santa on my kit that included my IFAK, 9 mags, camel back and medic run bag. Racking a round into the rifle chamber, I rolled around the back side of the van. I could hear automatic rifle fire descending on our position. Trying to ascertain where it was coming from, kneeling low on the ground, I could hear the rounds zip past like a bunch of angry bees. I couldn't see anything from here. Taking a chance and standing, peering around the back of the van, down the iron sights of my rifle - I still couldn't see shit. Then, *zip zip ZIP ZIP!* The rounds ripped past our position, just barely missing the van – I guess they saw me just fine. I was not in a good spot.

Baz yelled, "Move to the second floor!"

I popped out around the back of the van yelling, "Covering Fire!" I squeezed off one shot but when I squeezed the trigger again nothing happened. What the fuck? My rifle was misfiring??!!

"Goddamn it, not now!" Then, as if to make it less stressful, from another direction, new automatic rifle fire opened up on us. The sound of snapping twigs was coming from two directions. Rounds were snapping just over my head. *Zip Zip Zap.. Tink.. Crack...* Heavy machine gun rounds were mixed in with the deadly crossfire.

I called out loudly, "MY RIFLE'S JAMMMED! I AM OUT!" I fell back against the tire of the van, removing the upper receiver of my AK-47. I cycled the bolt and ejected the double stuffed round. It is a shitty feeling being attacked from two different directions and having a weapon stop working properly. What could I expect? My AK was made 45 years ago. I was ready for this peace of shit rifle to fuck me.

All of us were ready for it to go wrong. I knew, just looking at my garage sale rifle, that if I ever really needed it, I would be in trouble. To mitigate the crappy equipment, we had drilled, drilled and drilled. We had practiced the rifle jamming in contact, taking it apart and reassembling it. Dil Sause, after Shaddadi, started having contests to see who could do each drill the fastest.

My hands knew every part, so when it all went to shit, I was ready. Back in the fight, I stood near the back of the van. I looked down the sights of my gun toward the distant building, I didn't see anything. Screw it, I attempted to squeeze off three shots at nothing, anyway. Again, the rifle only fired once.

I swore loudly at it, "FUCK YOU!" I popped the mag back out and violently cycled the chamber twice, ejecting one and one. Slapping the mag back in, I racked it, leaned back out and fired again. "BANG! click," it only fired once and was jammed again. "FUCK!"

The Aussie yelled from the white house. "GO! TEKOSER!! WHAT ARE YOU WAITING FOR??!!"

I was the last one. My heart was pounding, my palms were sweating, and my mouth got real dry, real quick. I bolted across the open gap and made it to the wall. I scooted around the side and ran in.

The attack was intensifying, the gunfire sounded like beer-battered shrimp as they hit the oil and sizzle. Inside the white house, I ran across the debris-strewn floor and up the unfinished Y staircase. I came around the second story walkway and entered the side room. There was a good field of fire from here. Baz was also in the room, and we began trading rifle fire with the building next to the factory.

I still couldn't get my rifle to work properly. I could only fire one round at a time. It was just like shooting a single shot muzzle-loading rifle, but in a modern gun fight… it was all fucked up.

Super frustrated, I decided to fire it on full auto. I was not sure if it would work. I popped back out the window, completely exposed, but my rifle only went click when I fired it.

"FUCK!!" I ducked down again; I had forgotten to cycle a round into the chamber. I heard rounds striking the walls and tearing through the window where I had just been.

The building I was trying to fire on was about 200 meters away from our position. We had elevation, though, so I only set my range to the one. I stepped back to the window and tapped the trigger. *BWA.A WA. WA. WA!* The rounds ripped out in smooth perfection.

It's not ideal to be in full automatic, unless you're shooting into a crowd or in close quarters, because only the first round is on target; the next rounds are sent haphazardly after the first. The recoil of the rifle affects the accuracy.

Baz and I continued to trade fire with the building opposite us, ducking in and out of two different windows at random. Two mags down and, just as suddenly as it started on our side, it stopped. I didn't know what had happened.

Maybe we got them?

Maybe one of the others did?

Maybe they moved?

No way to know.

I was sitting there, my heart racing, bent over my smoking rifle. My eyes stung from the sweat dripping into them. I couldn't see any movement from. It made me feel anxious. It was easier when you knew where they were and bullets were flying. The unknown was the scary part. The silence was matched only by the loud ringing in my ears.

"Fuck this!" I moved out of the window. Looking around the room, my imagination was drawn back in, like a rock dropped on the ground.

On the other side of the building, I could still hear heavy fighting. Some hevals had arrived in our room and dropped a Bixy in the window. I headed out toward the sound of fighting on the other side of the house.

In the room where the gunfire was coming from, I saw Razon and Brusk. When Razon saw me, he looked like a kid at a theme park.

"Tekoser! The fire was coming from over there! I saw muzzle flashes from the door!" Razon popped up and squeezed off three more shots. *BANG.BANG.BANG!* Each shot was released as he came down off the last, and he dropped to a knee again. Turning to me, he had a giant smile on his face and, pointing at the wall where there was a cavernous hole, he yelled, "Tekoser look! That was for me!"

I had never seen anybody so excited or happy to almost get plugged. You can say what you want about the Mormon, but I can promise you this, when it comes to slinging lead? He slings it with the best of 'em! Maybe it's because Razon believes in something more than us, believes that he has somewhere special to go when he dies. I don't have that delusion though, so I plan on living as long as I can.

I joined in on the party and started firing at the low squat building Razon had pointed to. Since my AK-47 was on automatic, it was deafening in the small room. It seemed kind of funny to me at the time. That's the way it goes, though, when you're in the perfect gunfight and none of your friends gets hurt.

The tank showed up with the duska truck. Tanks are awesome. *BOOOMMMM!*!! It shot a High-Explosive (HE) cartridge and disappeared in a ring of smoke. The roof of the factory building was blown off.

The YPJ 30mm duska opened up in full auto, what a beautiful sound. *CHUHNKCHUNKC!* and then it got quiet. The assault on our position had ended as fast as it started.

The hevals jumped in their trucks and zoomed off toward the smoldering rubble. Today, Rojava's border grew by 300 meters; ten new buildings and five dead head-choppers... Hevals Sehid? Zero. Now that's a win right there.

Firing in automatic ate up my bullets though, and also made my rifle filthy. Later in the back of the van, alone, my ears still ringing and the adrenaline finally winding down, I cleaned my rifle. I finally had a moment to think about how lucky we had just been. The van door cracked open and a gentle breeze trickled through, licking my dirty, sweaty skin. My eyes were heavy; I was tired.

Baz came running up excitedly shouting, "Yes! Tekoser! We are moving up! You drive the ambulance; the Aussie will drive the van. Come, we must hurry!"

I bolted upright. "Fuck yeah!" Sleep was instantly gone from my mind, I was excited to be advancing, moving closer to the city and the fight.

I felt like we had been here forever, and forever is long enough. Long enough that is… until you get to the chicken factory.

The white house, as we all called it

CHAPTER 27: The Chicken Factory

I was in the ambulance. We were driving up to a large building. Baz was sitting next to me. There was a large hole in the wall where an HP tank round had penetrated it. We used this as our entrance point. I was following the truck tracks in front of us.

The hevals before us had quickly cleared the debris from the hole. The old 4x4 Ranger box truck ambulance had no difficulty clearing the crumbled wall.

Our best ally in Rojava, Hevala Jiyan, had helped Baz and Bagok secure the old ambulance a few months before. When we did get it, it took weeks to get it properly running. Finding Ford parts in Rojava was not exactly easy. That said, our hevals in the motor T were the most creative mechanics you ever knew. They figured out a way to fix the alternator and blown cylinder, giving us the only 4x4 ambulance on the western front.

As we entered, turning to the right, I drove down the factory road. On the left, there were two large three-story concrete buildings, each stretching a hundred meters or more back. On the right were two three-story office buildings. Between them was a large generator and oil-blackened ground. The signs of recent fighting were apparent everywhere. The old tenants' bodies, the dead Daesh, were piled up against the back wall, later to be dragged away and left unburied in the field.

Driving up, I took it all in. It was truly a scene from the end of days. With a sinking feeling inside, turning off the ignition, I paused before opening my door as if to somehow delay the inevitable. Stepping out of the ambulance, I had two horrible reactions, each as repugnant as the other. The first was the overwhelming stench of death and the second was a curtain of flies that had immediately begun to swarm me. They were so thick it was as if the flies were the very air itself. I could feel them all around me, swarming as if I was the future real estate for their eggs and children to eat, and perhaps I was.

"Oh, my fucking God!" I exclaimed in horror…

Now I must admit, I am grossed out by flies. I think flies are fucking disgusting. In my life I had never seen so many flies in one spot. I probably had not seen that many flies combined in my whole life. There were literally millions and millions of them.

"Oh no! We're not staying here!" I immediately told Baz.

He looked pissed, replying, "Tekoser this is our new home, Ja! So, no complaints about it!"

I shook my head back and forth in disbelief. He was always so serious. I couldn't believe it.

"Now you got to be kidding me! How are we supposed to treat casualties here? Flies all over them!?"

As I was talking, I sucked a fly into my mouth, gagging, spitting and choking! Baz started laughing at me, but I noticed he was careful not to open his own mouth too wide.

"Fucker!!" I tried to vomit the fly up, but it was no use; I had swallowed it! "AHHH GROSS!!"

My mind raced for an alternative to this hell. I suggested that perhaps we could return to our old position. The half-built white mansion now seemed luxurious. Baz did not like my suggestion; he just turned and stalked off.

Walking up to the ambulance, Brusk looked just about as horrified as I was. He was waving his hands back and forth, a pained expression on his face. Razon was still in the back of the van, as if he didn't want to get out.

Baz came back and summoned us all together, issuing us our marching orders. We were to set up CCP here. The commanders would not let us go any farther forward because the line was shifting too fast.

I started to protest. "But…"

Baz, interrupting me, said, "Don't worry, they're going to be taking medics out from here on the tracks and in the BMBs. For now, guys, this is where we are, and we got to make the best of it!"

Baz always was one for telling it how it 'is' very logically. I was getting close to invoking his temper as I started to protest again.

The Aussie, nudging me, gave me a wink, meaning, "Shut the fuck up, mate, before you piss off the boss."

So, I shut my mouth and just nodded. I raised my hand as soon as Baz stopped talking and volunteered to go out first. Brusk and the Mormon's hands also shot up as, simultaneously, they uttered the same thing. But first… is first!

The only one that didn't seem to mind the flies was the Aussie. Not one teeny tiny little fuck did Bagok give about them. He just smiled at us through his weathered blue eyes, beneath his bushy eyebrows, and said, "All right then, where should we set up the casualty control point? Let's do a walk-about and take a look."

As we walked around, it became clear what the place had been. Inside the large concrete factory buildings were a hundred thousand mostly dead chickens. Their cages were stacked floor to ceiling on some sort of massive, rotating conveyor system, and the eggs could be pulled out from a stationary position at the end of each line of cages.

Inside hevals with scarves tied around their faces were taking dead chickens out of their steel-caged graves. They piled their maggot-filled bodies on blankets and dragged the blankets out the back. Over and over, the process was repeated.

The air was black with flies; they swarmed like ocean waves. The stench was so overpowering that my eyes felt like they were bleeding. Gagging on the sweet heavy stench, I took it all in, repulsed by the vulgarity of the sight and smell.

In a testament to the tenacity and resilience of life, about every tenth cage had a live scraggy chicken, sitting on a bunch of eggs.

"God, those poor birds!" The hevals were putting the live ones in a large makeshift pen; they had scattered grain on the ground and the birds were eating it, like sharks in a feeding frenzy.

So much of the time we spend our reflective moments of war contemplating the human toll, but what I saw that day, that kind of carnage and suffering… I will never forget. I will remember it as one of the saddest things I've ever seen in my life.

What I loved about the hevals, what I admired so much, was that not one of them complained or looked pissed off doing this horrible job, this heart-wrenching, backbreaking, hot, sweaty, fly-infested, putrid, rotten, debauchery of all that's wrong with war. In fact, several of them exuberantly waved and called out to us through their scarf-wrapped faces, "Hello doctor. Welcome! Welcome!!"

I waved back at my hevals and turned and fled the interior. That was the first time in Rojava that I ran away.

Later, there were thousands of dead chickens piled in a massive heap, doused with diesel fuel, old tires stacked on top of them… and true to the motto, 'Will it Burn?' it burned! It smelled like a Texas roadhouse barbecue, mixed with mattress and burnt rubber.

The thick, black finger of smoke reached high into the sky as if to poke it in the face of Daesh/ISIS.

"Your eggs are now ours… Losers!"

The eggs were a very welcome addition. By this point, logistics had become a complete nightmare, as with the shifting lines and changing routes, it had been incredibly difficult for food/logistics trucks to make their way to the front. It had been weeks since we had fresh food other than what we could scavenge from the recently abandoned and war-ravaged buildings.

The Aussie had an awesome way to check eggs to see if they were good or bad, and later we sat and went through a large pile of eggs by putting them in a bucket of water. If they sank, they were rotten; if they floated, they were dinner.

So that night, for the first time in weeks, we each ate a giant meal of scrambled eggs. It was almost normal for a minute eating by the fire after dark, when the flies had finally gone away. Sitting under the stars, the five of us, felt as if we were on a camping trip back home. Even though we were all so far away, and we were from so many different corners of the world, the word HOME always had the same place in our hearts.

It's funny the things you miss when you're so far away. To me, minus the obvious, like my kids and stuff, I always missed American food the most. The taste of something familiar in my mouth with my eyes closed can transport me continents and years even... like in this moment, just the thought of ketchup up on my eggs made me think of home, and smile.

We laughed and joked around with the Mormon about how we were all going to crash his wedding. We concocted the perfect scheme to copy his Mormon card so we could sneak into the Mormon Temple and attend his wedding. Razon was often our muse when it came to humor because he was the only pure one of us. All of us ragtag, scrabble bastards had dirt and dirty jokes in common, except the Mormon Razon. Since we were such a sordid motley crew, it was only natural for us to greatly enjoy poking a little good-natured fun at the Mormon and his high values. In truth, perhaps we all secretly looked up to him a little, not for his beliefs, but rather for who he was, always principled. The whole time I served with Razon, I never saw him cuss, smoke, drink chai, coffee, or energy drinks. That's what made him so lovable, I suppose; he was something clean in a dirty world.

To me, peace was found in the simple moments, moments like that night, sitting under the stars, next to a fire free of flies, eating slightly burned scrambled eggs with no ketchup, all of us just sitting together, laughing and joking.

You know, those were the moments that made us hevals, the moments when we could shed off the layers of stress, fear and sorrow. The simple times where we were all just friends chalking it up by a campfire.

As I lay down that night, I thought about all that lay ahead for my friends here in Rojava. This place, where my privilege to leave after my six months was over, while my hevals could not, made me ashamed to say the word… "Home." It sounded so simple really, so humble. It seemed like something everyone should get to say and have, just a basic human right. In such a violent world, though, simplicity and right were found as far away as my heart…

At the edge of the end of life, where hope is all that's left to die for… HOME…

The chicken factory office building

The ground we walked on at the chicken factory

CHAPTER 28: The Dancing Hevals

On the way back to the front, I was sleeping in the back of the Heyva Sor ambulance. My dear friend, my heval from Til Tamer, Armang, didn't need the cot for the return trip. His leg was ripped off by an explosion.

I kept telling Heval Armang it was OK, but I knew it wasn't. He had lost a lot of blood. Even though I had a tourniquet on him and put an IV into him, he was fading the whole way, little by little. By the time we got to Sarin, he was barely conscious.

I passed him off to an ambulance that was headed to Kobani. I was hoping he could just make it ninety minutes more. My heart was heavy, wishing I could have done better for him; I'll probably never know.

Heval Adnan drove us the two and a half hours back to hell. One hope, shot across the black night. Speeding through ISIS/Daesh-held goonds, empty countryside, rolling hills and fields of wheat… I saw none of it.

I was lying on the gurney in the back, the same gurney that Heval Armang was just on. I lay there wondering when it would be 'my time' to look up at 'myself' working over 'me'… I wanted to tell my future self, trying to save my life, "It's OK," just like Heval Armang tried to tell me. In my fantasy, there was nothing I could do to save myself, and I knew this. I couldn't talk to my other self, not in this nightmare. I just had to lie paralyzed on my back, looking up at myself, working frantically, until the image faded to darkness…

I woke up, bouncing over dirt-washed homemade roads, in the back of the ambulance, confused and wondering where I was. Then it settled in on me, like a wet blanket. I was headed back to where the inferno burns the coldest, darkest, and hurts the most.

I was dropped off at the white house, where the Heyva Sor ambulances were now staged. The front had moved, and this was now the rear. I hitched a ride the rest of the way up to the frontline with some hevals who had been back on a resupply mission.

It was late or early, depending on how you feel about 0200. When I finally got back to our casualty control point, there was lots of activity.

An assault force was amassing. Truck after truck arrived, including mine. They were all packed with excited hevals, singing along to YPG morale songs that blasted through truck door speakers, their windows down.

At the rally point for the coming assault, the gathered trucks sat idling, and their headlights ignited the dust, like smoke on stage at a rock concert. My hevals got out of the waiting trucks and made a line together. Pinky in pinky, they danced.

The YPG music pulsated at full blast across the rooftops of the darkened city. Music of celebration and hope played through the door speakers of the ex-Daesh trucks. These were trucks we had killed to get, and Daesh knew this.

My hevals moved as one, all together, their shadows in step with them. The city's pockmarked lunar scape acted as the backdrop for 'the last party.' Our shadows disappeared, also together, where the darkness ate the light. The hevals were ignited by light but surrounded by darkness. We experienced joy in the face of terror, dancing with love in the shadow of death.

I smiled at the resilience, bravery and beauty of my hevals. Humbled by love and inspired by hope... I knew I had found my place in the world, even if only for this night or this hour. Even though I was tired, inspired by the energy in the air, I got up and joined in.

My friend, Hevala Berxwedana, was at the end and I joined in. She said, "Heval Tekoser! It is good to see you." She smiled at me, taking my pinky finger in hers.

I didn't get the dance steps right, but it didn't matter. The hevals didn't care; they just loved to dance together. When we (western volunteers) joined in, our bad dance steps and awkward blunders were ignored. We were all just hevals dancing into the night before the big battle started and we may never dance again.

The Kurds dance in a semi-circle and always have room for more to join in. Soon the line grew, and I was no longer on the end but in the middle. We moved in one giant single motion, as if we had 100 feet, not just two. There was an energy that I can't explain, as if a little electric current was running through all of us.

It was under the faint almost rose-colored sky of pre-dawn's early light that I found peace here on the edge of the end. This, the place where we celebrated life and died for hope.

Tired and knowing I had better be ready for this fight, I waved goodnight to my friends. Picking up my AK and medic bag, I stepped away holding my rifle high above my head.

I yelled as loud as I could, "BIJI! BIJI! ROJAVA!" The hevals cheered back at me, like we were at one of the bonfire-kegger parties I had been privileged enough to attend when I had been their age.

Excited voices rose high into the night, wild with wildness. I stepped away and back into the shadows, listening for a moment to their music and cheers over it. Their voices easily carried to the other side of the line, where in the cold and darkness, people cowered in fear and despair. Trapped, the city surrounded, unable to escape, hostages and Daesh alike listened. They had no choice. The hevals made enough noise for the entire city to hear. They sent all their joy into the darkness as cheers and victory songs, sung loudly, so all would know that freedom was coming with Jin! Jiyan! and Azadi! (Women! Life! Freedom!) coming for them all, the good and the bad. The voices exclaimed boldly, "Hear us celebrate! Daesh!! Hear our dancing, hear our joy, hear our freedom!"

The hevals dance

Daesh could hear for sure, because we were the frontline. They lay unseen, waiting to kill us only a few hundred meters away. Their conflict of human nature was knowing that deep down they were in hell already. As proof of their misery, there was no responding cheering or music from Daesh's side of the line, no joy or even a chant. From Daesh only came silence, fear and death.

Away from the lights and the music, away from the dancing and cheering, I scooted around the back between the concrete house and the concrete wall. Exhausted, I dropped my unit one bag. I got my kit laid out for immediate movement. I needed just a wee little sleep. Sitting down heavily, I leaned back against my body armor, propped there against the wall. I closed my eyes to let it all go... a little warm feeling inside from dancing with my hevals, a slight smile on my weary face.

Unspoken and just outside the consciousness was the reality that none of us would be going home ourselves… not the same, anyway. In the end, whatever freedom we fought for and sacrificed for belonged to others. That is why we say "Sehid Namirin!" (Martyrs never die)

Wherever peace and equality thrive, you will find a legacy of selflessness, a legacy left behind by those who would likely never see the fruits of their sacrifice, have families, or grow old. Age becomes permanently frozen in youth, a youth stolen by the horrors of war. Innocence is replaced by PTSD, life by death and the hard eyes of combat veterans. This is the only payment given to those who freely gave away their own lives, bodies and minds. That is why I know, the 'real heroes' never came home.

…Sehid Namirin…

CHAPTER 29: PTSD Dreams

Last night I dreamt I was running from them - like a cockroach running from the light. I climbed a bombed-out skyscraper. Up I went, with the wind so high the building swayed back and forth slowly.

Looking for a place to hide, I found the building's old gym. It was broken and vacant, ceiling tiles ripped out haphazardly, the windows broken, glass everywhere. I was thirty floors up and almost at the top of the decrepit skyscraper. The smoldering city lay below me, reverberating with the cries of the hearts slowly being devoured.

A few floors below me, I could hear the head choppers murmur, like the sound a snarling dog makes but way more sinister. Fighting back my panic, I hurried through a door. It closed behind me, just as I heard them come onto my floor. There was an old pool. It still had water, covered with a film of green algae. I took a deep breath, and the door opened behind me. I closed my eyes and dove into the water. I hit something cold and hard, and then something else bumpy and awkward, it had hair.

I swam down deeper and opened my eyes underwater. I was in a pool full of dead people in various clothing and stages of decay. I could hear the head choppers looking for me.

I had to swim under all the bodies to the other side of the pool… and up through them again. The cold slimy corpses bumped awkwardly into me as I swam through them. When I made it to the top and climbed out of the other side, the head choppers saw me, yelling. I ran out the door and shoved a broken weight bench in front of it. I ducked through a broken window and started climbing up again, climbing out into the wind, now tearing at me. Each step was tenuous, the height dizzying.

I don't like heights, but there was nowhere left to hide. I kept going, up into the mist and then above it. The higher I climbed, the scarier it got. The wind went from a whisper to a constant pull and then to a gale; its icy fingers ripped at me, trying to drag me off. My footing became tenuous. Still they came, the demons. Bullets snapped past me.

The howls of the undead head choppers emanated just below me. I could easily hear their fervor to torture and kill me. There was nowhere left to run, I was out of bullets, out of time, and out of lives. I stood up there and I leaned into the wind at the top. Up, closer they came, all clad in black, their skulls empty of eyes, because the dogs had already eaten them. With shredded lips and tongueless faces that pustulated, they howled for my soul. I wouldn't let them have it. The only way to save my soul is to kill my body!

"Well, this is it… this is the end." Just as the first rotten hand reaches for my leg… I jump….

But I am not in a building; I am in an airplane. It is split in half, spinning through the air. People are screaming all together in terror. I don't know why I am here. It doesn't matter. The feeling of falling is too much to bear… I am flung from the plane like so many little bits of confetti. I hang there suspended before I start to plummet back to earth.

There is moonlight sparkling through the clouds as I fall.

The water makes falling seem peaceful for a split second.

Ankles tightly crossed, I take a deep breath…

I hit the water… *BOOSSSSHHHHHHH*!!!!

Bubbles stream up like sparks from a fire…

Shafts of light penetrate deeper than me…

But there is no bottom.

Deeper and deeper I descend through the crystalline clear abyss…

I realize there will be no swimming up from this depth.

Sorrow that this is it…

I kick, but it's too late. It's over…

I wake up holding my breath, fists clenched, tight as a board. The morning light is just an idea in the window curtain. I lie there for a minute taking deep breaths in and out, feeling blessed and beyond grateful to still be alive.

All day, I am left feeling shaken and depressed by the dream, the fear of it clinging to me like morning breath. I wonder a lot about death, you know. What happens to us? Maybe because I've seen so much of it. Maybe because I am so scared of it. I am afraid of the unknown, fear beyond this body, beyond this ego. I used to be an atheist, then I became a Christian, and then I went to war and I just UN-became…

CHAPTER 30: The Devil's Belly

Overlooking the city of Manbij, I was crouched behind a low-cut wall on the roof of what was once a young couple's home. They had either fled, or more than likely, been murdered here. Below in the rooms, as evidence of their lovely life together, their possessions were scattered. Nothing, it seems, had been packed for their last trip, including all their photos.

Not long after we first took the position from Daesh, I was waiting for the others to arrive. While I waited, I poked around the house. It had been thoroughly tossed and everything lay scattered everywhere. I saw a photo book. Stooping down, I picked it up. Looking through the photo book, I saw pictures of a happy young couple. They looked very much in love. They had a large family: grandparents, parents, aunts, uncles, cousins.

I smiled for a moment when I found the classic bride glam photos celebrating their wedding. The lady was a teacher. There were pictures of her at a blackboard and him in a soccer jersey coaching children. They had lots of friends too, all smiling back at me from the colored paper.

My favorite pictures were the ones of the husband and wife planting olive trees together in the backyard. There was a sweetness to that moment. I looked through pictures of her with some dirt on her nose, holding the spade out playfully, him with his shirt off, leaning over a shovel. They were together, putting the trees in the soil. I skipped ahead a little in the photo book, past photos of dinners out and trips together. Three quarters of the way through the photo album, she was pregnant. She looked very excited and close to birth. I turned the next page to see the baby, perhaps, but the rest of the book was empty.

Putting the photo book down, my throat choked up and my eyes burned. I leaned against the wall, sinking down, just looking at the blank pages. Sitting on the ground in the room with its torn and tangled curtains drifting lazily behind the shot out broken glass windows, I sifted through the remnants of their life on ground in front of me. It was all mixed up together, shoved into a random and haphazard pile, at least twice looted already. I picked through the woman's tangled clothes, where colorful dresses, scarves and intimate items lay next to spent AK47 bullet casings, pots, pans, and bits of a broken crib.

I got up, upset, and walked out, closing the door to the room. Behind the door on the wall were two big brown stains, one a bit higher than the other, but next to each other nonetheless… There was an even bigger brown stain on the concrete floor… Blood dries brown.

What the fuck is wrong with this world? Why do I live in a world that has so much hate for sale so cheap? The love of blood money flowed here like water onto the ground and the sellers of death who had never seen this place couldn't care less that it existed. This is the place where all the bombs and bullets in the world end up, the place where murderers call themselves holy warriors. Supplied with all the newest guns and Gucci war gear, the scraggly-bearded head choppers are sent as the foot soldiers of profits, for the new god, money.

I tore my mind from thinking about the couple who used to live here, and I focused my attention on the task at hand, my 'watch.' Speaking of - I got my least favorite watch tonight, the 0200 to 0400; but the watch, unlike fate, rotated evenly.

My leg tingled from my kneeling position; I was trying not to make a silhouette with my head but still keep a watch. The road, dropped away, over a hill and reappeared a short time later, at the bottom. There it met the edge of the old city. A large moon hung in the sky, glowing like a crystal chandelier and bathing the land in a deceptively calm and peaceful silver light.

Fighting had been particularly heavy over the last few days. Our forces had been driving a wedge into the city to split it in half. The whole thing was like a football play, except it wasn't a game and there weren't any balls, downs, or timeouts. So… forward they sent us… and forward we fell.

Tonight, my watch had started out quiet for a change. I could hear the crickets chirping and an owl that always called out the same old question… "Whoo? Whoo?"

My hevals, my friends, were now out back, quietly piled on top of each other, individually wrapped in colorful blankets… but not for warmth.

I had tears in my eyes for this day. The metallic taste of battle mixed with exhaustion and sorrow. The quiet night seemed almost normal now; it was as if I was not actually here, but anywhere else.

I knew I would probably die here. It was with a great sadness that I accepted this reality, but if I didn't trade my life for love, then who would? Someone else? Should I have let another die for love in my place? Should we let greed and hate win?

Still, when I thought about dying, my heart was heavy with regrets, with so many moments not lived, so many beautiful potentials prematurely ended. My regrets were not just my own, but for all those who had already given everything I feared so deeply! I contemplated life, given away for 'the good,' in a place of bad.

My fear of death made me feel like a coward. I might have been able to hide from Daesh, but it was impossible to hide from myself. My AK was useless to protect me from my own fear.

Looking out over the rooftops, I stared into space until the dots got blurry and my vision fuzzed darkly. I saw the mixing of two worlds here. I was on the rim of a precipice, on the edge of infinity. It was as if the two worlds were two pieces of paper pressed against a bright window. The translucent glow allowed one to read both pages at the same time, but it wasn't light there, the abyss was so dark, so devoid of light, it created a new color, the lack of any. As if the sun was blackness instead of lightness… I stared, unblinking, into a place just beyond the vision of the human eye. The quiet moment didn't last… it never lasted long here… the sound of a sniper's rifle pulled me from the darkness.

CRACK! and again, *CRACK*! *CRACK*! There was a pause, as if the night held its breath.

"Was that it?" the night seemed to ask hope…

Hope answered back with an automatic burst… *BWAAAAA..AAAAAA* .... a long pause.

Jiyan/Life let her breath out slowly and evenly… shadows running, she palmed the trigger.

BAWWAAAAAA BAWWAAAAAAAA! Everything disappeared in white and yellow as fire belched ten feet out of her flame-tipped lance. Three 30mm Duska rounds were set free… at 5,400 feet per second and a few pounds each. The shadows disappeared before the blinding muzzle flashes, leaving the retinas over-exposed and seeing nothing but hot spots. Another long automatic burst stabbed back through the night.

KAABA WOOOMMM!!! Mayhem showed up to the party with a car bomb. The crickets were no longer singing, and the owl flew away.

I was looking hard down the road now; the battle had intensified. Talking rifles spat hate back and forth.

Our position had already been cut off once today. Hevals covered in concrete dust using sledgehammers had punched holes through walls. The fighting was fierce, building to building, room by room. In the end, this time the hevals had pushed Daesh back. In payment for their efforts, six of our friends fell Sehid (KIA). They traded their lives for us to get a few hours more; then two more fell, then two more and three. We sent sixteen back to Kobani with serious injuries and four to Sarin field hospital with minor... Thirteen hevals were still awaiting transport; they were piled on top of each other out back and had to wait until later to go... it seemed I was the only one who minded though.

That was the day, well, until now. Jesus! Was today a new day? 0241... Does midnight count as a change-over when it's all just one long episode?

The fighting continued to intensify about a half klick from me. The city had a growl to it, but not like any city growl you have ever heard. There was an inner mixing echo of small arms fire, heavy weapons, and rocket-propelled grenades reverberating through the debris-strewn, abandoned city streets.

I guess Daesh was pissed that we took so much from them yesterday, 'cuz tonight it was jumpin' off. There was a repugnant beauty to battle at night. The tracer rounds, like Roman candles on the 4th of July, drifted back and forth across the night sky. They crisscrossed in the air like shooting stars passing, but these stars didn't end in dreams coming true. The only wishing made on these stars... was that they would somehow miss.

It was not only Daesh/ISIS in the city. Many civilians had also been trapped with them, to be used as human shields against air strikes. The city still had to fall, though, one way or another. Painstakingly slow: house by house, block by block, apartment buildings, shopping centers, schools, mosques, hospitals; we traded life for land.

My position was illuminated in a series of large flashes. I could see sparks fly outward, but it was silent for just that moment - as if the sound on the TV was muted. It's wild how much faster light is than sound. Then like thunder, but way more sinister, the sound came.

KaKaKaRUNKAAA! In the distance, I heard faint screaming, almost inaudible, but it clung there like the aftertaste of bad water. The haunting murmur spoke of a pain so deep, there was only one conclusion.

Then, much closer, the sound of automatic gunfire erupted. The assault was picking up tempo as it pushed in. I watched as the battle grew in size.

Then I saw something on the road, a shadow? I blinked hard twice. The shadow glided down the street away from me, past our position. It was floating up and down over buildings and the road. It was going in a straight line toward the fighting. Shadows from all over were flying into it, and the shadow grew into a large, rolling black mass. I shook my head and looked away before looking back.

When I did, I could see, high above the entire city, there was this blackness with long black tendrils. It looked like the legs of an octopus caressing downwards, growing bigger and bigger and bigger. It feasted on the terror of thousands. It was not of this world, except for surely, it must have been of this world. Was it a mistake the human eye wasn't supposed to see? I couldn't really explain it because I had never seen anything like it. But I am telling you, it was there, and it was as real as you… or me

Below the city, the ground was like a giant slow turning whirlpool as if I was looking into the devil's gullet, the place where souls were consumed. The black fire wasn't hot, but cold. It twisted and growled hungrily.

Good/bad, it didn't matter, as the giant above wove tendrils of death back and forth like underwater sea grass, pulling to and from in the waves of terror. The shadows boiled over the agonized, like thousands of maggots feasting on carrion before the soul was sucked down into the devil's belly.

The devoid emptiness twisted and grew until the very moon was red and then disappeared. It was so big and massive; it was as if the whole galaxy could fit in the chasm. I had found the quantum space opening up to war and mayhem.

Everywhere, shadows were feasting on terror. Their spawn-like, fanged faces buried in, ripping and tearing, until the soul was completely drained, ragged, a translucent grey. Discarded, like a used plastic bag, slowly going down the drain, the empty soul swirled into the infinite blackness of hell's belly to be digested.

There was no justice here, just hell on earth. I closed my eyes, trying to shut it out, but even though I shut them to this sight, it was as if my eyelids were made out of clear glass and I saw right through them. I say to you, I swear on my life, I saw these things... it was as real as the world you are sitting in right now.

In the distance, coming out of the blackest part of the blackness, a light flicked on and then off. The sound of automatic gunfire followed it. Sparks flew at the escaping lights, but they did not stop.

My radio crackled; a voice came over the other end, "Doctor! Doctor! Galc binindar," is all that was said.

I keyed the radio in reply, "We are ready for you."

The lights got closer and as they did, I could see shadows chasing after them, as if the lights were fish escaping a feeding frenzy. The shadows tried to pull glowing, white-hot souls out of the back... but they were stuck there... clinging onto hope... and they would not be pulled away.

A hand slapped me on the shoulder. I was startled. It was the old man, Pops, who had just recently joined the unit. "Time to go, Doc, there are wounded on the way." I peeled my eyes away from the spectacle.

He said, "Don't worry, I will finish your watch for you, mate." I got up to go; a shiver passed over me. But maybe it wasn't a shiver at all, but one of the shadows feeding on my own fear and exhaustion.

I have no worldly explanation for what I saw that night, but I know this: It made me want to live a good life, every single day.

Fighting at night

Tank round hits a building

The city burning by moonlight

CHAPTER 31: Hevala Berxwedana

I had been sleeping on a concrete sidewalk next to a bombed-out house. I was tired. Something woke me. I wasn't sure what. Lying there, adjusting to my surroundings - the sun had reached me, it was hot. I guess that's what woke me up.

I sat up, feeling groggy, like the day after partying all night, except my headache wasn't from drinking too much but rather too little. Groaning and rubbing my face with my hands, I felt dazed and confused. I couldn't remember where I was. Looking around for clues to my location, I hoped it would come back to me; I was sure it would. It was scary for a second, because what if I was left behind when they pushed up? Or worse, they retreated, and I would be left in no-man's-land alone? My heart took a few extra thumps...

It was the afternoon. There was not a lot to delineate from. I was between a concrete wall and a house. My bed roll and all my gear were laid out, ready to go at a second's notice. I was as pre-packed as one can get. I had slept in my body armor, so I knew I was in a dangerous place.

Then in the near distance, I heard the sound of a sniper's solitary *CRACK*! ……. And then again *CRACK*. Then automatic gunfire opened up, *BWWA>>AAAA>>AA*! It echoed across the city. There was a long pause.

I looked at my hands; they were battered and bruised, but clean. My camo BDU blouse was stained in blood from the sleeves to the chest. It came back to me now, like a tidal wave returning to the sea. My memory was dragged back to me, whether I wanted it or not.

Getting up, I looked around. This part of the city used to be a very wealthy neighborhood. We had been here for a few days now. Our house was at the end of the street. A beautiful two-story sprawling home with olive, apricot, and pomegranate trees sat in the back. It was all surrounded by a large concrete wall. The house, which had been ransacked and fought through multiple times, was but a shattered and broken ghost of its former self. Bullet-pockmarked walls and shattered glass were strewn everywhere. Inside, we had flipped the couches back over. Perhaps the previous owners had fled, hoping they would have a house to come back to. Perhaps they were now refugees in a camp, or fleeing to Europe? Perhaps they were murdered here by Daesh. There was a whole city of houses like this - empty only of people. We wouldn't be staying here long.

The sound of fighting was all around now, near and far. A not too distant *BOOOOOMM* rattled the walls... That was definitely an airstrike! The sound drifted into my ears, across the empty streets, topless trees, destroyed schools, and empty parks. It also traveled across the ears of those poor souls still there, huddled in fear, unable to escape and with nowhere safe left to hide.

Outside the wall, I heard a truck zoom up. There was a commotion. Someone was yelling, "Binadar embichem."

Baz came running up to me, not in a panic or a loud voice, more tired than that. He just said, "Tekoser, we have casualties inbound." He turned back around the corner and out the door of the courtyard.

My eyes burned from lack of sleep, lack of hope, and malnutrition. Grabbing my medic bag and AK, I stuffed my rucksack cameras and laptop under the concrete porch to be retrieved later. I trotted around the house through the gate and into the square cul-de-sac parking lot.

It didn't take long for the BMB to roar up. I landed just opposite the German as the door was opened for our casualty to be brought out of the dark interior. I leaned in to help remove our injured heval.

Inside the belly of the homemade armored truck, cigarette smoke filled the air, shafts of light crisscrossed inside from a Daesh 50-cal plugging holes through it, like shooting a can with a BB gun...

The thankless job of the panzer driver? Day in and day out, it escaped with the injured and returned with the replacements, a never-ending rotation.

"Goddam! What a world!!" A cigarette hung out of the driver's mouth. A melancholy song, 'Beritan,' was playing through the one paper speaker by him in the door.

Our injured comrade was wrapped in a blanket. Grabbing the corner, I was careful not to bump our casualty on the way out of the small hatch. Outside, on the gurney, I unfolded the blanket. It was my friend Berxwedana. Quickly, I looked for injuries. She was spotless, except her curly black hair was all wet and sticky. She was twitching.

"Oh no, this isn't good!" I muttered to Baz. My heart sank in my chest.

One of the hevalas who came in with her said, "Look, she is moving! Help her, Doctor! Please!!"

I didn't know what to say. I looked back down at our friend Hevala Berxwedana. Her hair was not wet from a shower, but wet from the end of hope. What could I do? How could I save what had already been taken away?

Baz looked at me and nodded, saying, "Tekoser, we have to try!!"

But I already knew this, so I just agreed vapidly. There were no words to say.

Baz said, "I have to go get the…. whheeezzzzzdfkjhfbbzzzzhggghhgg," But it was as if he was speaking into a wind tunnel. I didn't understand a word he said.

I looked back down at my dear friend Berxwedana. She was just a kid, you know. Fucking snipers! They liked to shoot the YPJ because the sexist fucks believed if they were killed by a woman, then they wouldn't make it to paradise.

I knew why Berxwedana was twitching. It didn't matter that I knew she wouldn't make it. Sometimes we do things that might not make sense to someone not familiar with a combat medic's creed, but they made sense to us.

If you bring your best friend to us hurt and too messed up to save, we're still going to give it hell anyway, because of loyalty, hope, and, most of all, because of love! I took an oath; I promised all of my hevals before we left, I would never quit on them. In my heart, I wanted them to believe in that last moment that I still thought they would make it, even if I knew they would not. I always wanted them to know I was fighting for them, so they knew they were not alone at the edge of the end. I always wanted them to know Doc Tekoser was working to keep them alive, no matter what. Because of that refusal to quit, I've seen the lights go out many, many times. I've seen the look of fear, peace, then... nothing.

The eyes of my comrades, the eyes of civilians, Daesh... They all look the same when they're dead... Gone.... I hoped our efforts mattered somewhere, other than to just my memory and your ghosts...

Looking down at Hevala Berxwedana as I wheeled her away from the BMB on our gurney, it was as if for just that second, I was looking down at my own daughter lying there dying. I knew I couldn't save her no matter how much CPR I did.

What do you do? ... What do you do?

I started doing chest compressions... 1, 2, 3; I saw Berxwedana as a baby in her mom's arms; she was looking down at her, tickling her cheek as she giggled... 4, 5, 6, 7, 8, Berxwedana was a year old and walking around on pudgy little legs, giggling, chasing the cat who was not entertained to have his nice nap disturbed. 9,10,11, her first day of school, her dad and mom waved to her as she went inside. They looked so proud. Inside, Berxwedana walked into the class confidently, smiling and excited about this new adventure... 12, 13, 14, she was winning an award for good citizenship at middle school... 15,16,17, the war had started and she was saying goodbye to her mother and father. Her mom looked at her with so much love. She reached out her hand and caressed her daughter's cheek one last time, just like she did when Berxwedana was in her arms as a baby. 18, 19, 20, 21, tears in her momma's eyes. Berxwedana smiled like the sun at her. "Don't worry! I will be back soon," she seemed to say, though there were no words spoken.

I leaned up from the chest compressions to give her a breath, a breath of my life into her. She had vomit on her mouth. I wiped it away and gave her the breath anyway, but it did not return life to her, no matter how much life I sent it in with. It just came back to me, a gurgle, an empty trickle of air through her still pale lips.

I was now crying. 22,23,24,25,26, I knew I couldn't save her. Hope was always the last to die. I am angry at the unfairness of Berxwedana's sacrifice, while my own daughter goes to college. 27,28,29,30, with a new car, boyfriend, and an opportunity to grow old in a free land. 31,32,33,34, but not Berxwedana! Berxwedana was shot in the head and it didn't matter how much CPR I gave her. 35,36,37,38,39, 40, she wouldn't make it today.

Wiping the puke off her pretty young face again, a face that would never know age, wrinkles, or time, I give her another breath. Berxwedana's friends bent over with grief as they comforted each other in shock and disbelief, as if somehow, they truly believed she would be OK too.

I kept doing chest compressions and breaths until Baz made it back with an airbag and the van. My vision blurry from tears, I didn't know how long it had been. It seemed like it was forever; we loaded Berxwedana into the back of the ambulance and I climbed in with her.

When we drove away, Berxwedana was looking up at nothing, so I closed her eyes for her, one last time.

I looked out the dirty back window of the van as her four friends grew smaller and smaller, just kids that wouldn't ever get to be kids... left behind, to wait their turn, at the edge of hell. The four remained standing there, then, one at a time, they turned back toward the city... all but one.... she stood there until she was just a speck, and then we dropped over the rise and were gone.

"I remember that last day, I held your hand, brother. I closed your eyes, sister. I wrapped you in a colorful blanket, away from the mud, the cold and dying, away from the ideals that led us all here, away from the commanders who order such things day after day. I put you in my heart where one keeps such treasures safe. Sehid Namirin hevala min"

Sehid Berxwedana

CHAPTER 32: For a Few Hours More

Midmorning, DAY 3: Somewhere in front of all of us was the end point. The undeniable truth: life ends, so no matter how much good I did now, the past was its own and did not belong to today.

I guess I always knew there was a good damn chance of getting killed here. But now I saw it the other way around. I would be very, very lucky not to get killed here. Home had never seemed so far away.

A jet, low and fast, came shrieking across the rooftops, ripping right overhead and then there was a massive explosion. *KAAAAABOOOOOOOOMMMMM*!!!

The building I was in shook violently, everything disappearing in dust particulate. I was completely coated in it, like an asbestos-dusted sugar cookie. A part of the room behind me crumbled.

"Fuck! Not again!" How many times could one man get lucky?

Sand, like in an hourglass, trickled onto me. The already crumbled building hung there for a moment… deciding if it wanted to collapse or not. More debris, insulation, drywall and roof debris came down around me. I was afraid to move. The building settled back in.

I scrambled to my feet and scurried down the blown-open hallway, down a flight of stairs, and out a hole blown through the outer wall. Once outside the building, I felt better, taking a breath as if experiencing the cutting of the umbilical cord. I felt like a zombie, numb, detached, not myself, but still myself, like a ghost. Maybe I was dead? Maybe it was my ghost running right now and not me at all?

As I got back toward the old line and the rally point, I ducked around a corner to where a bunch of hevals were gathered waiting in the shade of the wall. My hevals saw me covered in dust and dirt and were concerned.

"Doctor, tu bosn?" (Are you OK) they wanted to know…

I lied and tell them I was OK, making the universal sign of the dead, a finger drawn across my neck. "Daesh dead! America!! Jets!" I pointed skyward with pride, smiling.

My SDF hevals love America, and they all gave a cheer! Our jets had helped turn the tide of this war against Daesh and it had saved countless SDF/YPG lives.

Down here in the city, trying to avoid death was the main objective. Live long enough to find and kill your enemy before you yourself were killed, one block at a time. Urban warfare is as cruel as it is random: faces, arms, legs, blown off… left blind, disfigured, buried alive for days, until dying is the only hope left… "Please death, please come to me!"

Shot by snipers never seen…

Blown up by a missed air strike, drone, car bomb, grenade, RPG, IED…

Friendly fire… that's not so friendly.

A shudder passed over me at the grim thought.

I didn't know how many wounded hevals and civilians we had treated and sent back, 450? 550? I lost track.

I didn't lose track of what happened yesterday, though. I extra hated yesterday… By now in this war, I hated a lot of days…

Yesterday, though, had left me with a deep regret and sorrow in my heart. Yesterday I had screwed up and let my guard down… GOD DAMNIT!

Back up the street I could hear a gunfight start up. It was another position getting hit though and not mine… Not yet anyway!

The automatic rifle fire was like hail on a tin roof. My nerves were shot. I felt raw and at the edge of panic. I pushed it aside, preparing my mind for the next assault. This was no place to come apart but coming apart I was anyway.

A BMB pulled up, its brakes squealing loudly. The door banged open and the driver stepped out, waving to me.

"Doctor!"

I couldn't avoid him.

"Heval Tekoser. Doctor, you have to come with me, now!"

I started to protest. "I can't leave now. I am the only medic down here."

But he just shook his head and opened the back door of the BMB. Motioning at me to get in, I had no choice.

Afternoon, DAY 1: Commander Baz got orders to send two medics deep into the city to stay with the advancing assault. The commanders knew it was going to be the bloodiest push of the engagement. Baz chose Razon and me to go. I was glad Razon was my co-medic; he was an Iraq veteran and a calm hand in bad spots. We both knew we were going deep into hell and there was an excitement in the air because of that.

When Heval Razon and I entered the city, it was under a dinner plate moon. The hevals stormed a multi-story apartment building. Razon and I set up for casualties in the lobby of a building just down the street.

It was just us waiting there in the darkness of this vacant building, waiting for our jobs to begin and hoping to skip it this night.

I kept a watch out the back for movement and Razon watched the front. Our side was still, but every once in a while, wild gunfire would erupt from the four-story apartments that the hevals had just stormed.

A grenade blast ripped out a wall midway up; it sent a fireball out the window and into the blackness, night momentarily interrupted by the ball of fire. I could hear the sound of falling glass and someone screaming in pain. "AhhhhAAAHHHhhaaaaa!"

More gunfire. *BWAAAABWAAAABWAAA*!

The screaming stopped.

WACKaaa.WACKaaa.WACKaaa! I could hear the sound of hevals' sledgehammers, methodically pounding on more than one wall at the same time, breaking our way in. No way out today, Daeshy Daesh.

There was a danger here, unseen but extremely deadly. Always waiting there, the threat hung unseen in the air until it struck.

WHACK! It was the last sound ever heard. You never knew from what window, or hole, the sniper's bullets would come.

Since logistics, other than ammunition and moldy nan bread, had not gotten through in weeks, Heval Agir's tabor had sent him down the line to scavenge food and water. They were all starving; that's not a figure of speech, but a literal description. That's how it was down here in no-man's-land. If you wanted to eat, you had to find it. It was exceptionally hard to find food in a city where people were already starving, a city ravaged by war and plundered by every possible scavenger, including us.

The situation was getting desperate, but as we pushed deeper and deeper into the city, eating anything only became more and more difficult. Hunger was more than just an irritation; it began to cloud judgments too.

Just after 0000, DAY 2: Two casualties showed up, one walking who could wait and a hevala that was carried in who was in serious condition. Our hevala had been shot in the leg and abdomen. I put pressure on her leg to stanch her blood flow. It came out through my fingers and onto the long, dulled, marble floor of the upscale building.

It was extra dark in the inner city, with no power at night. My little red head lamp made everything look monotone. Having wrapped her leg with a pressure bandage, I applied steady pressure on her abdomen while getting the dressing out of my bag one handed.

Blood is black in red light. White is red. The floor beneath my hevala had a large black puddle. It looked like the negative filter was flipped on. I blinked hard, shook my head, and got the abdominal dressing on her.

The IV bag connected, Heval Razon squeezed the bags into her. It took a few minutes, but she stabilized.

Her life was saved for now. There was no guarantee we could get her out of here. This was the real zombie-land. Night would help her odds of getting transportation. She would keep bleeding until she could go into surgery and there was nothing I could do about that here except try to find her a ride. STAT!

Dragging a dirty blanket from one of the shattered apartments, we wrapped her in it for warmth. I was happy we had gotten to her. Had we not been down here so close, she wouldn't have had a chance. Our hevala would have bled out for sure. So, even if in two days my uniform smelled rotten from all the old blood on it, that wouldn't be so bad, for the trade of a life lived.

Razon stepped outside and I could hear him call out that we needed transport right away.

A few minutes later, Heval Agir (Levi Shirley, Colorado USA) poked his head into the dark lobby Razon and I were in.

"Hey, is that Razon I hear in here?" Heval Agir asked, standing framed by the moonlight in the doorway.

Razon was instantly happy, "Heval Agir? Is that you?" He stood and the two old friends greeted each other, laughing and hugging.

I let the two friends reunite while I finished up our casualties. I gave her some Ketamine. It was not enough, because we never had enough, but some, and some is a lot better than none. She finally started to relax as the drugs worked their way into her. I eased off a little too. I finally let go of the knot I always felt inside when I was working on a casualty. The knot any combat medic worth their sand knows: Sometimes… it's better to be lucky than good.

I got our hevala ready to move outside. Heval Razon and Agir stooped down to help me, each of them grabbing a top corner of the blanket. I got the lighter bottom. We carried her outside to join the other heval who had been injured and was also waiting for transport to the CCP.

After we got her down, standing up, Razon turned and said to me, "You know Heval Agir?"

I nodded my head in the moonlight. "Yeah, we met once briefly after Shaddadi." Sticking out my hand, I said, "Heval Tekoser."

Heval Agir had a good grip. You can tell a lot about a person in how they shake a hand.

Turning and kneeling down to finish up, I took out my sharpy and wrote my treatments on our hevala's upper arm. Quickly going through the pockets of her BDU top, I found some pictures and slipped them into a small bag. I tossed away the destroyed uniform. I taped the bag to her arm with silk tape so it wouldn't get lost. If she made it to the hospital alive, those pictures might be the only family visit she would get.

Razon handed me my AK47. The BMB pulled up out of the dark and some hevals came to help us load up our casualties. After we got them all loaded, the armored truck left. Heval Razon, Agir and I ran up the street, zigzagging randomly to avoid snipers.

Getting to the building the hevals had just cleared, we moved up our own little CCP. We waited there for some time. It was just the three of us. The hevals pushed up to the next apartment building. A flare was shot into the night sky; it made our shadows dance, wall to wall, as if they had a life of their own.

Heval Agir was dusty from sledgehammering through walls. Being American and broad in the shoulders, he had a knack for wall punching with the ten-pound sledgehammer. He had on beat-up body armor, was loaded down with AK47 magazines, and had a bandana tied around his head and an old Marine Corps BDU blouse under it all; there was danger in his eyes. A flicker lay just beneath the surface and it was from more than just the flare that was drifting back to earth. I could see why the Kurds had named him Fire (Agir).

CHA.AA>A CHA CHA! New fighting started. The 30mm tracer rounds skipped off or through buildings; they ricocheted high into the dark sky, as if they could shoot down the very stars themselves.

While we waited, the two old friends talked. Heval Agir had been surprised to see Razon down here in the city, because Razon had initially come to Rojava from Utah not to fight but to do I.T. for the YPG. Razon's goal was to set up an internet radio station and he also wanted to teach kids how to write apps with iPads.

It was Heval Baz who convinced Razon that since he was an ex-Army trained combat first responder, he should join our team – the Tactical Medical Unit/TMU.

When you meet another American volunteer in Rojava, there is an immediate shared connection. No matter why you both ended up here, the result is the same: you're here. The foreign volunteers that ended up here in Rojava with the SDF were an eclectic group of people; they ranged from super left-wing Antifa to Anarchist to conservative Republicans, from Internationalists to Communists. Here, our political views didn't matter that much. What counted here was that we stood, side by side, shoulder to shoulder, and faced our common enemy together, like the family we all were.

I was exhausted from lack of sleep, malnutrition and constantly carrying sixty-five pounds of gear. I settled into a place where I could naturally drift off to sleep but also be ready to jump at a moment's notice. My AK was draped in front of me, naturally pointing at the hole in the wall. I settled into a half sleeping nap state and listened to the conversation between friends.

Agir had been here for ten months and this was his second tour here. He said that fighting had been extremely heavy for his unit the past week.

They had taken quite a few Sehids already; about half his unit had been killed or injured so far. Agir was not thrilled to go back and he said as much to Razon.

I sat up and interrupted their conversation. "Yo, Razon, we could use him for security when we treat casualties if he wants to stay here and help us. I might even be able to talk his commander into a more permanent loan of him to the TMU. What do you guys think?"

Razon was excited by the idea "Yeah! We get left alone a lot here. Look at now, there is just Tekoser and me. If you weren't here Agir, usually it's just the two of us!"

Agir looked surprised, but also stoked. "Really?"

I nodded, "Yeah, we would be happy for another gun to watch our backs while we treat hevals or are waiting by ourselves for the next wave to arrive."

Heval Agir lit up at the idea that maybe he didn't have to go back to punching holes in walls, room by room, fighting ghosts in a tangled web of destruction that wants to kill you. I also felt good looking out for Agir.

Agir asked, "Can you write me a note? I'll take it to my commander."

I laughed, "Yeah, but I can't write Kurdish. Just go back and tell your commander we are here and need your help! Here, take a radio and call us."

Handing Heval Agir my short-range radio, I told him, "Razon has the other one; either way, you have to bring it back to us, so we will keep you for a day. What are they gonna do… send you to the front?!" We all cracked up at that. Agir was stoked. He took the radio and left.

It didn't take long for the radio to squawk to life. Razon explained our need for security to his commander while we treated injured hevals. Agir's commander agreed to loan him to us for security for the next three days.

When the radio went off, Razon smiled, saying, "That was easy!"

I felt good too. I knew there was no guarantee here, but I felt like we had gotten Agir a break. I laid back and fell asleep almost instantly.

I awoke with a start; it was still dark. Heval Agir was there with his AK, keeping watch. He just nodded to me, saying, "Don't worry Doc, I got your six."

Then, as if on cue, a BMB pulled up. We heard the familiar call of "Binidar!" We all jumped up and ran out to the street to get our injured hevals, but the BMB was already speeding off before we could treat our casualty. It could be frustrating, but I didn't blame the BMB driver after having been in so many rocket magnets myself.

The battle was always the worst just before dawn. The casualties had started coming in a constant stream: head wounds, gunshots, a blinded YPJ, a few amputees and ten or so sehids. I lost one hevala; she had been shot in the head. She started out awake but slipped in and out of consciousness, making little suckling sounds with her mouth. I packed cool scarfs around her, but we had no ice. By the time the BMB made the trip back to get the next load of injured fighters, she had been rolled in a blanket and gently set out back with the others waiting to go, but no longer in a hurry.

Heval Agir, true to his word, pulled security for us and also helped us get casualties out of trucks. Every once in a while, he took fire from some unseen window or building, but he just smiled and shrugged it off as no big deal.

The fighting was getting heavy again. When we got so many injured at once, in the end they all kind of ran together. In the blur of an exhausted brain and broken heart, sometimes it was hard to remember any of them individually.

Somewhere just before first light, the fighting stopped. With the first dusk of color in the sky, the Daesh call to prayers reverberated over the devastated city. I don't know what the prayer is for. It seems twisted to pray to God after killing all night, but I was happy nonetheless for a pause in the fighting.

I had a sour taste in the back of my mouth, sandpaper in my eyes, and a wicked headache. I looked at Heval Agir and Razon. They also looked ragged; I made a decision.

Getting up, I suggested, "OK let's roll it up and get over to our little hideaway. Maybe we can get lucky and get a few hours of sleep. Sound good?"

They both looked happy at my suggestion, and Razon said, "Yeah, let's go! And let's eat a little breakfast before we sleep!"

Agir looked surprised. "You have food?" he asked Razon - who, for his part, got a mischievous twinkle in his eye and nodded yes.

We packed up. Getting to the doorway leading out onto the street and sniper alley, Agir said, "OK, I am gonna advance to that wall right there." He pointed across the street with all five fingers to a low wall. "I will post up there and cover you two so you can go straight to the far hole. Then I'll roll in behind you."

With that, Agir was out the door at a medium trot. Once across the street, he dropped down at the crumbled wall. He waved us out. Razon and I jogged up the street, ducked around the corner, and went in through a hole in the wall that led to the back courtyard of a four-story apartment building. The back was surrounded by a high wall and our temporary staging area.

A few moments later, Agir came jogging up and in. We rolled a big satellite dish in front of the hole. It was less for ballistic protection and more for sight blocking and noise making.

Back in our little hideaway, I uncovered the sea bag we had stuffed full of supplies. I needed to refill my Unit One Bag and so did Razon. Agir's IFAK was lacking, so we set him up with some better bandages, a little foot powder, and a tourniquet. Hooking up a little swag for helping us out was the least we could do.

"Food?" I asked.

Agir nodded up and down excitedly. I rummaged around in the bag and came out with a few cans of beans, but Razon shook his head,

"No! Heval Tekoser… Let's have the other one." He nodded down to the bag with a twinkle in his eye. I knew exactly what he was talking about.

I grinned, not because I was happy, but because I knew it would go down like this. "Fucking Mormon!"

He was not a big talker, but what Razon said he meant. So, in the end I just smiled and obliged his wish. I reached into the sea bag and pulled out a 'Menu 2, MRE,' (Shredded Beef and BBQ). I handed it to the Mormon, who handed it to Agir, saying, "Here you can have my half. You can share it with Tekoser."

I shook my head, saying, "Naaa let him have the whole thing!" Following the Mormon's lead, I continued, "Besides, I got these." I pulled back out the few cans of beans and some very stale goondie bread. I winked at my heval.

Agir was floored. He hit the roof with excitement.

"WHAT? NOOO WAYYY!!!???" His face lit up like an eight-year-old kid at Christmas. Revealing true joy, unexpected and out of the blue, Agir became over-animated. He waved his hands around, still in disbelief, and started talking like Nicolas Cage, "Cause obviously you have a tendency to OVERREACT!"

Razon and I started laughing. Agir looked at the MRE, turning it over and over in his hands like it was a big sack of money. Smiling from ear to ear, Agir asked, "Hey, where in the world did you get this?!!! The SoCom guys?"

Razon, smiling, a glint in his eye, said nonchalantly, "Yeah, we got it from DELTA."

Agir wanted to know more. "Really? How's that? They just give you MREs?"

Razon answered, "One of our guys traded them ISIS flags and some intel for one full box of real MREs."

Agir looked very intrigued. "So, if I know where a Daesh flag is or something even better? If I give it to you… you can get it to him, and he can trade it for me?" Razon nodded hesitantly at his friend's excited question. Sensing, perhaps, that this was going in a direction he didn't feel that comfortable with, he offered, "Yeah…? Maybe?"

Agir looked serious for a moment. "In the building we cleared yesterday there was some stuff we could trade heval! We can go look after breakfast."

Razon shook his head. "I don't think that's such a good idea. Are you sure the building is clear?"

Agir insisted, "No, for sure we cleared the whole thing yesterday."

I shook my head, not liking the idea, saying, "I know it's tempting but we gotta stay put here because if any casualties arrive, we're the medics and we got to be where they know we are." And that was that.

Agir very carefully opened the MRE. Someone who has never witnessed starvation might think when you're starving, you will tear at food and devour it in great big bites. Actually, when someone is starving like Agir, time is taken with great care to savor each bite, morsel, and moment of eating. The look, smell - and only then the taste. Looking up, smiling, Agir said, "Oh man! Homemade food!!"

Razon laughed, "Hold on now, that isn't exactly homemade!"

When Agir was done eating, licking his fingers like a cat after a meal, he leaned back against the bullet-pockmarked wall, rubbing his swollen and very full belly. He had a deeply satisfied look on his face. I smiled too. Agir cracked the quiet with a large belch. We all laughed.

Razon wasn't done with his surprises yet, though. He took out two fake juice packages and some powdered milk. Taking a water bottle, he started mixing the juice milk in it.

Agir looked on quizzically at Razon, asking, "What are you making, heval?" Razon wouldn't say, as was often the Mormon's way when he had a trick up his sleeve. He just twinkled his eye and shook the drink up. When it was done, he handed the bottle to Agir and said proudly, "Here heval, strawberry milk!"

Agir laughed, "Haaaahaaaaa!! NOoooo Waaaayyyy! That's like my favorite!... The Nesquik one!"

I laughed too, because I knew how good Razon's secret strawberry milk recipe was. It tasted uncannily like the real thing. So, when Agir sipped it for the first time, he almost spat it out, but sucked it right back in. I laughed at the comic gesture. Agir was funny. Even here, even with all this going on, he had made us laugh more in these last few hours than in months.

You know, when you're so far away from home, in such a crazy place, separated from anything familiar, in a world gone psychotic crazy, a taste, a smell… these things can trigger a flashback just as real as the PTSD flashback you will get later, at home.

Agir drifted off there for a moment, savoring sips of the milk, his eyes closed, head tilted back. It was like a mini vacation, a momentary escape. Even the fighting had stopped for the time being.

Looking back down and breaking the silence, Agir said, "I miss my family, man! I kinda skipped out on them the last time, you know."

I shook my head. "No. What do you mean?"

"Well, I was here before, but I went home. I didn't fit in back there anymore, you know. I kept thinking about my hevals here and that they needed me. So, I came back… Shit's been real this time, man!" he said with a serious undertone.

I nodded. "Yeah, reentry can be difficult, no two times are the same. Take it from me. I've had three hard trips to the Middle East before this one. But I had to come back too. You know, sometimes we have to follow what's right over what's easy."

Agir nodded. "Yeah, I know what you're saying. That's why I had to return. I kept seeing my friends getting hurt here. I feel bad I lied to my mom, dad and little sister. Mostly my little sister, Kate. We were always really close, heval… but I just couldn't you know…" He fell silent, looking down to the right for a moment before looking back up and continuing, "Anyway, I just left. I didn't contact them until I was already back in Rojava. I think it was harder on them this last time. I didn't tell them because I didn't want them to try to stop me, you know, because my mind was already made up. I didn't want them to worry longer than they already had to. It's bad enough they have to worry about me while I am here. Might as well not make them worry before I leave too!"

Razon agreed knowingly, nodding up and down at a shared commonality. "Man, I totally relate. When I made up my mind to come to Rojava, I didn't tell anybody in my family either. In fact, I told them I got a job on the east coast, in computer programing. I also told my mom that the job provided me an apartment, so my mom would not try to look for one for me. I felt bad, but I am with you Agir, it would have just made them worry longer than they had to, I was coming either way."

I laughed at Razon, "I can't believe you told a lie!" I said in mock horror at this most un-Mormon gesture.

Agir laughed heartily, and then said deadpan, "Yeah, Razon won't that, like, bar you from Mormon heaven?"

Razon laughed… looking sheepish for a moment, but then he took on a more serious look. "Well, I do feel bad, you know, but it was necessary. So, I am sure God will forgive me." As if to answer, down the street gunfire erupted back and forth, followed by an RPG exploding. The gunfight was intense for about five minutes and then ceased as fast as it started.

Morning, DAY 2: I started to get my medic bag ready. Then from down the street I heard someone call out "BINDAR!"

Agir went first; his AK poked out of the hole left, right. He scooted out and disappeared from sight.

Once outside, Agir dropped to a knee by the opposite wall, his AK up. He called out, "All clear!"

Razon and I climbed out of the hole and ran down the street. We crossed sniper alley and made our way to the tall apartment building from the night before. We waited there, providing back cover, and Agir came running up.

Smiling again, Agir said, "So now that we are already up and out, let's stop by the building my taboor cleared yesterday and see if what I saw is what I think I saw. If it is, we could trade it for a whole crate of MREs and then I can share it with my taboor too!... We are all starving, man. Fucking starving!" His speech drifted off there.

I shook my head, irritated at the idea. "No, it's not a good idea. Sorry, heval, but we gotta keep here at the rally zone."

Heval Agir said, "BMB en route!" Standing up, he exited the shelter - his rifle up, pointed in the direction of the Daesh snipers, shooting a few rounds at the not-so-distant buildings to keep their heads low. *BANG!BANG!BANG!*

The BMB stopped abruptly, the door flying open. Heval Agir helped get the casualty out of the back. It was one heval; he had been shot through the chest and was in a bad way. I recognized him. We had been to his taboor to train them some months before. Upon seeing Razon and me, I could see relief in his eyes. He was struggling to breathe and tapping his chest, gasping for air. Our friend was not going to make it if we did not intervene immediately.

Once out of the line of sniper fire, Agir gently helped him sit down. Not allowing him to fall over, I quickly got out a chest seal and tore it open. Razon cut off his shirt. *Ziiiipppppppp* it fell to the ground. The sticky dressing open, I pressed it onto the front of his exposed chest. I put it directly over the bubbly, frothy, little red angry hole. Unlike a tire, there were no spare lungs out here for our hevals.

Each breath he took only made it worse. I got out combat gauze and Razon leaned him forward with Agir's help. I quickly packed the hole in his back, blood all over my hands. We didn't have any more gloves. I wiped my hands on my pants. There was nothing else, niceties didn't matter anymore. It was either save or let die and I was not willing to do the latter. It worked. His bleeding had slowed so the new chest seal would stick. It was the last good chest seal I had. I slapped it over the much larger, gaping, exit hole. My wound packing was already soaking red with blood.

He would need immediate transport to the hospital. Agir helped me lean him up and I plunged the needle decompression into his chest. It was a good stick; I could hear a *hissssss* and our heval immediately started to improve.

It was a good clean save. It had taken three minutes from start to finish. All sealed up and able to walk on his own now with a little help, we loaded him into the BMB.

Agir again provided much-needed cover for us, as we were exposed while loading our casualty in. The BMB sped away.

KKAAAAABBBOOOMM!!!

I dropped to my knee, my gun coming up.

"What just happened?"

The BMB that had just left was now blown up. The vehicle was stranded about 150 feet from us. It was between two berms and completely exposed to enemy fire. The driver and gunner escaped, but our casualty was trapped in the back as it was repeatedly shot by snipers and rocket-propelled grenades. The BMB was half on fire and full of more holes than could be healthy for any occupant.

Razon wanted us to go get the casualty out. There was some cover to the BMB, but to get into it and get anyone out, we would be exposed to the snipers and the RPG fire it was still taking.

In short, without a full rescue effort by the YPG/SDF, there was no way to safely get our casualty out. I thought about our friend trapped in the armored truck.

My heart hated me for the decision I had to make, but I could not justify risking our three lives for his one. I didn't want to say no, but I did. I also didn't want to think about our friend being trapped in the back of the armored truck, as bullets passed through it and rockets exploded into it, but I did. Our poor heval was left out there to die. I shuddered to think of what was going through his mind now at the realization that he was not saved after all. "Fuck!" It ripped me up.

I got angry and snapped at Razon, "Look, fine! - You want to go get him out hero? Then go do it! But I ain't doin' it because if we do that, we will be shot or killed! There is no safe way to get him out without the SDF sending troops on a full-blown rescue attempt!"

Agir agreed with me and tried to convince Razon that it was a bad idea too. I didn't blame Razon for pushing back. We all felt like he did, but it was my call to make, so I made it.

I didn't like it one bit. It actually broke my damn heart, to leave our friend out there to die, but there was nothing we could do. It didn't seem to bother anyone else but the three of us.

What a cold, hard place this is. I shook it off; it was my job to get Razon and now Agir home alive. Caring can be a real mind-fuck sometimes.

The all-foreign volunteer unit '223' showed up. We were in the last building, looking out of the murder holes over no-man's-land at the sad situation. Razon hit them up to see if they would give us cover to get our stranded casualty. Their commander, Servan, refused, pointing out the same thing Agir and I had. There was no safe way to get a casualty out, even if he had survived all the rockets and bullets still hitting the BMB. Agir spoke to the room, "Hey, if you guys got any Daesh shit, the medics can trade them to DELTA for MREs!" I spoke up immediately, "Well, that's not exactly what we meant. What happened was Brusk traded some swag he had to a guy who gave him a box of MREs, but it was on the super down low and the only one who knows who it was is Brusk. So, when you see him, ask him, but please don't go bugging those DELTA dudes. They got enough shit going on without all of us pestering them for shit they can't give."

I was even more grouchy now. It wasn't that I didn't want to share the hookup, but DELTA didn't like the foreign volunteers around them, except the medics. We earned a spot there because we had treated Daesh prisoners that we later handed over to them. More important than the food, DELTA gave us medical gear. Before we were using paper and glue to hold these kids together. We still did a pretty damn good job, considering. But the real medical supplies DELTA gave us were indispensable. The last thing I wanted was for this to get around, but it was already too late for that.

I was pissed at myself for letting it get this far. A massive explosion rocked the BMB and it burst into a red fingered blow torch and the flames seared any hope of survival our friend had. I felt a sense of loss that hit me deeply. I felt like it was my call that ended our friend's only chance.

What if we had been able to get him out with no one getting hurt? Fuck! No way to know. I knew one thing though. It was almost noon and we needed to get some rest before our work started again. We said goodbye to the '223' dudes and rolled out.

At the door just before we hit the street and had to run, Agir asked again, "Hey you guys want to check that building for the Daesh/ISIS shit?"

Razon said, "I ain't sure that's such a good idea. I mean, what if Deash/ISIS went back since you cleared it, you know?"

Agir started to protest, but I broke in, still upset about our heval who died in the BMB. "No! We're going back to the building and we're getting some rest before we get more casualties."

Razon stepped out onto the street and Agir followed him. It sounded like he was still trying to convince Razon to go with him.

I looked back out of the murder hole in the wall one more time, at the burning BMB. Did I make the right call? Could we have gotten our heval out? I felt like a coward for leaving him out there.

Just then, Heval Engin stepped in the door. Seeing my shoulders drooped, he looked concerned and stopped. "Heval Tekoser, you good bro?" He flashed his big smile at me and gave me the operator's thumbs up.

I smiled, though I didn't mean it, saying, "Yeah, I am good," but he could tell I was lying. Patting me on the shoulders, he said, "Sometimes we all have to make that call, brother! You did the right thing, you can't save em all Doc!" With that, he turned and was gone.

Up the street, we ran across the rubble, under perfectly clear blue skies with puffy little white clouds. A gentle breeze blew today. If we were anywhere else in the world, we would have described this day as idyllic.

Then, from behind the sun, dropping out of nowhere, low and moving fast, two jets tore open the sky, just over our heads. They rolled hard to the right and disappeared as fast as they came. The ground shook in a massive explosion.

KAABOOMMMMMM!!! Everything rattled from the massive explosion. We ran back up the street and into our own building. That was the first time in a long time I wasn't worried about snipers.

Inside, in the back, I was tired. I lay down against the wall. The sun shone through my closed eyelids. I tried to shut out this world, all of its fear, anger, and death, to shut out the cruelty and madness of this place. I was too tired to dream, even too tired to sleep. So, I just lay there unmoving.

My eyes burned through clenched, shut lids. The sun was blocked. I opened my eyes a slit. It was Razon and Agir.

Razon said, "We're gonna go next door now. You want to come?"

I gave up. I didn't want to let go of sleep. I didn't want to fight it anymore. I closed my eyes again. "No, I don't want to go. I told you it was a stupid idea, but since you insist on doing it anyway, go ahead and go."

Razon happily said, "OK then, are you sure you don't want to come?"

I shook my head, eyes again closed. As they turned to leave, without opening my eyes, I said, "Hey, if you two find any Daesh media, grab it for me."

Agir responded, "Yeah, you bet! Come on Razon, let's go!" I didn't look back up. I let my mind clear and the world disappear. Sleep came to me…

KAAAAAABOOOOOOOOOMMMMMM! The walls rattled; this was not an air strike. I bolted upright. What was that?! I heard yelling in Kurdish, someone saying, "Embichem." Agir's commander hurried past me.

He said, "Doctor! A mine, a mine." He pointed out toward the street! "Stay here, I will check."

Quickly he went across the courtyard, stepped out of the hole into sniper alley, and disappeared. I stood up, shaking. I had a sick feeling of dread in my guts.

I was all saddled up when, a few minutes later, he poked his head back in the hole.

"Doctor! Hurry!" is all he said. He disappeared back through the hole again.

I grabbed my rifle and ran out behind him. We trotted up the street and out onto the main drag where we took a left. The ground here was strewn with rubble, shredded trees, burned cars, and not a living soul… just rubble for as far as the eye could see.

One block up on the left, a smoking hole had vomited new debris out onto the street. Another heval was inside, his back to me. I couldn't see what he was doing, but I could see Heval Agir. He was dead. He had been separated from the waist down. His dust-covered face didn't have a scratch on it. His eyes were closed, his face to the side - he had a peaceful, quiet expression. I could see each eyelash perfectly coated in fine dust. Motionless, he lay there like he didn't have a care in the world.

My eyes were torn away by Razon yelling out "AAAAHHHHHHHH!! AAAAAHHHHH!! WHAT HAPPENED???!!! AAAAAAAAHHHHHHHH!"

My mind was crushed by this scenario. "Ahhh FUCK!... My friends!" Coming around the hole to what used to be the front door, there was another massive hole blown through it. Out of the direct line of fire of snipers, I dropped my bag. "Quick, get him out of the hole! I'm the medic!"

It looked like Heval Agir and Razon had entered the building through the door where I was standing and had continued in and around into the next room, a utility-type room with building piping and janitorial stuff. It looked like Agir had gone into the room first and made his way to the back wall, where he was facing the wall. Razon had entered the room but for some unknown reason had turned around and was facing out.

The explosion itself had been massive. It blew two holes each in opposing walls and in the corner. I will never know what Heval Agir saw. There was nothing left in the room to see but the aftermath. It didn't matter now; sAgir had died instantly. Heval Razon had been in perhaps the only spot that could have saved him. sAgirs' commander dragged Razon out of the hole to me. My hands were shaking as I fixed the ketamine. Razon lay at my feet, still recovering consciousness, groaning. I was sick with this! I was furious! It was my fault! Fuck! I should have stopped them! I didn't!!!

So, what do you do when you are wrong, and someone dies because of it? "FUCK!" I yelled at Razon, "God damnit, Mormon! Look what you two went and did! Now your friend is blown in half! He's fucking dead, Razon!" I was inspecting Razon the whole time. His vest was gone; who knows where? His back legs were riddled with shrapnel. His back was weirdly untouched, but the back of his head had a large hole in it from shrapnel. I flipped it up, and I could see his pearly white skull; it was covered in blood, but it did not appear to have a hole through it.

Razon screamed, "MY HIP HURTS! AHHHHHHH!"

My eyes were tearing up. I needed to work quickly, inspect him, and move him out of here. In this position we were all completely exposed to Daesh. Razon was disorientated, which isn't a good sign. It's bad because when someone has a 'traumatic brain injury' (TBI), the brain swells; confusion is an early indication of a TBI. To treat brain swelling, you want to ice the head immediately. If the bleeding in the brain becomes too bad, you have to drill the skull to relieve pressure. There are no guarantees when it comes to your brain. I didn't have anything for any of it. My poor heval! "FUCK!" I was so angry at myself for letting this happen.

Dazed but awake, Razon kept saying in a chillingly confused voice, "What happened? Whatt HapppennnnneD?!" Then he started wailing, "WAAAHHHAAAA IT HURTS!!! My LEG aaaaahhhhahaaaaaaaaaa!" sAgir's commander patted me on the shoulder to go. My guilt at seeing both of them all blown up was beyond description. Shaking, I didn't know how to handle it. I felt like my brain had also exploded. I was shaking, I was furious at myself. WHAT HAD I DONE!!??? I let them go!! FUCK!

"Doctor, we must hurry! Daesh." He pointed up the street. In the near distance, I could hear the sound of automatic rifle fire.

"Fucking Daesh! I fucking hate Daesh!!"

I looked up and said, "OK, heval, let's move him now!" Using a shredded old blanket, we rolled Razon onto it and half carried, half dragged him out of the building across the rubble. We carried him as fast as we could between us back down the street and away from the oncoming automatic rifle fire. We had to leave sAgir where he lay for now, because on this day there was only time to save the living.

We made it back around the first corner and then, running as fast as we could, we crossed 'sniper alley.' Razon's AK painfully banged into my leg; my medic bag, camera and broken heart all dragged along with us. I looked at my friend and my anger started to boil over again. It was like a wave washing over me.

Breathing hard, at last we reached a safe building. I needed both hands because Razon was heavier than he looked. He was crying out and very confused. His piteous cries hit like daggers in my heart. His blood on my hands was, literally, a reminder that I fucked up. I let them go. I knew better, and I didn't stop them. "FUCK!" His blood dripped down my arm off my elbow. It felt like dishwater going up my sleeve, but instead of dishwater it was the life of my friend running out.

I got him down on the ground; out came my scissors and off came his clothes. He was still howling in agony. "AHHHHAAHHHH! What happened? AHHHH!"

I ignored his piteous howls and began on the backs of his legs first. His cries were not like an adult's, but more like a little kid's. I was sure that was because the TBI had already put tremendous pressure on his brain. I knew it would probably kill him here. I shoved it from my mind. Hands shaking, I stayed on task to fix what I could fix and get him transported STAT!!

The backs of his legs were peppered with shrapnel. The angry little red holes oozed blood, there were hundreds of them. In some instances, it was not too deep, I could see jagged pieces of metal poking out of his flesh. I knew better than to pull them out. You never knew how deep it went or what would be damaged if it were removed.

I took out the broad-band antibiotic. Breaking the water vial, I filled the syringe and then squirted it into the powder side. Mixing it, I injected Razon in the ass.

He screamed again "AHHHHHHH! It hurts!"

I pushed my finger inside the enormous gaping hole in his back leg. I couldn't feel any shrapnel with my fingers, so I took out the CLOX from my own IFAK and packed it into the wound, and again he screamed.

"AHHAAAHHAAHHAAHH!"

I wanted to shut him up, but I couldn't! His screams hung in my ears like fingernails on chalkboards.

Finishing his legs, I wrapped his head gently. He was babbling incoherently to me. He kept asking what happened but couldn't understand my responses. He was severely confused. The clock was ticking. I was powerless to really do shit. I used my penlight to check his eyes; they stayed dilated, which was not a good sign because it meant his brain was swelling for sure.

Where would they send him to cool his head? This is the western front, there is no ice here, no way to stop the clock.

I got more and more upset with myself. I FUCKED UP! I knew better than to let them go. I was tired. I let my guard down. I didn't stop them.

FUCK! The more guilty I felt, the blunter I was. I told Razon again that sAgir had been killed, but he didn't understand me.

He screamed, "AGGGGRRRAAAgggggaaaaa WHERE AM I??"

I shut my ear to his pain. I used my anger to cover his suffering. I yelled at him, "You fucking killed your friend! Shut up! Just… SHUT UP!" I was crying. I didn't realize I was crying until my eyes bleared over.

Finishing, I called out shaking, "Heval!!! LET'S GO! HE'S BAD!!" The driver of the BMB ran over and started the BMB. That was the first time I had ever seen that man run to his BMB for me. Black smoke spilled violently from the stacks into the sky. The BMB reversed wildly toward us, sliding to a stop. We loaded Razon in with two other casualties I hadn't even noticed, who climbed in behind Heval Razon.

Just before I shut the hatch, I told the gunner on the inside, "Tell them Heval Tekoser is OK! Understand!? Heval Tekoser is OK! I am staying here for the next assault! Tonight!"

He nodded at me and gave me a thumbs up. I slammed the door of the homemade armored truck and it sped away, but this time no Daesh rockets or IEDs blew it up.

Razon was off the front, headed back to the dudes in TMU but without a very good outlook. I assumed he would probably die from his TBI or be mentally handicapped from it. The closest hospital was three hours away. That's a lot of swelling for a long, hot, bumpy ride.

I was still standing there where I had last seen the BMB speed off. I felt defeated; my rifle hung limply in my hand. A hevala came over and handed me Razon's bullet-proof vest. I took it from her and looked at the shredded article. The level 4 plates were powdered, which is why his back had been saved. I know a lot of guys here don't wear a vest at all, but if Razon lived, it was only because his vest had taken the majority of the blast. In all my combat time, I had never seen high quality plates like those turned into dust and crumbs.

"Fucking Hell man!" I held the shredded article in my hand, shaking my head slowly back and forth. I whistled low under my breath.

"Poor Razon!" I felt bad for yelling at him. It wasn't his fault, it was mine. I was the one in command. I was the one they asked to go and I was the one who let them go. I messed up. "FUCK!"

I found sAgir's commander and asked him if we could get him now; his commander said we had to wait until dark because of Daesh. I stepped back out onto the rubble-strewn street. I didn't have cover, and I didn't care. I trotted a half a block, then I sprinted across sniper ally and up to our old building.

I entered the side and moved the big metal door that scraped loudly. I called out, "Heval Tekoser!" But there was no reply. I stepped in and dragged the door back shut behind me. The sound grated on my nerves, like Freddy Kruger's knife fingers. I called out again, "Heval Tekoser is here."

From upstairs, a heval called back, "Dembos Heval Tekoser," but I didn't see anyone.

I made my way through the building toward the back. The sound of fighting was much quieter here. It was still heard but muffled and so somehow removed from the present chaos before me.

Down the dark hallway in front of me I found exploded doors, walls, and interiors. People's clothes and all their worldly possessions lay vomited out, randomly strew around and picked over.

We had figured out where all the citizens had gone and why they had not packed a thing. It was because there was no need for suitcases when you were a human shield, dragged out by Daesh to protect the cowards from air assaults.

Erie pools of daylight spilled into the hallway's darkness as I made my way down it. The light spilled through the various holes, made by missing upper floors, broken walls, and windows. Climbing through another hole and passing through the kitchen of an apartment, I stepped over pots and broken chai cups, a busted spice rack, an exploded counter, and a rotten smelling refrigerator. Broken glass crunched underfoot; I stepped through someone's innocence, traded for dollars on the world's gun markets.

I didn't like being alone here, but what else was I supposed to do? Leave? Then no medics would be down here on the front. Fear? Fear is a smell I was used to by now. 'Heartbroken' is more than a word, more than a feeling; it is a physical pain in my aching chest.

I stepped outside to the back courtyard where we had all been lounging around just an hour before. I sat down against the wall. The sound of automatic rifle fire was louder here than it had been inside. It came from nothing, just ripped into the silence, tearing at the misery that was in my heart. These were outgoing rounds. Sent from the upper floor of my building, I hoped the heval had hit what he was aiming at.

There was a pigeon here; it looked thirsty. I *coo*ed at it and it came closer. The sound of fighting from far away rippled across the back courtyard again, not heavy, just intermittently; it seemed like harassing fire.

The little pigeon pulled me from my dark thoughts. "What a pretty bird," I said to it. I guess it didn't like the sound of fighting either, because it jumped, a little startled at a particularly close machine gun burst. "Pretty scary huh, little bird… Here you want some water?" The pigeon looked at me, cocking its head to the side for a moment before it hopped over to me, but it stopped a few feet away. I had a tiny bit of water left in my water bottle. I poured it into the cap. I pushed it toward the little bird. It looked at me and then at the cap of water. Then the little pigeon hopped over the last few hops and thirstily drank. Every so often it looked at me sideways, as if just to check me out.

The pigeon drank the cap down to the last drop. So, I gave it two more capfuls. It was a very handsome little bird, and I am sure once, not long ago, it was someone's prized pigeon. It was very tame and had a fine plume. The bird fluffed out its feathers and started preening itself, looking back at me all fluffed up, as if to say thank you very much! I smiled sadly, alone.

My smile faded and a sob racked my body, but it was put back in by a second, long machine gun burst. *BWWAA WWAA WAAA WAAAAA!*

No time for regret here, Daesh was close again. The heval's automatic burst was answered back by Daesh, who was three buildings away and just as fast as the rounds went out they were returned. I could hear the incoming bullets smacking the outside wall. I palmed my AK, keeping an eye out. I sat alone and guarded the back entrance so if Daesh did try to come in the rear, they would get a belly full.

The fighting down the street intensified noticeably and so did the bixie fire that was coming from my building. An air strike hit across the street and it bucked the ground, as if slapped by the hand of God. I didn't flinch, but the pigeon flew away in fright.

I sat there for who knows how long, just staring at the sky and the puffy clouds. I guess I fell asleep. After some time, I woke up; I was disorientated. I could hear the back-door scrape loudly on concrete, then someone inside the hallway through the blown-open doors. I was instantly alert and scooted back with my rifle by the far wall. My AK was aiming from my hip nonchalantly at the door. I fingered off the safety and waited, my heart racing. I was hoping it was Daesh; I wanted to blow him back to hell! The crunching got louder and then… sAgir's commander poked his head through the door, asking, "Heval Tekoser? Hello? Doctor!"

I stirred and said, "Yes, heval, I am here."

He looked over. Seeing me, he smiled with sorrow, something my Kurdish friends here all had mastered. "Are you ready? We can go get sAgir now"

I stood up stiffly, rubbing the sand out of my eyes. How long had I slept? The sky was dusted rose and magenta, a sunset for the ages, or was it sunrise? I didn't know anymore. It didn't matter.

Outside, the shadows were long and deep. We made our way up the street and around the corner. I had the eerie feeling of being watched the whole way. The hair stood up on the back of my neck. We made our way back to the hole from the explosion; it was almost dark. sAgir was lying just as we had left him. His commander carefully looked around his body, taking his time to make sure Daesh hadn't come back and planted another booby-trap.

I put down the blanket. I inspected him for clues. He used to have on a ballistic vest; it was no longer on him. I rolled him over. The vest lay tangled with one of his legs. There was very little blood, so I knew he died instantly. With that amount of damage to his body, if he did not die right away, his heart would have pushed all his blood out, making a huge pool. Under sAgir was just a small puddle of blood and body fluids from where his body had been separated.

"Poor sAgir!" I was just trying to get him a break off the front - not get him killed! There was no place to hide my shame, my dereliction of duty. sAgir was covered in dust. I just wanted to dust him off, but I knew that was stupid. Choking back regret, I focused on the task at hand. I grabbed his shoulders and slid him onto the blanket. I took his leg off the tangled wreckage overhead and set it next to him in the blanket. Heval Sores folded his other leg on his chest. You never want to see your friend this way EVER. He was just a young man, a brave young man who would never grow old. Fuck!

"I am so sorry heval," I told his still, cold form.

Once sAgir was all in for the ride, the two of us carried him outside. We each held one arm and gripped the bottom of the blanket where his legs should have been. sAgir's blood, unlike Razon's, was cold. There were other fluids, too… I don't want to talk about it.

When we got sAgir back to the rally point, we set him down. heval after heval came by and would say something quietly to him. Many of them were crying. Often, they would touch me on the shoulder as they left and say "Sehid Namirin" as they made their way back into position for the coming blackness and assault.

Sehid Agir

Heval sAgir helping with casualties

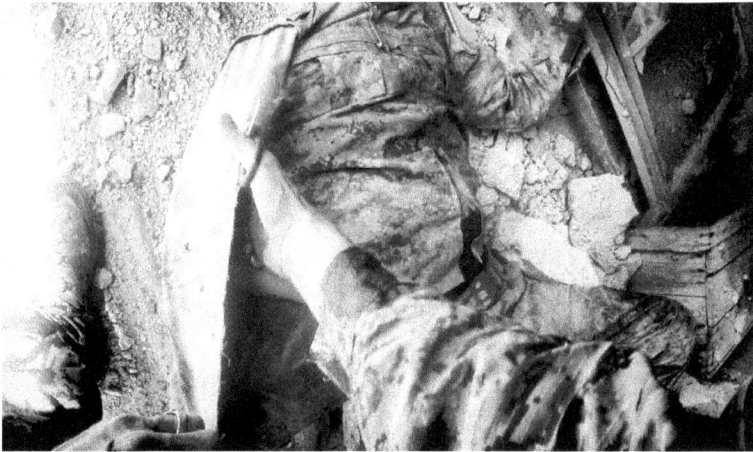

Patching up Razon, cutting off his BDU top and giving him pain management

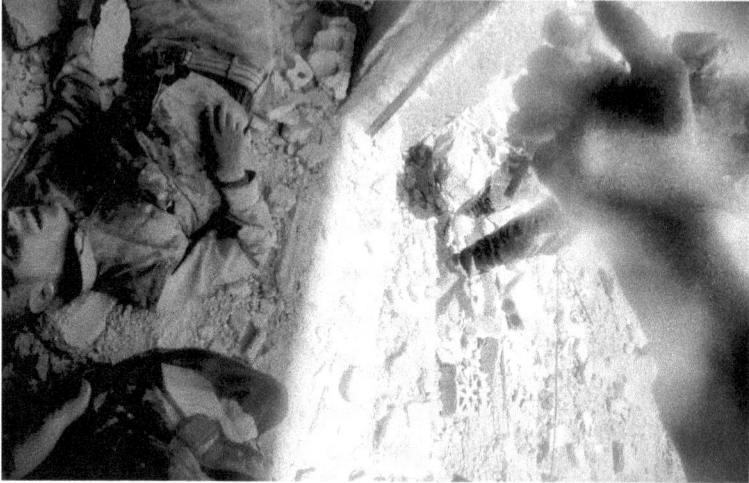

Getting Razon evacuated, you can see the fighting in the near distance.

The last time I saw sAgir was when we loaded him onto the back of a pickup truck around midnight. The back of the truck was already full of our Sehids. They were all similarly wrapped in various blankets and sheets. Sent in alive, dragged out cold, they were stacked on top of each other like cordwood. A small drizzle of black-colored fluid in a constant rivulet trickled out of the back tailgate. It ran across the corner of the dented back bumper and down onto the thirsty, dark ground.

The truck was shoved into gear and sped away. The retreating brake lights flashed on and off as it disappeared into blackness toward the rear and toward safety and at last home… but this no longer mattered to the passengers in the back.

Middle of the night, end of Day 2: Poor sAgir. My heart was heavy as I wondered when it would be my time to get stacked in the back of the same truck. Probably not long, I concluded.

I felt a deep sorrow at the reality that in the end I couldn't save enough to even save myself. I couldn't kill enough to make it stop. I couldn't hurt enough to take away the pain and I wouldn't live long enough to say this to anyone. There was no way out, but in. I turned away from the darkness toward my hevals gathering along a wall, preparing to assault deeper into the city.

I felt like a robot. I made my way back to the little courtyard to collect what was left of my medical supplies, back to the same place where we had all been eating and joking just a few hours before. The place where Razon had sung a beautiful rendition of the Star-Spangled Banner and 'Heaven, where art thou?' We had shared a beautiful moment there with our hevals, who also sang in Kurdish and Arabic, songs of home and loves left behind, love given up for hope, freedom, and a day when we could all just live in peace.

Some of these same friends from last night were also sent back under sAgir. I did not get to see them clearly at the time, though, wrapped in blankets as they were.

In the back of the building, I moved the rubble off the sea bag of medical supplies. It was almost empty anyway. Quickly, stuffing as much of it as I could in my Unit One bag, I went back out to the street.

Running across 'sniper ally' to where the hevals were now gathered, waiting to assault forward, I sat down to wait.

Hours had passed when we were, at last, sent forward. I moved up to the wall, following the hevals. I felt only dread. My hevals around me had eyes full of excitement, the same excitement I used to have. They shared the same heroic jubilation and naivety, still thinking war was heroic.

I stared blankly down the line - my eyes unfocused. No one really truly pictures themselves dying or being blown to hell… until they stand at this wall, that is. Then, there is no illusion about one's fate… and fate was about all I could picture anymore.

I shivered at the coming doom. I was pulled from my dark thoughts by a heval patting me on the shoulder and saying kindly, "Doctor, we must move forward… it is time!"

The commander at the front of the line ordered the taboor to move up past him and into the darkness. There was no more time for regret, no more time for feeling sorry. I was the only medic down here and damn it, I would keep after it until commanders forced me back in.

I felt a numbness that comes from crying too hard and caring too much in a place where life is casually poured out onto the ground.

War doesn't give a shit about your tears.

Crouched low and moving up the street with the hevals, all my sorrow had gone, replaced by fear.

Into the darkness of the twisted cityscape we moved like ghosts… and perhaps we already were. Only our memory moved up the street. Perhaps we were all already dead. All who remember this night, killed, so, 'this' ceases to have ever been.

I tried to think myself into becoming a shadow as we ran deeper into the darkness. As I did, I became conscious of the black tendrils I had seen in my hallucination, moving over the city, caressing the back of my own neck. The demons were all around me, feasting on my misery, drinking my fear.

It was quiet, minus the sound of our feet. Someone stumbled, quietly cursing. The owl was back out calling "Whoo?…Whoo?…" so I knew the devil was close. I could hear my heart louder than anything else.

Then, like a hammer to your finger, the sound of gunfire erupted just up the street.

BWWAAABPPAAA! A light, like a little star, makes me think, "Twinkle, twinkle little star, how I wonder what you are?"

Bullets ripped down the street past us.

Zzpppa, zzzzee, zzap. Zpawwwwwouu.ffweettt..ffett.fettt. Somehow, they missed us.

I dodged left through an open doorway. I hoped I was not going to trigger a mine. Cringing, as if that would help, I pushed it out of my mind and kept going.

Jumping over a crumbled back wall, I followed the hevals in front of me as they ran up to the next street - flanking the gunfire. They cut back in through the belly of a destroyed building.

New gun fire erupted from close by. I had no idea who was shooting at who. Or who was who. "Fucking fuck!!" The darkness ate everything but terror.

There was no way to tell what was going on! One of the hevalas had a bixie. She dropped it down on a crumbled wall, then in the distance she saw shadows running. She said excitedly, "Daesh!!"

BWAAAABWAAABAAAA!! Her gun belched fire like a flame-tipped lance as she started feeding Daesh lead.

The rest of the hevals were getting ready to push past the wall. There was more gunfire from the street where we had just come from, and then I heard a hevala back behind me, calling, "Doctor! Bindar!!" So, I ran back through the building, to the street, where another gun battle erupted.

Hevals ran out, one at a time into the road, unloaded half a mag, and then ran back. Two of them were shot in this process; they were pulled to the side and around the corner.

I patched them both up in a hurry, working in the light of the now burning city all around me.

Two more casualties were brought to me. I had run out of everything. It's not like we had enough to start with. I used what was around me. I stuffed my fingers into wounds with rags I dragged from the smoldering ruins and used sticks from broken chairs, cribs, and walls for splints. There were no more bandages, no more antibiotics, no more NPAs or chest seals, no more pressure dressings, CLOX or anything for pain management.

Surprisingly, there was more useful stuff buried and scattered around than one might think. Moving past a heval who had been shot in the neck,

I saw he was almost expired. I couldn't save him here. The hevala next to him was a right arm amputee. I used his blood-soaked scarf to make a tourniquet for her. He wasn't moving anymore. She looked like the hevala who had been shooting the bixie not too long before. Tying the scarf into a square knot, I used an AK cleaning rod to twist it until her bleeding stopped. She had lost a lot of blood and wouldn't make it unless we got her out quickly. A heval radioed it into the command.

The heval who volunteered for the suicide mission to rescue our injured drove his little pickup truck like one of the boys right out of 'Dukes of Hazard.' He came tearing up the street, swerving around rocks, craters and debris in the road, bouncing over the busted=up median.

It was a small miracle for him to find us in the chaos and darkness. The bullet-riddled truck screeched to a halt in the cover of a wall just behind our position.

I saw the lights wash across the back wall and then go off. A great sense of hope washed over me as we loaded our injured friends onto the back of the truck. By now, the front line had already pushed up another block, and the hevals were pushing hard to secure another city block tonight.

Our casualties all loaded up, a less seriously injured hevala rode shotgun. Her AK pointed out the window, she was ready to rock and roll. The truck ground down to reverse and careened backward out into the street and the line of fire, which was also the only way out. The hevala riding shotgun fired her AK into the blackness. *BWWAAAP…BAWWWWAPPPP….BWAAAAPPPPP…* Her automatic fire tore out of the truck window, sparks like a deadly kaleidoscope as each round exploded out of the tip. A tracer round tore back down the street in reply, but the truck already shifted down into first and was fishtailing away, turning right away from the gunfire to safety.

After the truck left, I could still see the muzzle flashing from her fire burned onto my eye. The heval with me grabbed me by the shoulder and said,, "Doctor. Embichem." He motioned for me to follow him. We moved up another two buildings. Two hevals rounded a corner, coming toward us low and moving fast. Then two more arrived and then a duska truck came zooming up out of the apocalyptic landscape. Stopping, it began firing with its large 30mm cannon.

The fighting was pushing forward quickly. More and more hevals poured into the city and ran through the streets. Machine gun fire tore at the sky overhead, reverberating off concrete walls. Then honking started and it was coming quickly closer...

Bbeep **beeeeep** *BEEEEEEPPP!* We all knew what that meant... car bomb. FUCK, I ducked down behind the wall cowering. A rocket was fired from behind my position. I heard it streak down the street past me. *wwWEESSSHHHHHAAaaaa.*

Then, about a block away, a massive explosion rattled the walls, and the ground seemed to buck beneath me. I could feel the explosion through my teeth. *KKKAAAAABOOOOOMMMMMM!!*

We heard the sounds of concrete and metal bits falling back to earth all around us, *Klink.thunkthawap. Klink.kink. Tink.. Tinktinktink.... CRUNK.* The engine block landed. I cowered, trying to make myself, not... just hoping none of it landed on me. What a lucky rocket shot. Thank God.

Just around the half-destroyed wall, out of the smoke and back-lit flames, hevals emerged one by one, like in a Hollywood movie on the back lot.

The rocket - a perfect hit - struck the VBID just behind Daesh lines. All that was left was a half a city block that isn't there anymore.

More hevals came around the corner to move up the now silent but still burning city street.

A casualty was brought to me. She was in a bad way. Her top was stained red. My hands were shaking almost uncontrollably, but I knew what needed to be done. There is a simplicity in focusing on a task in a crazy shit-gone-sideways world. Like it was a way out. Just focus on my casualties, get them home, and move on. Getting my black scissors out, I cut the camo netting the hevala used for her mags. They fell to the side. She was not moving much, but she was still gasping for air, so I knew where I had to go first.

Zzzziiiiiiiiiipppp! I cut up the side of her YPJ camo blouse. It peeled open easily before my scissors. Off came her top, though it wasn't her wedding night. Her bloody undershirt and bra were pulled away, exposing her breast; there was a bullet hole in it. "Fuck! Knew it!" Rolling her to her side in the recovery position, I peeled the rest of her tunic back. There was a gaping, meaty exit wound. She had been shot from elevation downward. The small entry and large exit told me it was definitely a 5.56.

If the unlucky were lucky, her lung had not been destroyed, but only winged. As if getting shot in the chest wasn't bad enough, she also had a large piece of her upper arm missing, and it was bleeding profusely. It was not pulsating, but still she had lost a lot of blood from it. I had nothing left. My mind moved quickly to solutions to this problem. I did have 4x4s still, and they had a plastic back. I tore two open. I pulled her forward off the caved in wall and stuffed the gauzes into the exit hole. I used the plastic backing from one and her blood to act like the tape. I stuck it over the hole, then I leaned her back on the bandage, sitting up and against the wall. She was fading. I had to get the pressure off her heart fast. Taking the second plastic wrapper for the entry wound, I did the same thing. I cut the bloody sleeve of her YPJ blouse. Cutting it in half, I tied the two parts together. I tied her wrist with one end and then I crossed her hand over her breast and the bandage. I wrapped it around twice and tied it. It held her hand on the bandage. Since I didn't have a needle decompression kit, I made a personal call. I did have a large IV cannula that I had for myself. Fumbling in my IFAK, I took out the large-gauge needle.

My hands followed her collarbone halfway across her chest. I pushed the huge needle in. It pushed through her skin straight about ¾ of the way. The needle made its little *pop* and *hisssss* as the air pressure was relieved from her chest cavity.

"Fuck Yeah!" That would help for sure. I had just bought her a chance. There was no guarantees here, but fucking hell, it was a chance. She started to improve almost immediately as the air compressing her heart was alleviated. Getting stronger, she was able to help hold her hand on the entry wound, where it was already tied.

"Thank God!"

I cut her scarf in three strips down the middle. Wadding one up, I shoved it in the hole in her arm. She squeaked - she didn't have enough energy to scream. Wrapping the other bit around her arm, I tied a stick in the middle of it with a square knot. I twisted it three times. She screamed now, and then passed out. Using the third bit, I tied the stick in place. It crushed my heart, but it was the only way to save her. The homemade pressure bandage stanched the bleeding. I slapped her in the face gently.

"Wake up!" She didn't wake up, so I slapped her harder.

"WAKE UP!" I barked at her.

It worked. Her eyes fluttered open. "No razin!" I tell her (No sleeping!) She was really struggling to stay awake. Making sure she was propped up OK, I called out, "Bindar embichem nequshani!! ZOO! ZOOO!!"

A heval with a radio called it in again. Then, a short time later, two hevals stepped through the shattered doorway, motioning for me to come with them. We carried our injured hevala out to the BMB.

The sky was rosy colored in dawn's early light. Daesh's call to prayers followed us down the street. There were also three new walking wounded I had not treated. "Shit, I didn't even know about them!"

By the time the BMB left, it was full daylight. I turned doggedly back toward the building. The casualties I kept alive had the best chance they could have. My battle was over… for now.

I climbed the stairs to the second floor to find a room to take a nap. Heval Sores was there.

"Heval Tekoser, I am sorry about your friend." He put his hand on my shoulder.

I shook my head, "It's OK, heval."

There is no rest for the undead, though, and Daesh was pissed about how much we took off him last night. So, from across the street, we started taking automatic fire. It was not to my floor, but up above us. Heval Sores quickly turned to go. I started to follow him, but he said, "No Tekoser, you stay here. Watch the building across the street and the stairs." He pointed left through a crumbled interior wall, down a long hallway to the staircase that was going down to the street level.

"If Daesh tries to flank us, that is where they will come up. They will be easy to kill there. Let them get all the way into the hallway and then send them all to hell, heval!" And with that, he took off for the upper floor.

My sorrow instantly gone, I cycled a round into my AK, keeping my eye on the building next to us and the exposed hallway leading to the stairs.

The gunfight above me picked up intensity. Then, out of the corner of my eye, I caught movement in the building across the street. Calmly, without hesitation, I palmed my AK from about ten feet deep in the room.

I started shooting at where I saw the movement. *BAAAWWAABBAAAA…. BWWWAAAAAAA*! I leveled two automatic bursts into the opposite building, just letting Daesh eat shit, eat it for all this pain and suffering, loss and regret.

I didn't want to get shot in return, so I scooted to the left and got down on my belly. It turned out to be a good move because bullets tore back in reply through the window and walls. The room instantly filled with dust.

I started laughing. Scooting up to another window, I stood, bringing my rifle up, and I let out another automatic burst.

BWAAAP.. BWAAAP. WAP. WAP! I felt free at last! As I fired, I yelled at Daesh across the street, "FUCK YOU DAESH!" Ducking in and to the right, I moved back to watch the hallway again. It was only a matter of time before they would come at us now.

Late Morning, Day 3 When the driver of the BMB told me I had to go back to the CCP, I was not surprised. I saw it coming. I tried to protest one last time. , "Heval, I can't return! There is about to be an assault and I am the only medic down here!"

The BMB driver just looked at me and, *tisk, tisk, tisk*ed. Shaking his head side to side he said, "No, heval! Your commander is ordering you to return. I must insist! The jets just destroyed Daesh in the building that collapsed. Our friends will be fine here now. Come. Come!" He motioned toward the door for me to get in.

Having no choice, I climbed into the open hatch, pissed. "Fuck!" I said to no one who cared.

I knew Baz wouldn't send a replacement. There just weren't enough of us. It wasn't Baz's fault… it was the world's fault.

The door shut and, just like that, the outside world disappeared into the rolling, jolting, jarring, terrifying ride through hell. I was finally headed back in, back toward the impossibility of a hope I no longer had.

The BMB were escaping the inner city to the outer edge where our CCP was set up - the door opened. The bright daylight streamed in and people talked too loudly, seemingly all at once.

I climbed out of the BMB, and Baz yelled, "TEKOSER! GET OVER HERE!!"

"Ahhh shit! Here it comes!" I thought. I turned around as Baz came up to me, not waiting for me to get all the way to him. He was pissed.

"WHAT THE FUCK MAN! WHY DIDN'T YOU COME BACK IN WITH RAZON?!!!" He was even more furious than I figured he would be. I had to stay down on the line, there was no one else.

I just shrugged at him. No matter what I said, he would be pissed. Baz was red in the face with anger.

"What do you think, this is a JOKE TEKOSER?! When you sent Razon back half dead and they said another American was killed! I thought for sure it was you man! YOU FUCKING! FUCKA!!" He pokes at me in the air with his index finger while seething. "Then yesterday they sent back a body bag! I wasn't gonna look because no one had heard from you, so I was sure! I WAS SURE!! It was YOU!" His voice was shaking. "But then you FUCKER!! We started getting casualties all bandaged up! Nice dressings too! AND chest seals! AND then even the improvised bandages were tight-n-tidy, and they all made it! YOU FUCK!!" Baz waited - looking at me furiously.

I didn't say anything …

"So, I thought then maybe you were still alive?!" He jammed his index finger at me, red in the face, his voice trembling. "So, who was killed?! We didn't know!? So Bagok and I opened the body bag you fucker! To check! To SEE if it was you or NOT! YOU HEAR ME! WE OPENED THAT BAG BECAUSE WE THOUGHT IT WAS YOU! YOU FUCKER! How could you do that to US! - just staying down there?! You should have brought back Razon!" Baz was legitimately pissed.

I wouldn't apologize. Fuck that. Because what was going to happen now was what would have happened then and that was before the big push. How many casualties had I gotten out? I didn't even know.

I retorted, "There was nothing I could do for Razon! Baz, I did what I could. Why the hell would I come back? That would have left no one down there! Just like right now! There's no one!"

Baz shook his head furiously, yelling, "SOPs Tekoser! S.. O…Ps!!! How dare you put me through that! Why did you not ride back with your own?! Fucking Razon was seriously hurt man! The DELTA crew flew him out on a chopper for a TBI! They drilled his fucking head to relieve the pressure!! He almost didn't make it!! And YOUUU!"

Again, he was ramming his finger at my chest. "And YOU just sent him back on his OWN!!!! HOW DARE YOU!!! ONE OF OUR OWN!!! TEKOSER!"

I just shook my head, speechless for a moment, before I said, "I am needed at the front. Way more than here!"

Baz was beyond furious! He lost his shit "NOOO YOU ARE NOT!! You are needed ALIVE back HOME!!! DAD!!"

I shook my head. "There is no fucking home! Baz!! FUCK!!" I yelled at him angrily.

Baz wasn't having it. He said, "Tekoser, you're GROUNDED! You will be working the CCP until further notice!"

I tried to protest, but there is one thing for sure about Baz. When he makes up his mind it's made up.

CHAPTER 33: Where is Ser?

I wanted to leave you with an epic ending and pontific conclusion that both uplifted and inspired you. I wanted to end this book with the chapter of all chapters about hope, heroism, and war, but then this book would not have ended honestly.

So, in the end, it was two weeks after sAgir was killed and Heval Razon was injured that I left Manbij and Syria permanently. Baz did not send me back to the front anymore, so I volunteered for ambulance service.

I ferried casualties back to Sarin, or Kobani hospital. Following the thin red line on the blank GPS screen, across dark nights and what seemed like to me even darker days, I didn't tell anyone I was coming apart, having nightmares, depression, fits of rage, panic attacks. My nerves were shot. I retreated deeper and deeper.

The night before I left for the last time, we made a big feast. One of the new volunteers, Heval Erish, brought back a whole chicken from Kobani, so I cooked a big stew and fed all the hevals one last feast. We savored potatoes, eggplant, bread, sweets and chai.

Just as we sat down to eat, Daesh hit us with 155 artillery shells. They screamed overhead, smashing a building close to us.

Bowls spilled and utensils clattered to the ground as everyone hit the deck and then scrambled for rifles and the door.

So much for dinner.

The building that got hit was in ruins. It was twenty-five meters, two buildings, and a low wall away, the only difference between alive and not.

The 155 acted as a stark reminder to me; I was not out of here yet. It was a reminder that shook me with panic.

I felt like my mind was in a strait jacket. Like suffocating slowly, I just wanted to go home, but I didn't know where that was anymore. I wanted to forget the pain of it all, but the pain now defined me.

I thought about my decision to come here even as I was hoping to run away from here. I felt guilty. The job was not finished. Could it ever be? Suddenly, the six months I stayed didn't seem long enough.

In the morning, when the sun touched the horizon, I got up. Bagok came in; he looked tired. He had been driving all night.

"Well mate, I guess this is it. I'll drive you up to Derik and you can get your own way from there to the border as you asked."

I grabbed my rucksack, leaving all my supplies and Unit One Bag for the TMU to use as needed. I walked out of the room and onto the street.

Driving away from the insanity, it felt bizarre, like some other-worldly moment, imprinted in my mind, clear as crystal glass. The imagined moment, at long last, had arrived.

I stared out the window at the passing landscape. We passed through village after village that we had liberated, land we had killed and died to free. We passed the Euphrates River crossing, Sarin field hospital and Kobani, back through Shaddadi and Til Tamer. The mud-painted van flew down the M4, over the golden hills rolling through Qamishli and finally up to where Derik lay, nestled just below the majestic mountain peaks that surrounded it.

I said goodbye to Heval Bagok, one last time. Getting my bag out of the back, I closed the trunk and, turning without looking back, I walked into the hotel.

In the morning, I was getting a taxi to the Iraqi border. Everything was all set. I was going to be on a jet home in less than twenty-four hours, almost home free! What a strange word to hold in the mouth of my mind. Home… The place where it all starts to get better. I imagined hugging my little girls, having a house-sized jalapeno bacon cheeseburger and a cold beer. My mouth was watering at the thought. My heart pulled me forward, away from all this pain, darkness and suffering.

I thought about the coming day. I was assured everything was all set. Barzani's Iraqi border guards had all been paid off. I would just cross and be picked up by some company guys and taken directly to the airport in Sulaymaniyah, Iraq. There was already a plane ticket waiting for me.

Outside my hotel window, the peaceful city of Derik bustled with daily life. It was thriving in the newly re-founded country of Rojava (Western Kurdistan). It was like a new flower the first morning, opening its petals to the dawn of a new day... called hope.

In Rojava, every household had more than one beloved who had given their life for this chance of freedom and independence. There is a difference to the taste of freedom when it is tasted through tears, shed for blood, spilled in her name. That's why the streets here were adorned with posters of the fallen: daughters, sons, fathers, mothers, aunts, uncles and best friends; all had traded their lives for this dream called Rojava.

Down the street, painted on the side of a building, I looked up at a large mural of Abdullah Öcalan (Apo), the originator of Democratic Confederalism, the concept that was working so well here in the newly liberated Daesh lands.

It's a crime against humanity that Apo has been locked up in a Turkish prison for decades. I imagined his eyes, imagined him seeing this land independent and free, as he had fought his whole life for. My own wish to go home must be but a shadow passing his cell window, from a cloud, on a windy day. Again, I started to feel guilty.

"What is wrong with me?" I shook my head, refocusing, looking again outside at the Sehid posters hung on the lampposts over the street. Then, I saw a Sehid poster of someone I knew very well – sAgir. It took me by surprise. I looked at it like a stranger, as if I didn't know that face. In the picture, he was much cleaner and fatter than when I had known him. In the poster he was frozen, forever in youth. My eyes teared up. I looked away in shame.

My heart was too heavy to drag around anymore. I was too scared of getting blown up, buried alive or shot; my nerves were shot. I was running away because I could, because I am from paradise, where the Pacific Ocean meets the land, peaceful and free already. Most of all, I was running away because I was naïve, and I still thought I could escape this time and place.

What I know now is: there are no heroes in war, because war is not heroic. There is no luck to be found in war, because no one in war is lucky. There is only hell to be found in war, and once you go there, you can never come back, not the same anyway.

So, if you asked me today. "Where is Ser? ... Where is The Brave Lion?" I would say, "I don't know? He never came home."

THE END

Heval Agir poster

AUTHOR'S NOTE

When I finally made it back to the United States from Iraqi prison, I came back homeless. I had nowhere to turn and nothing left. Emotionally bankrupt, I drove away from that long dreamed-of ending in my old RV with whatever I could fit in it. A shadow of a person… a ghost…

The Future of Rojava

Rojava is currently in grave danger and under siege by hostile Turkish forces hell-bent on extinguishing freedom in Rojava. There has been a civil war happening in Turkey for over forty years now against the minority Kurds there. Over 1,200 towns, cities and villages have been destroyed in this civil war. The autocratic government in Turkey is led by a man named Erdogan; he does not want to see a free Rojava. Freedom in Rojava is a seed of hope to all of Kurdistan, much of which is located in modern-day Turkey where they are not free. Democratic Confederalism is a potential model for peace for all of the Middle East. Hope and freedom are the greatest threats to dictators, despots, and tyrants. Rojava needs international support to ensure democracy and peace can spread and grow there.

Over 12,000 YPG/YPJ/SDF laid down their lives to beat back ISIS/Daesh. Untold more were wounded, both from the seen and unseen ravages of war.

List of foreign volunteers killed in action fighting Daesh/ISIS:

1. Emir Kubadi 2014 IRAN
2. Ashley Johnston 23 Feb 2015 AUS
3. Kosta Scurfield 2 Mar 2015 UK/GR
4. Ivana Hoffman 7 March 2015 GER
5. Mihemed Kerim 5 May 2015 IRAN
6. Keith Broomfield 3 Jun 2015 USA
7. Arnavut Karker. 26 June 2015 AL

8. Reece Harding 27 June 2015 AUS
9. Kevin Jochim 6 Jul 2015. GER
10. John Gallagher 4 Nov 2015 CAN
11. Gunter Hellstern 23 Feb 2016 GER
12. Mario Nunes, PTSD suicide, 3 May 2016 POR
13. Jamie Bright 25 May 2016 AUS
14. Levi Jonathan Shirley 14 July 2016 USA
15. Dean Carl Evans 21 July 2016 UK
16. Martin Gruden 27 July 2016 SLO
17. Firaz Kardo 3 August 2016
18. Jordan MacTaggart 3 August 2016 USA
19. William Savage 10 Aug 2016 USA
20. Michael Israel 24 Nov 2016 USA
21. Anton Leschek 24 Nov 2016 GER.
22. Ryan Lock 21 Dec 2016 UK
23. Nazzareno Tassone 21 Dec 2016 CAN
24. Paolo Todd 15 January 2017 USA
25. Albert A Harrington 25 January 2017 USA
26. Robert Grodt 6 July 2017 USA
27. Nicolas A Warden 6 July 2017 USA
28. Luke Rutter 6 July 2017 UK
29. David Taylor. 16 July 2017 USA
30. Orhan B N Ozanyan 14 Aug 2017 ARM
31. Fred Demoncheaux 7 September 2017 FR
32. Memhet Aksoy. 26 September 2017 UK
33. Jac Holmes. 23 October 2017 UK
34. Ollie Hall. 25 November 2017 UK
35. Abraham Hassan 5 Dec 2017 LEB
36. Samuel P Leon 10 Feb 2018 Galacia
37. Kendal Breizh 10 Feb 2018 Breton
38. Baran Sason. 12 February NL
39. Jake Kilpsch. 5 Jan 2018 USA
40. Haukur Hilmarsson. 6 March 2018 ICE
41. Anna Campbell. 15 March 2018 UK
42. Dr. Lêgerîn Çiya (Alîna Sanchez) AR
43. Farid Medjahed. 6 Oct 2018. FR
44. Giovanni Francesco Asperti (Hîwa Bosco)

7 Dec 2018. I

45. Lorenzo Orsetti (Heval Tekoser) 18 March 2019

46. Alex Moreau PTSD suicide

Tactile Medical Unit (TMU/YPT)

Calak (Brennan Phillips) was the first person who ever talked to me about making a medical unit in the YPG. That was in September 2015 in Kentucky, before either of us left for Rojava. I brought the first Unit One Pack into Rojava that I know of and Baran the Brit raised money for the first 300 IFAK kits to get into Rojava.

The Tactile Medical Unit was first formed in early February 2016. The first unit to see combat was when three of us hitchhiked to the Battle for Shaddai from Til Tamir. Dil Sauz was the first battlefield commander of the Unit. Firat got the unit its first nocta and first vehicle, a white minivan. Baran went for permissions.

The unit treated 368 seriously injured SDF/YPG/YPJ casualties; we classified 'serous' as any life-threatening injury. In the Manbij operation, we did not keep track of the non-life threatening, or civilian, casualties we treated. That number was astronomically higher, by more than five to one.

T.M.U. Combat medical training: Calak, Baz and Firat first translated and recreated the US Army's TCCC course into an adapted Kurdish version. The first training curriculum from it was created by Baz. Additionally, Baz, Razon, Firat and I acted as instructors in teaching those courses to SDF (Syrian Democratic Forces). I also taught a special IV course with Firat. The T.M.U. collectively gave access to hundreds of SDF hevals in basic medical training during the first half of 2016.

Hevala Jiyan, YPJ, got the unit's permission to take the first ambulance that Baz and Bagok found. She also cleared the way with the medical board to get us medical supplies down from Manbij, which remains the system in place to the current day. Hevala Jiyan has helped more than any single one of us to create a complete culture shift in the Syrian Democratic Forces and YPG/YPJ. As a result of this change, we all contributed, too, championed for years now by her and others like Jabs Canada combat medics, who are being placed into each unit.

In Manbij, at the start, there were four of us combat medics on the front, four of us for 7000 actioned troops and 50,000 civilians. Others joined as we rotated out. People like Hevala Jiyan, Heval Adnan, Carlos Hoddi, and countless others laid the groundwork for the future combat medics in Rojava.

The original members of the Tactical Medical Unit in order listed were:
Dil Saus, Tama (New Zealand/UK)
Calak, Brennan (Kentucky/USA)
Beran (UK)
Tekoser, River Rainbow (California and Hawaii, USA,)
Firat Kabak, Kendal (Kurdistan/Sweden)

After Shaddadi, the unit was able to grow and others were able to join the T.M.U. They included:
Arges, Jeff Kupp (Illinois, USA)
Big Botan (UK) sServan (Canada)
Baz (German)
Bagok Bagok (Australia)
Jiyan (German)
Farzad (Iran)
Razon, Porter Goodman (Uta, USA)
Brusk (Florida, USA)
Olivia Mefras (Sweden).
Agir/Levi Shirley (Colorado/Texas)
The Irishman Josh Malloy (Ireland)
Pops (UK)
Erish, Michael Makuch (Germany)

"Life is traded for dollars that are placed against the head of freedom and she is executed there on the side of anywhere but where the guns are made." *Sehid Namirin*

SPECIAL THANKS

YPG, YPJ, All the people of Rojava. My three amazing children; Arcata Rainbow, Alyna-Rose and Mariluna Sunset. Elissa-Reiko Yamamoto *for thirty years of friendship.* Moms Storyteller *you helped me do the second copy edit this book, line by line. I learned so much, and for that help I am very thankful.* Dad, Ron Hagg, *thanks for the first copy edit to get the ball rolling. That was no small task.* Uncle Coast Chris Dehnert *you were always my hero growing up and from you I learned I could do this kind of thing,* Bro Song O'Mahoney *always there for your brother 100% the best kind of brother a brother could want,* My sister Sunrise O'Mahoney *thanks for the dresses... LoL.* Dr. E.Momeni *for insisting that I write this book.* Ricky Schroder *for helping spring me from Iraqi prison and making "The Volunteers" documentary with me and always having my back.* Jake Simkin *the last Kabul Knight for making it all possible to get into YPG.* Kendal Derbasiye Heval Firat Batman *because yo without you my brah were always the Key to the TMU making it and saving life.* The Families of our Sehids: Susan Shirley, Chris Scurfield, Raven Cienfuegos, Connie Israel, Fred Savage, Chelsea Niehaus and kids, the Tailors, Angie Blannin, Peter Holms. Wes Davis *always took me surfing as a grom and taught me that "it's what I make it."* Bone-Tony Deeter *because you always been down, since day one.* Ben Burnett *keeping it real as real in the ocean flow my bro.* Doug Harms *my brother from another and grill master,* Jax Harms *growing up to be a fine young man.* EggB-Arron Edgar *sorry about the bad tattoo.* My counselors at the Vet Center, Nancy Chapman, Felipe and Denise *thank you for all your help.* Next Steps Service Dogs and Gina Esoldi *for helping Doc and me open up the world,* Doc Stella *the dog the best best best ever!!!* Kathy Pacheco from Annie's Bar and Grill *you helped me to become me, without your help... Wow, thank you for the job and all years of friendship.* Blare Paulsen *for my first camera gig.* Ethan Van Thillo and the San Diego Media Arts center, *for giving a young storyteller a job to start it all from.* All my Topanga and ocean Ohana, Ryan Krouse

Jr you got this, so proud of you bro! Alex Roe *charger and artist who goes easy and makes me laugh to Brexit reggae…* Wade Lawson *there is only one, GO WADE!!* Dennis Crispin *thanks for taking me to Mav's that time and years of advice,* Doc Russ Kino *Doc you are the best of Topanga down under!* Mitt and Frankie Seely *the Honey Badger clan… F around and find out!!* Michael Bihari *one of a kind genuine soul,* Casey Engelhardt… *Deadses..i But for real tho you R 1 Epic human my bro,* Hideo Oida *soul sensi,* Nikos Batanides *eat cookies,* Jacob Samuel *thanks for the inspiration both in the water and out,* Jessica Monty *(Chef) Beautiful and Free!! You go Girl!!* Richard Evens *that stlyle!!* Steve Rabino *1-kind person, thanks for the shirt!* Carolyn Day, Gaston Wurth, Kyle Ruddick, Paul Harman, Leigh Kennedy *thanks for all the years of sic surfboards and taking me surf the ranch!!* Barbra Kennedy, Gordon Forbes 3rd RIP, Nick Savander *you got so much talent thank for your awesome eye!* Matt and Molly Silver *Matt the funny guy molly the sweet so happy for you two!* David Kneiss, LTC Linsey Colvin aka Charley *you are a badass and a true American hero,* Cico Silva *for letting me film you playing the USA national anthem in Red Square and getting away with it,* John Preston *always all your brothers keeper #carrytheload,* Pete and Hugh Peterson *two EPs with souls,* Rob Dorfman *for always having my back the advice and friendship,* Shannon Ehinger *your sweet and tuff thanks for the support and tuna tail,* Heval Adnan *one badass Kurdi hero,* Marjan Dhoker *an advocate for peace and justice.* Jake Simkin, *yeah again, for getting me the number bro*!! Brennan Phillips *because you got the biggest heart and you introduced me to chicken and waffles,* Jeff Kupp *you always keep us alughing,* Tama aka Dil Saus *the brave big heart!* Big Botan England, Botan England, Jayson Pihajlic *baddest of the bad and glad your on our team,* Joe Akerman *OG sabatoge crew with more courage than 10 men and a heart of gold,* Stephen Kerr *he might be small but he is mighty fuck around and find out,* Artiaga Arges *one good eye is all you ever needed 223 Sniper,* Heval Sores Norway *thanks for helping us get to the fight!,* Hanna Bohman *proof more than looks kill, YPJ sniper,* Alex Moreau RIP *miss you bro.* Olivia Mefras *-straight bad ass Daesh killer-* , Michael Enright *(let's get him home!),* Baz *the fearless, because we were a motley crew to lead but he did it the best!* John Foxx *who was always ready to help TMU,* Anderson Bryant *because you are the real deal when it comes to walk it like you talk it.* Kato Matthew Hughes *you're the toughest person I ever met!!!* Bobby

Wisconsin *always had a smile*, Jordon Mattson *the controversial 1st American to go and for kicking down the doors to start.* Michael Makuch, Caveman Rob, Heval Sasson, Heval Jonser, Hevala Gul Cyia, Heval sArmang, Heval Sores, Hevala Jiyan *still training medics in Rojava and my personal hero!,* Wil Okken, Sean Murphy, Matt and Molly Silver *best sound guy around and also a great shooter*, Cuz Jack and Maybe Abbott, Mike 'Mr. Pacheco'-(RIP), Johnny Rotten and manager Rambo Stevens, David Kniess friend and fellow Navy vet, Scott Warner *for brawling with me in HS and becoming life long friends*, Dave Carraro, Paul Herbert, TJ Ott, Bubba Ott, Sr and all the Otts! Nick and Chrissy Gowitzka, Cpt Greg Frenzy Henni and Billon, Jake Griff, Greg Gibbs, Captain Ralf, Capt Dave Marciano, Davira Shain, Aunt Mary Burris, Dave De Angelis, Steve and Tawn Jones, Scott Warner, Geana Kanoa Miura and family. Da crew at Honali'i for welcoming me home; Kaynan, Casey, Kahea, Chad, Greg, Travis, Bertrand (Bert), T' Ted (Da-Mayor), Brada George, Uncle Ken, Uncle Ronnie Bowls, Jr Bowls Sara, Jason aka 'Da Boss, Brahma, Brada Ranz, Chef Ernie, Popi, All the Uncles who raised me right, Deb Zuchowski, Dr Fares Hamo, David Morgan, Jessy Brady, Brenda Jabs, Jabs Canada *another huge hero of mine*, Chris Shaw, Albert Bain, Liz Dobbins, Buddy Mickle, Marc Graham, Paul Maty, Steve Korkis, Monroe, Ben and Blake Burnett, Matt Getz, Chris Serra, Jason Martinez, Grady O'Donnell, Matt Crocco, Shey Gladstone, Heval Ceko Tolhildan.

Extra **BIG** thank you, Krista Carlson, *for the amazing copy edit. I wanted to give you your own line, because you did this while on your Hawaiian vacation and it saved my bacon. You Rock! ROCK! ROCK!*

Names as they appear are in no particular order.

ABOUT THE AUTHOR

River Rainbow O'Mahoney Hagg is a disabled American combat veteran, writer and a documentary filmmaker.

In 2016, he went to Rojava, Syria, to make a documentary on the conflict against ISIS. To accomplish this, River volunteered for the YPG as a combat medic. His documentary, The Volunteers (part one and part two), purchased by AT&T, aired on Audience Channel as an AT&T Original series, and is now available on Vimeo, and YouTube for free.

River has been interviewed or appeared in: *LA Times*, *Washington Post*, *Variety*, *Business Insider*, *Lost Coast Outpost*, *CNN-News Room*, *TED Talk*, *CNN-Brooks Baldwin*, *RT-Ruptly* and *CNN United Shades of America*.

His latest project *Where is Ser (the Brave Lion)* is a memoir of his time Rojava, Syria.

NOTE FROM THE AUTHOR

Word of mouth is crucial for any author to succeed. If you enjoyed *Where is Ser*, please leave a review online—anywhere you are able. Even if it's just a sentence or two, it would make all the difference and would be very much appreciated.

Thanks!
River Rainbow O'Mahoney Hagg / Tekoser Azad

We hope you enjoyed reading this title from:

BLACK ROSE
writing™

www.blackrosewriting.com

Subscribe to our mailing list – *The Rosevine* – and receive **FREE** books, daily deals, and stay current with news about upcoming releases and our hottest authors.
Scan the QR code below to sign up.

Already a subscriber? Please accept a sincere thank you for being a fan of Black Rose Writing authors.

View other Black Rose Writing titles at www.blackrosewriting.com/books and use promo code **PRINT** to receive a **20% discount** when purchasing.

Lightning Source UK Ltd.
Milton Keynes UK
UKHW020640070422
401231UK00009B/394

9 781684 339198